Family-based Interpersonal Psychotherapy for Depressed Preadolescents

PROGRAMS THAT WORK

Family-based Interpersonal Psychotherapy for Depressed Preadolescents

CLINICIAN GUIDE

LAURA J. DIETZ

REBECCA J. WEINBERG

LAURA MUFSON

OXFORD
UNIVERSITY PRESS

OXFORD
UNIVERSITY PRESS

Oxford University Press is a department of the University of Oxford. It furthers the University's objective of excellence in research, scholarship, and education by publishing worldwide. Oxford is a registered trade mark of Oxford University Press in the UK and certain other countries.

Published in the United States of America by Oxford University Press
198 Madison Avenue, New York, NY 10016, United States of America.

Library of Congress Cataloging-in-Publication Data
Names: Dietz, Laura J., author. | Weinberg, Rebecca J., author. | Mufson, Laura, author.
Title: Family-based interpersonal psychotherapy for depressed preadolescents: clinician guide / Laura J. Dietz, Rebecca J. Weinberg, Laura Mufson.
Other titles: Treatments that work.
Description: New York : Oxford University Press, [2018] | Series: Treatments that work | Includes bibliographical references.
Identifiers: LCCN 2017058869 | ISBN 9780190640033 (pbk. : alk. paper) | ISBN 9780190640040 (updf) | ISBN 9780190670122 (epub)
Subjects: | MESH: Depression—therapy | Family Therapy—methods | Child | Interpersonal Relations
Classification: LCC RJ506.D4 | NLM WM 171.5 | DDC 616.85/2700835—dc23
LC record available at https://lccn.loc.gov/2017058869

About ✓ PROGRAMS THAT WORK

Stunning developments in healthcare have taken place over the last several years, but some widely accepted interventions and strategies in mental health and behavioral medicine have been brought into question by research evidence as not only lacking benefit, but perhaps, inducing harm (Barlow, 2010). Fortunately, other strategies have been proven effective using the best current standards of evidence, resulting in broad-based recommendations to make these practices more available to the public (McHugh & Barlow, 2012). Several recent developments are behind this revolution. First, we have arrived at a much deeper understanding of pathology, both psychological and physical, which has led to the development of new, more precisely targeted interventions. Second, our research methodologies have improved substantially, such that we have reduced threats to internal and external validity, making the outcomes more directly applicable to clinical situations. Third, governments around the world and healthcare systems and policymakers have decided that the quality of care should improve, that it should be evidence-based, and that it is in the public's interest to ensure that this happens (Barlow, 2004; Institute of Medicine, 2001, 2015; Weisz & Kazdin, 2017).

Of course, the major stumbling block for clinicians everywhere is the accessibility of newly developed evidence-based psychological interventions. Workshops and books can go only so far in acquainting responsible and conscientious practitioners with the latest behavioral healthcare practices and their applicability to individual patients. This series of treatment manuals and companion client workbooks, Programs *That Work*™, is devoted to communicating exciting, effective interventions for children and adolescents to clinicians on the frontlines of practice.

The manuals and workbooks in this series contain step-by-step detailed procedures for assessing and treating specific problems and diagnoses. But this series also goes beyond the books and manuals by providing ancillary materials that will approximate the supervisory process in assisting practitioners in the implementation of these procedures in their practice.

In our emerging healthcare system, the growing consensus is that evidence-based practice offers the most responsible course of action for the mental health professional. All behavioral healthcare clinicians deeply desire to provide the best possible care for their patients. In this series, our aim is to close the dissemination and information gap and make that possible.

This volume, *Family-based Interpersonal Psychotherapy for Depressed Preadolescents*, presents a developmental adaptation of Interpersonal Psychotherapy for Depressed Adolescents (IPT-A), used to treat adolescents aged 12–18. Additionally, IPT-A has shown success in treating young people diagnosed with dysthymic disorder, depression not otherwise specified, and adjustment disorder with depression mood; it has also been successful in the treatment of depressed young people with comorbid anxiety disorders and related internalizing diagnoses.

Anne Marie Albano, Editor-in-Chief
David H. Barlow, Editor-in-Chief
Programs *ThatWork*™

References

Barlow, D. H. (2004). Psychological treatments. *American Psychologist, 59*, 869–878.

Barlow, D. H. (2010). Negative effects from psychological treatments: A perspective. *American Psychologist, 65*(2), 13–20.

Institute of Medicine. (2001). *Crossing the quality chasm: A new health system for the 21st century*. Washington, DC: National Academy Press.

Institute of Medicine. (2015). *Psychosocial interventions for mental and substance use disorders: a framework for establishing evidence-based standards*. Washington, DC: National Academy Press.

McHugh, R. K., & Barlow, D. H. (2012). *Dissemination and implementation of evidence-based psychological interventions*. Oxford: Oxford University Press.

Weisz, J. R., & Kazdin, A. E. (2017). *Evidence-based psychotherapies for children and adolescents* (3rd ed.). New York: Guilford.

Accessing Programs *ThatWork* Forms and Worksheets Online

All forms and worksheets from books in the PTW series are made available digitally shortly following print publication. You may download, print, save, and digitally complete them as PDFs. To access the forms and worksheets, please visit http://www.oup.com/us/ttw.

Contents

Part Three Middle Phase of FB-IPT

Part Four Termination Phase of FB-IPT

Part Five Implementation of FB-IPT

Appendices

Family-based Interpersonal Psychotherapy for Depressed Preadolescents

PART ONE

Background and Rationale for FB-IPT

CHAPTER 1 Introduction to Preadolescent Depression

Prior to the 1970s, the existence of childhood depression was not widely accepted in the psychiatric community. The prevailing view was that children's immature cognitive, social, and emotional development protected them from experiencing depressive symptoms that required more introspection and psychological orientation, such as melancholia, worthlessness, hopelessness, and suicidality. Depression in children was hypothesized to be "masked" and was expected to manifest in more age-appropriate disturbances of behavior as opposed to other symptoms of depression. Early epidemiological and clinical studies examined depression in children and adolescents (Graham & Rutter, 1968; Kovacs, Feinberg, Crouse-Novak, Paulauskas, Pollock, et al., 1984; Kovacs, Feinberg, Crouse-Novak, Paulauskas, & Finkelstein, 1984; Puig-Antich, Blau, Marx, Greenhill, & Chambers, 1978; Rutter & Graham, 1968). Sir Michael Rutter's epidemiological studies of psychopathology in the Isle of Wright (Rutter & Graham, 1968) revealed the existence of depressive symptoms in children that were similar to adult depression in the presence of mood disturbance and neurovegetative symptoms. Puig-Antich (1982) presented some of the first pilot data demonstrating that depression in prepubertal children could be indexed using unmodified research diagnostic criteria for diagnosing major depressive disorder (MDD) in adults. The majority of children endorsed symptoms of dysphoric mood, sleep disturbances, inappropriate guilt, and thoughts of suicide, similar to presentation of depression in adults. These studies validated the existence of a depressive phenotype in children.

Decades of subsequent research on depression in children consistently support these early findings regarding the similarity of depressive symptoms in children and adults. Depression in children and adolescents manifests in

- a persistent low mood or lack of interest or enjoyment in usually pleasurable activities (anhedonia);
- sleep disturbance (trouble falling asleep, staying asleep, or early morning wakening);
- impaired or distorted cognitive ability (such as poor concentration and thoughts of guilt and hopelessness);
- a negative sense of self (such as low self-esteem); and
- a range of suicidal ideation, from passive death wish to suicidal ideation with method and intent. Recent studies indicate that preschool children and school-age children experience rates of suicidal ideation similar to those of adolescents (Bridge et al., 2015; Bridge, Greenhouse, Weldon, Campo, & Kelleher, 2008; Whalen, Dixon-Gordon, Belden, Barch, & Luby, 2015).

However, depressive symptoms in youth differ from those observed in adults in several significant ways:

- Youth often demonstrate irritability when experiencing a significant disturbance in mood rather than a melancholic depression often described by adults (Birmaher & Rozel, 2003).
- Depressed mood and anhedonia in youth also appear to be more reactive to external situations than in adults, with periods of euthymic mood occurring during a depressive episode (Williamson et al., 2000).
- Early clinical studies on childhood-onset depression do not reflect the 2:1 female preponderance evident in adult and adolescent-onset depression. Rather, childhood-onset depression affects both girls and boys equally, with some studies citing higher rates of depression in boys (Kovacs, Feinberg, Crouse-Novak, Paulauskas, & Finkelstein, 1984; Puig-Antich et al., 1985a).
- Suicidal behavior and completed suicide are typically low among preadolescent children, and reach rates similar to those seen in adults by adolescence (Dervic, Brent, & Oquendo, 2008).

Prevalence

Depression affects between 0.4% to 2.5% of preadolescent children (Birmaher & Rozel, 2003). However, these prevalence rates may underestimate the number of preadolescents who present for outpatient treatment with clinically significant depressive symptoms and functional impairment but who do not meet full diagnostic criteria for MDD. Angold, Costello, Farmer, Burns, and Erkanli (1999) argue that preadolescents with impairing subthreshold depression have psychiatric illnesses that are often underdiagnosed and untreated.

Comorbidity

Joaquim Puig-Antich (1978) once noted that finding a "pure" case of MDD in children was "a futile effort." More than 30 years of research has emphatically documented that comorbidity in depressive disorders in children and adolescents is the rule, rather than the exception. Up to 70% of children and adolescents with depression have comorbid psychiatric disorders (Avenevoli, Stolar, Li, Dierker, & Ries Merikangas, 2001; Costello, Mustillo, Erkanli, Keeler, & Angold, 2003; Kessler, Avenevoli, & Ries Merikangas, 2001), with anxiety and disruptive behavior disorders being the most common.

Anxiety

Comorbid anxiety disorders affect an estimated 30% to 58% of children and adolescents with depression (Costello et al., 2003; Kovacs, Gatsonis, Paulauskas, & Richards, 1989). The most common anxiety disorders in children with depression are separation anxiety disorder followed by generalized (overanxious) anxiety disorder (Kovacs et al., 1989). Although comorbid separation anxiety disorder decreases with age, generalized anxiety disorder continues to remain a significant comorbidity for children with depression (Costello et al., 2003). Comorbid anxiety disorders complicate and, in many cases, worsen the prognosis for treatment and recurrence. Children and adolescents with depression and anxiety disorders demonstrate increased severity and duration of depressive symptoms, increased suicidality and psychosocial problems, and poor response to psychotherapy (Brent et al., 1998; Cheung et al., 2010; Goodyer, Herbert, Secher, & Pearson, 1997).

It is not surprising that anxiety and depressive disorders are highly comorbid in children. Indeed, both depression and anxiety disorders in children share some of the same symptoms, such as fatigue, difficulty concentrating, and sleep disturbances. Community, clinical, and school populations repeatedly demonstrate high correlations between self-report measures of childhood depression and anxiety, ranging from .40 to .80 (Brady & Kendall, 1992; Muris, Van Brakel, & Meesters, 1998). More recent studies on childhood depression and anxiety have found that anxiety disorders often precede depressive disorders in children and adolescents and may serve as a "gateway" to depression in affected children (Axelson & Birmaher, 2001; Silk, Davis, McMakin, Dahl, & Forbes, 2012).

Disruptive Behavior Disorders

Disruptive behavior disorders, such as conduct, oppositional defiant, and attention deficit hyperactivity disorders, are also common in children and adolescents with depression, and affect an estimated 21% to 83% of depressed youth (Angold & Costello, 1993). In an early paper, Puig-Antich (1982) identified a diagnostic subgroup of children with depression and conduct disorder (roughly one-third of the sample) in a cohort of prepubertal boys clinically referred for treatment for depression. Kovacs, Paulauskas, Gatsonis, and Richards (1988) documented a prevalence rate of 16% for co-occurrence of depression and conduct disorder in their sample of depressed children. However, conduct disorder occurred secondary to depression in children, possibly developing as a complication to the mood disorder. Comorbid disruptive behavior disorders are significant predictors of a more persistent course of psychiatric disorder in children (Goodyer et al., 1997).

Course of Childhood Depression

Longitudinal studies that have tracked clinic and community samples of children across the lifespan have informed our knowledge-base about the course of childhood depression. Long-term follow-up studies of clinic samples of children diagnosed with depression have been important for understanding whether or not childhood depression predicts depression in adolescence and adulthood. Kovacs' groundbreaking studies of childhood depression (Kovacs, Feinberg, Crouse-Novak, Paulauskas, Pollock, et al., 1984; Kovacs, Feinberg, Crouse-Novak, Paulauskas, & Finkelstein, 1984) were among the first to outline the course and correlates of depressive disorders in children, as well as to investigate rates of recovery in children diagnosed with major depression, dysthymia, double depression, and adjustment disorder with depressed mood. In their sample, an earlier age of onset for depression predicted a longer recovery from the initial episode; hence, older children recovered from their depression more rapidly than did younger children. This finding suggested that early-onset depression in children was associated with a more protracted course of the disorder and was a deleterious marker for severe psychiatric outcomes in adolescence and adulthood (more so than later onset of depression in children and early adolescents). These studies demonstrated that depression in children was not a relatively benign and transient problem and suggested the continuity between childhood-onset and depression into adolescence and adulthood.

The Maudsley Hospital studies of early-onset depression in a sample of clinically identified children and adolescents with depression followed these youth into young adulthood to determine whether childhood-onset or adolescent-onset depression was more likely to predict depression in adulthood (Fombonne, Wostear, Cooper, Harrington, & Rutter, 2001a, 2001b; Harrington, Fudge, Rutter, Pickles, & Hill, 1990, 1991; Harrington et al., 1993, 1997). Although both childhood-onset and adolescent-onset groups were at high risk for depression as adults, those diagnosed with depression in childhood did not experience higher rates of depression as adults when compared to nondepressed children or depressed adolescents. Indeed, there was a trend for the adolescent-onset depression group to have an increased likelihood of depression in adulthood. Methodological problems related to the retrospective diagnosing of childhood depression from medical records and the small number of identified cases have complicated the implications from the Maudsley Hospital studies. Nevertheless, these investigations were significant in furthering debate about the discontinuity of early-onset depression and suggesting an etiological distinction between childhood and adolescent-onset depression.

Weissman and colleagues (1999) conducted a follow-up study of Puig-Antich's original sample of children with prepubertal-onset depression (Puig-Antich et al., 1985a, 1985b) when they were young adults. Although they evidenced increased social impairment, psychiatric treatment utilization, and suicide rates compared to controls, individuals who experienced prepubertal depression were generally not at an increased risk for depression in adulthood. Closer examination of the sample revealed heterogeneity in cases based upon comorbidity and family history of depression. A subgroup of children with depression experienced recurrent episodes of depression into adulthood. These cases were more likely to have a family history of depression. A second subgroup, those with childhood-onset depression and conduct disorder, evidenced adult psychiatric outcomes marked by a twofold increased risk for alcohol abuse/dependence and a fourfold increased risk for conduct disorder compared to controls. Childhood cases with depression and comorbid conduct disorder also had a significantly higher rate of antisocial personality disorder than cases with childhood-onset depression alone. Thus results from Weissman et al.'s follow-up study supported earlier findings on the course of childhood-onset depression being moderated by comorbid conduct disorder and family history of depression.

A 10- to 15-year follow-up of Puig-Antich et al.'s (1989) sample of children with prepubertal-onset depression presented additional evidence that childhood-onset depression can be continuous or discontinuous with adult depression based upon family psychiatric history (Wickramaratne, Greenwald, & Weissman, 2000). While the majority of children with prepubertal-onset depression did not have recurrent MDD into adulthood, those children who went on to have recurrent depression had significantly higher rates of MDD in their first-degree relatives than those who did not. That is, the continuity of MDD from childhood to adulthood was associated with a strong family history of MDD. Similar to findings from high-risk studies, these data support the continuity of course for childhood-onset depression in cases where there is significant familial loading for depression.

The handful of prospective longitudinal studies that have tracked the course of depression across different phases of development provide some of the best evidence regarding the course of childhood-onset depression. For example, the Oregon Adolescent Depression Study prospectively assessed a community sample of youths over a 12-year period to identify antecedents, correlates, and course of MDD in children and adolescents (Lewinsohn, Rohde, Seeley, Klein, & Gotlib, 2000; Rohde, Lewinsohn, Klein, Seeley, & Gau, 2013). Their findings suggested a strong degree of continuity for depression across childhood, adolescence, and early adulthood. Incident of childhood depression doubled the risk of experiencing depression in adolescence, and adolescent depression strongly predicted depression in early adulthood. In the Great Smoky Mountains Study, preadolescent girls who met diagnostic criteria for MDD, minor depression, or dysthymia between the ages of 9 and 13 were approximately 20 times more likely to manifest a diagnosis of MDD by age 16 (Copeland, Shanahan, Costello, & Angold, 2009; Costello et al., 1996; Shanahan, Copeland, Costello, & Angold, 2011). Thus these two separate population-based studies provide support for the continuity of childhood-onset depression into adolescence and early adulthood and further the case for the predictive validity of childhood-onset depression.

Other prospective longitudinal studies using community samples of youths have also examined subthreshold symptoms of depression in preadolescent children—elevated depressive symptoms that are not extensive or severe enough to warrant a diagnosis—as predictors of later MDD diagnoses in adolescence and early adulthood. Keenan and colleagues' (2008) study of depressive symptoms in preadolescent girls provides strong evidence for subthreshold symptoms of depression during the preadolescent period predicting a later onset of MDD. Using diagnostic interviews, researchers studied depressive symptoms and depressive disorders in a cohort of preadolescent girls across a three-year period, from ages 9 to 11. Not only did they find a high degree of stability of subthreshold and threshold levels of depressive symptoms in girls during this developmental period; they found that higher depressive symptoms at ages 9 and 10 significantly predicted a nearly twofold increase in risk for a later depressive disorder in these preadolescent girls. In fact, 78% of all girls meeting criteria for minor or major depression at age 11 had at least one depressive symptom at age 9 (Keenan et al., 2008). Other studies have also found that elevated symptoms of depression at earlier developmental periods were strong predictors of a later MDD diagnosis in both children and adolescents (Johnson, Cohen, & Kasen, 2009; Rohde, Beevers, Stice, & O'Neil, 2009; Wesselhoeft, Sorensen, Heiervang, & Bilenberg, 2013). Taken together, these studies support the more continuous course of depression across development, including during the preadolescent period.

Preadolescent Development

Significant developmental changes in physical appearance, cognitive processes, and reciprocal interpersonal relationships occur during the preadolescent period, roughly defined as between the ages of 7 and 12 years. It has been a more highlighted aspect of "middle childhood" over the past decade primarily due to the well-established trend that puberty, particularly in girls, is occurring at earlier ages than in previous generations (Graber, 2013). Pubertal maturation has been associated with an increased interest in and gravitation toward social relationships. During puberty, the human brain undergoes a significant shift in the social, affective, and attentional processes that underlie this increased orientation toward interpersonal relationships (Dahl & Gunnar, 2009; Dorn et al., 2006; Forbes & Dahl, 2010). Brain regions associated with socioaffective processes undergo a period of increased plasticity (Nelson & Guyer, 2011; Nelson, Leibenluft, McClure, & Pine, 2005), specifically those involved in the regulation of social distress, including the amygdala, subgenual cingulate, anterior insula, as well as the ventromedial/ventrolateral and dorsolateral prefrontal cortical regions (Silk et al., 2014). Preadolescents' interpersonal experiences shape and strengthen neural pathways in these regions of the brain associated with social and affective processing. Preadolescents begin to engage in interpersonal relationships that require new and more sophisticated social and problem-solving skills as they develop closer relationships with peers and begin to individuate from their parents.

In both community and clinical samples, more preadolescents are presenting with issues associated with the "storm and stress" once attributed to adolescents. Parent–child conflict may increase during this time, as preadolescents begin to assert independence and experiment with individuating from parents (Steinberg & Silverberg, 1986). Increased sensitivity to peer rejection accompanies this developmental period, and unstable peer relationships can contribute to high levels of interpersonal stress (Connolly, 2000; Degirmenicioglu, 1998).

Why "Preadolescent" Depression?

Depression during the preadolescent period is an increasingly recognized public health concern. Preadolescent depression interferes with normative social and emotional development at a sensitive developmental period that increases the risk for recurrent depression into adolescence (Asarnow et al., 1988; Emslie et al., 1997; Goodyer et al., 1997) and adulthood, particularly when there is a strong family loading for depression (Weissman et al., 1999; Wickramaratne et al., 2000). Marked interpersonal impairment has been associated with depression in preadolescents (Birmaher & Rozel, 2003; Geller, Zimerman, Williams, Bolhofner, & Craney, 2001; Hammen, Rudolph, Weisz, Rao, & Burge, 1999; Hammen & Rudolph, 1996) and appears to be one of the mechanisms for recurrent depression in adolescence and adulthood. Depressed preadolescents experience frequent negative interactions and more distant relationships with parents, as well as more problematic (e.g., teasing) and fewer close peer relationships as compared to nondepressed preadolescents (Puig-Antich et al., 1985a). Unfortunately, depressed preadolescents remain at risk for interpersonal and social impairment even after their symptoms remit (Kovacs, Feinberg, Crouse-Novak, Paulauskas, Pollock, et al., 1984; Puig-Antich et al., 1985b), as they continue to experience significantly more difficulties in interpersonal relationships with parents and peers than do preadolescents with no history of depression. Hence preadolescent depression appears to not only interfere with normative social development during a formative period but also results in residual impairments in preadolescents' interpersonal functioning, which may increase their risk for recurrent depression into adolescence and adulthood.

Family and Interpersonal Risk Factors

Studies of depressed preadolescents and preadolescents at risk for developing depression identify several psychosocial factors that are commonly associated with depression in preadolescent children. Understanding family and interpersonal risk factors that accompany preadolescent depression can inform treatment strategies and may suggest antecedents for future episodes of depression.

Family Risk Factors

Adverse family environments marked by high levels of family discord, conflict, and criticism are more strongly associated with preadolescent depression than with adolescent depression (Fendrich, Warner, & Weissman, 1990; Nomura, Wickramaratne, Warner, Mufson, & Weissman, 2002). Clinical studies of depressed preadolescents revealed that their families were significantly less cohesive and more disengaged compared to the families of nondepressed children (Puig-Antich et al., 1985b). Preadolescent depression is associated with high rates of depressive disorders in parents (Harrington et al., 1990; Weissman et al., 1984). This finding is consistent with studies documenting the increased risk for developing depressive disorders during childhood and adolescence in children of depressed parents (Beardslee, Versage, & Gladstone, 1998; Weissman et al., 1997). Children of depressed parents experience severe and recurrent courses of depression, with high rates of interpersonal impairment and suicide (Beardslee, 1993; Weissman & Klerman, 1992; Weissman et al., 1997). The high rates of parental depression in these preadolescents' families are likely to contribute to negative family processes. Negative family interactions, such as poor parenting behavior and harsh/critical interactions with children, are factors related to parental depression that may increase children's risk for depression (Campbell, Cohn, & Meyers, 1995; Goodman & Gotlib, 1999). When parents are depressed, they may model maladaptive strategies for controlling emotional distress and coping with problems. Preadolescents socialized in these families may develop poor emotional regulation skills and passive coping strategies that place them at higher risk for depressive disorders, complicating their adjustment to loss and life transitions, and creating problems within their interpersonal relationships (Keenan & Hipwell, 2005).

Interpersonal Impairment

Preadolescent depression is associated with impairments in social interactions, poor emotion processing, and difficulties taking the perspective of others in social interactions. These difficulties in interpersonal relationships may precede the onset of preadolescent depression and are consistent with profiles of children of depressed parents. For example, children at high risk for developing depression are more likely than low-risk children to demonstrate heightened negative affect in distress inducing protocols (Forbes, Cohn, Allen, & Lewinsohn, 2004), lower positive affect when engaging in pleasurable tasks (Dietz, Birmaher, et al., 2008; Olino et al., 2011), and difficulties regulating negative emotions (Silk, Shaw, Skuban, Oland, & Kovacs, 2006). High-risk children also demonstrate difficulties correctly identifying emotion in others (Joormann, Gilbert, & Gotlib, 2010; Joormann, Talbot, & Gotlib, 2007) and may demonstrate a bias toward negatively interpreting others' affect and behavior. These difficulties in emotional processing may further impair communication and problem-solving with parents and peers, increasing the preadolescents' experience of conflict in their relationships with others.

Although depression in preadolescents is associated with social withdrawal, anhedonia, and increased sensitivity to rejection, the high rates of comorbid anxiety disorders further complicate depressed preadolescents' interpersonal relationships. Similar to the effects of depression, comorbid anxiety may impair depressed preadolescents' ability to engage in social situations or interpersonal relationships (Allen & Badcock, 2003; Brown & Harris, 1978; Coyne, 1976; Gilbert, 1992). Because preadolescent depression and anxiety often co-occur, it is difficult to distinguish the independent effects each has on social withdrawal and loneliness. However, continued anxiety symptoms may contribute to preadolescents' residual interpersonal impairment in relationships with family members and peers and their ongoing social isolation even after their depressive symptoms remit (Cyranowski, Frank, Young, & Shear, 2000; Leadbeater, Blatt, & Quinlan, 1995; Ruble, Greulich, Pomerantz, & Gochberg, 1993; Rudolph, 2002).

Peer Stressors

Peer exclusion and rejection are consistent predictors of elevated depressive symptoms from middle childhood to early adolescence (Brendgen, Wanner, Morin, & Vitaro, 2005; Hazel, Oppenheimer, Technow, Young, & Hankin, 2014); chronic experiences of peer rejection and peer victimization (e.g., bullying) have been associated with poor mental health outcomes in young adulthood and suicidality (Copeland, Wolke, Angold, & Costello, 2013). These stressful experiences evoke feelings of loneliness and low self-esteem that may intensify depressive symptoms (Joiner, 1997; Joiner, Lewinsohn, & Seeley, 2002) and increase social withdrawal. Rejection sensitivity, anxious expectations of interpersonal rejection (Downey & Feldman, 1996), may increase depressed youths' attention bias to negative affective cues in peer relationships and increase their fear of peer rejection. However, positive parent–child relationships may buffer preadolescents from the stress in peer relationships. In close parent–child relationships, parents actively model effective communication skills and problem-solving strategies (Alloy, Abramson, Smith, Gibb, & Neeren, 2006). The quality of parent–child relationships appears to moderate the effects of peer rejection on preadolescents. For example, preadolescents were more negatively affected by peer rejection when they felt less accepted by their parents and were less sensitive to peer rejection when parental acceptance was high (McLachlan, Zimmer-Gembeck, & McGregor, 2010). Similarly, studies find a stronger relationship between peer stress in middle childhood and depressive symptoms in early adolescence among preadolescents who report poor relationships with their parents (Hazel et al., 2014).

The accessibility and use of technology and social media also present new stressors regarding peer relationships in preadolescents. Since cell phones have become increasingly affordable, accessible, and necessary, the age of first acquisition has been steadily decreasing—a trend that will no doubt continue. Many preadolescents, especially those between the ages of 10 and 12, routinely use cell phones to engage and interact with peers, both individually and in groups. Having a cell phone allows the preadolescents access to social media (e.g., Facebook, Instagram, Snapchat, FaceTime) that provides further opportunities to interact with peers outside of school or extracurricular activities. Peer interactions on social media can be sources of stress for the preadolescent. There are increased opportunities for conflict, oversharing sensitive information, and feeling excluded by peers (e.g., friends posting pictures of a get-together to which the preteen was not invited). Developmentally, preadolescents may be at increased risk for impulsivity when texting/posting pictures and may have trouble disengaging from interacting with peers on social media (e.g., FOMO = fear of missing out). They may also feel pressure to present themselves as older or more sexualized on social media to appear "cool" or garner positive feedback and attention from peers (e.g., Likes, Followers, Friend Requests). Parents differ in their degree of monitoring and in their knowledge of how to monitor their preadolescents' activities on social media. This generation gap can often leave preadolescents with tremendous amounts of freedom in their cyber interactions.

Treatments for Preadolescent Depression

Although there is extensive research on psychosocial treatments for adult and adolescent depression, clinical interventions for preadolescent depression are less studied. At present, the field lacks usable and effective treatments for depressed preadolescents. While there is well-established support for the efficacy of cognitive behavior therapy (CBT) relative to no-treatment control conditions for treating community samples of preadolescents with elevated depressive symptoms (David-Ferdon & Kaslow, 2008), the few studies of depressed preadolescents randomized to either CBT or to an active treatment comparator have found no differences between CBT and relaxation training (Kahn, Kehle, Jenson,

& Clark, 1990) or supportive, nondirected therapy (Vostanis, Feehan, & Grattan, 1998; Vostanis, Feehan, Grattan, & Bickerton, 1996). Two CBT treatment protocols, Taking Action (Stark, Streuand, Krumholz, & al., 2010) and Primary and Secondary Control Enhancement Training (PASCET; Weisz, Thurber, Sweeney, Proffitt, & LeGagnoux, 1997), have demonstrated promise in effectively treating children with elevated depressive symptoms as compared to wait-list control groups, but studies have yet to compare these interventions to active control conditions. However, a recent efficacy trial comparing PASCET and client-centered therapy, a supportive and nondirective treatment that closely approximates the standard of care for pediatric depression in community mental health, in preadolescents with irritable bowel disorder and elevated depressive symptoms found no differences between the two treatment groups on posttreatment outcomes (Szigethy et al., 2014).

Developmental Considerations for Psychosocial Treatments for Depressed Preadolescents

Interventions for preadolescent depression must match therapy tasks to the developmental competencies of preadolescents. There is great heterogeneity in preadolescents' social, emotional, and cognitive development because of the developmental transition from childhood to adolescence. Despite the increased focus on interpersonal relationships, preadolescents still experience less sophisticated cognitive processing than adolescents do, particularly as it relates to metacognition or the awareness of one's own thinking. The equivocal efficacy of CBT protocols for preadolescent depression may highlight the developmental limitations of this treatment model. CBT-based treatments emphasize cognitive restructuring to identify and modify automatic negative thoughts that affect behavior and contribute to depressive symptoms. Because younger children often have difficulties employing these more abstract skills given their developmental competencies, this approach may be less effective when treating depression in younger children. Hence, interventions such as CBT that focus on identifying and restructuring negative automatic thoughts related to depressed mood and vegetative symptoms may be less effective for this age group. Cognitive skills related to success in interpersonal relationships, such as perspective taking, are aspects of intervention that are accessible to preadolescents' developmental stage and consistent with their increasing social motivation. Teaching depressed preadolescents more sophisticated communication skills and problem-solving skills, such as negotiation and compromise, may be helpful to improve relationships with family members and peers both concurrently and after remission of the preadolescents' depressive episode.

Parental Involvement in Treatment of Depressed Preadolescents

A developmentally appropriate treatment for preadolescent depression must focus on the family environment and peer relationships, the two primary interpersonal domains where preadolescents experience stress and support. Preadolescents experiencing stress in their family or peer relationships are vulnerable to disturbances in mood and self-regulation as their age and developmental period leave them firmly entrenched in these interpersonal contexts and less able to create their own social support networks. As children are dependent upon their parents for nurturance, support, and assistance (Hammen et al., 1999), parental involvement in treatment for childhood depression is a critical developmental concern.

- First, parent involvement in preadolescents' treatment allows for a more nuanced understanding of stressors in the family environment that may be contributing to the preteen's mood symptoms. Parental divorce, job loss or change, financial difficulties, the birth/illness/impairment of a sibling, a move to another location, and parental psychopathology affect preadolescents' mood and functioning. However, preadolescents often do not explicitly understand the link between these issues and their depressed mood and symptoms. Routine meetings with parents allow therapists to gain a broader understanding of the preteen's family context and the circumstances or issues that may be contributing to the preadolescent's depression. Therapists can use this information to identify key issues to discuss with the parent and preadolescent, or guide parents in how to best support their preadolescent in negotiating issues with others.

- Second, routinely involving parents in their preadolescent's treatment allows parents to have a good understanding of the focus of their preteen's therapy, enabling them to support their child's practice of new skills and strategies for handling stressors in his relationships. Parents are more likely to support their preadolescent's use of new communication skills or negotiation and problem-solving skills if they understand that their child is practicing what he has learned in therapy. Similarly, parents may also model these skills and strategies in their interactions with their depressed preadolescent. Parental rehearsal of skills may improve parent–child interactions and increase preadolescents' willingness to implement new skills in situations outside of therapy sessions. The therapist's ability to share the new communication and problem-solving skills with parents and to obtain their "buy-in" for trying out these skills at home increases the likelihood of these skills generalizing to the preadolescent's relationships with family members and peers.
- Third, *parents may actually benefit* from learning different ways to communicate with their preadolescents. Hence, strategic parental involvement in the preadolescent's therapy is an opportunity to intervene on both child and parent levels of influence and increase the likelihood of changing dyadic patterns of communication in the family.
- Finally, there may be negative consequences for not involving parents in their preadolescents' treatment. When parents are not involved in the process, they can become confused, disappointed in the efficacy of their child's treatment, and less committed to bringing the child into sessions.

Parental Psychopathology

Involving parents in their preadolescent's therapy allows therapists to informally assess parents for their own current depressive symptoms that may be negatively affecting their interactions with their preteen and discuss the possibility of seeking their own psychiatric treatment. Parents of depressed preadolescents are highly likely to have a history of depression or other psychiatric disorder. As a result, they may model less effective communication and problem-solving strategies in their interactions with their child. Oftentimes, parents' untreated depression and impaired parenting behavior may contribute to family stressors that influence preadolescents' depressive symptoms. Recent studies indicate the benefit of treating parental depression on the long-term improvement of psychiatric symptoms in children (Swartz et al., 2016). Therefore, identifying and supporting depressed parents is a strategy for promoting the mental health and well-being of depressed preadolescents. Although therapists can broach the issue of parental psychopathology and individual treatment without involving parents in their child's treatment, this approach has the potential to increase parents' defensiveness and mistrust of the therapist. In our experience, encouraging parents to pursue their own treatment is most effective when it involves a conversation that progresses over time. Parents may be more willing to consider the therapist's suggestion of pursuing treatment for themselves when they feel that their child's therapist understands the challenges in the family context and can link parental treatment to supporting their preadolescent's well-being. This is possible only if the therapist has a collaborative relationship with parents.

Comorbid Anxiety Disorders

Appropriate interventions for depressed preadolescents must also address the high rates of comorbid anxiety disorders among this age group and the potential for this untreated anxiety to increase social withdrawal and interpersonal avoidance. The effects of social isolation can be detrimental to depressed preadolescents both during and after a depressive episode. Depressed preadolescents who avoid social interactions and have anxiety about initiating peer relationships may have prolonged courses of disorder and miss opportunities to rehearse, practice, and implement any new interpersonal communication and problem-solving skills learned in therapy. In the absence of depressive symptoms, continued social anxiety and interpersonal avoidance may contribute to preadolescents' residual social impairment and social isolation—factors that may increase their risk for recurrent depression in the future. Therefore, a psychosocial intervention for preadolescent depression must address any comorbid social anxiety and work to decrease social withdrawal and reluctance toward initiating with peers.

Early Intervention and Secondary Prevention

The preadolescent period presents a window of opportunity for early psychosocial intervention for depressive disorders and for addressing risk factors associated with recurrence. It is important to address depressive disorders in preadolescents when treatment has the potential to be most successful, when suicide rates are low, and when comorbid substance use disorders are rare. It is also important to treat preadolescents' depressive symptoms prior to early adolescence (ages 13–15), when dramatic increases in rates of depression occur, particularly for girls. Effective clinical intervention for depressed preadolescents could decrease the burden of illness on youth during a sensitive period of social and neural development. Treatments that target preadolescents' interpersonal impairment with parents and peers may also reduce risk for depression recurrence during adolescence. Empirically supported treatments that target poor interpersonal functioning need to be validated for this high-risk group. The area of early psychosocial interventions for preadolescent depression remains open to the development of effective and family-based protocols that provide alternatives to pharmacotherapy and address interpersonal risk factors in preadolescents related to continued courses of depression (Tompson, 2008; Tompson, Boger, & Asarnow, 2012).

Summary

Preadolescent depression is an important public health concern because it is often a "gateway" condition that increases the risk for recurrent depression in adolescence (Asarnow et al., 1988; Emslie et al., 1997; Goodyer et al., 1997) and adulthood, particularly when there is a strong family loading for depression (Weissman et al., 1999; Wickramaratne et al., 2000). Marked interpersonal impairment has been associated with depression in preadolescents (Birmaher & Rozel, 2003; Geller et al., 2001; Hammen et al., 1999; Hammen & Rudolph, 1996) and appears to be one of the mechanisms for recurrent depression in adolescence and adulthood. Depressed preadolescents experience frequent negative interactions and more distant relationships with parents, as well as more problematic (e.g., teasing) and fewer close peer relationships as compared to non-depressed preteens or psychiatric controls (Puig-Antich et al., 1985a). Unfortunately, depressed children remain at risk for interpersonal and social impairment even after their symptoms remit (Kovacs, Feinberg, Crouse-Novak, Paulauskas, Pollock, et al., 1984; Puig-Antich et al., 1985b), as they continue to experience significantly more difficulties in interpersonal relationships with parents and peers than do non-depressed children. Preadolescent depression not only interferes with normative social development at a formative period but also results in residual impairments in preadolescents' interpersonal functioning, which may increase their risk for recurrent depression into adolescence and adulthood. Effective interventions for depression in the preadolescent period that target family and interpersonal risk factors may reduce risk for depression recurrence in adolescence.

CHAPTER 2 IPT and IPT-A

Core Components and Evidence

Interpersonal psychotherapy (IPT) was originally developed by Gerald Klerman and Myrna Weissman as a brief, time-limited psychotherapy intervention for depressed adult outpatients (Weissman, Markowitz, & Klerman, 2007). IPT has its theoretical foundation in the work of John Bowlby, Henry Stack Sullivan, and Adolf Meyer whose writings emphasized the link between the quality of interpersonal relationships and mental health. They highlighted the influence of relationships on mood by identifying the role of insecure attachment and depression (Bowlby, 1978), the role of maladaptive communication in relationships and psychiatric illness (Sullivan, 1953), and the importance of social support for coping with life stressors and understanding interpersonal context to understand psychiatric illness (Meyer, 1957). *The basic tenet of IPT is that depression occurs in the context of interpersonal relationships and there is a bi-directional relationship between mood and relationships. That is, relationships impact mood and mood impacts relationship health. Therefore, the focus of IPT is on reducing the depressive symptoms and improving the state of the client's significant relationships that appear linked to his mood symptoms.*

Research on interpersonal risk factors for depression provides evidence for the strong role interpersonal problems play in the onset and/or maintenance of depression symptoms for both adults and adolescents. In adults, marital distress, reduced social support, social isolation, or excessive need for emotional support from others all have been identified as antecedents to depression (Barnett & Gotlib, 1988; Hames, Hagan, & Joiner, 2013). Individuals with depression often engage in communication that elicits poor responses from others. This cycle of impaired/ineffective communication and poor responses from others often perpetuates depression in adults (Hames et al., 2013; Joiner & Metalsky, 2001). For adolescents, problems with family members and peers increase risk for depression (Hammen & Brennan, 2001; Sheeber, Davis, Leve, Hops, & Tildesley, 2007). In general, a paucity of close relationships seems to be a significant risk factor for adolescent depression as outlined in Bowlby's attachment theory. Within the family domain, relationship problems commonly associated with adolescent depression center around conflictual and unsupportive relationships with parents or other primary caregivers. Increased conflict with parents during this developmental period is a common consequence of adolescents negotiating their individuation from their parents (Sheeber et al., 2007). Depressive symptoms are also associated with adolescents' peer relationship problems. Rejection, peer victimization, and poor communication patterns are all associated with depression in adolescents (Allen et al., 2006; Galambos, Leadbeater, & Barker, 2004; Klomek, Marrocco, Kleinman, Schonfeld, & Gould, 2007; Nolan, Flynn, & Garber, 2003).

IPT: Basic Principles

As delineated in IPT, clinical depression is conceptualized as consisting of three components: (a) symptom formation, (b) social functioning, and (c) personality (Weissman et al., 2007). IPT interventions target symptom formation and social functioning and do not focus as much on making changes in personality, given its short duration. To accomplish the goals of reducing depression and improving interpersonal relationships, the IPT therapist's tasks are to

1. identify a specific focused problem area;
2. identify effective communication and problem-solving techniques to use with the problem area; and
3. practice the skills with the clients in session, and eventually support practice of the skills outside the session, in the context of a focused problem area.

IPT is a time-limited treatment consisting of 16 to 20 sessions in the adult model with three phases of treatment (initial, middle, and termination). The initial phase is focused on assessment of depression symptoms, confirmation of the depression diagnosis, examination of significant interpersonal relationships, and construction of the interpersonal formulation, which includes identification of a problem area for the treatment focus. The four problem areas include grief, role transitions, interpersonal role disputes, and interpersonal deficits. The middle phase of treatment focuses on helping the client develop more effective ways of communicating and problem-solving within the identified problem area. During termination phase, the therapist and client review treatment gains, discuss generalization of strategies to future situations, and assess need for further treatment.

IPT-A

Overview

Interpersonal psychotherapy for depressed adolescents (IPT-A) is a developmental adaptation that is designed to treat adolescents, ages 12–18 years, with depression. It was initially developed to treat major depressive disorder but has been expanded to treat adolescents diagnosed with dysthymic disorder, depression not otherwise specified, and adjustment disorder with depression mood. Depressed adolescents with comorbid anxiety disorders, attention deficit hyperactivity disorder, and oppositional defiant disorder also have been successfully treated with IPT-A, although IPT-A is most effective when depression is the primary diagnosis. IPT-A is not recommended for adolescents who have intellectual disability, active suicidal or homicidal thoughts with a plan and/or intent, psychosis, or bipolar disorder or who are actively abusing substances.

IPT has been selected for use with adolescents based in part on its success with adults and most importantly because the focus on relationships and skills-building seemed to be developmentally relevant for adolescents. Like the adult model, IPT-A is structured, includes a large psychoeducational component, and focuses on using the therapeutic relationship to aid in the acquisition of better interpersonal communication and problem-solving skills. As treatment progresses, the adolescent is encouraged to take an active role in applying new strategies to the identified interpersonal problem area. To ensure progress in a short period of time, the IPT-A therapist identifies both interpersonal strengths and weaknesses of the individual; the therapist focuses on addressing the difficulties while continuing to enhance and generalize the strengths of the individual to additional relationships. The goal is to give adolescents the tools to appropriately increase their independence and negotiate the developmental shifts in dependence on their significant relationships. Thus IPT-A supports the task of individuation and increased autonomy that is so important to adolescents while helping them to maintain supportive family and peer relationships.

Modifications for Use with Adolescents

Although the overall goals and problem areas of IPT-A are the same as the IPT adult model, several modifications have been made to increase the model's relevance for treating depressed adolescents. The interpersonal problem areas in IPT-A have been modified to take into account developmental tasks including individuation, establishment of autonomy, development of romantic relationships, coping with initial experiences of death and loss, and managing peer pressure. The problem area of role transitions incorporates a specific discussion about transitions that are due to family structural change (e.g., divorce, separation, remarriage) for adolescents because these are common and present specific challenges adolescents. The model addresses the interpersonal challenges and difficulties that are associated with such family transitions and its demonstrated link to depressive symptoms (Mufson, Dorta, et al., 2004). The techniques used in IPT with depressed adults also have been modified to use with adolescents. To assist with mood monitoring, therapists teach the adolescents to rate their mood on a scale from 1 to 10 which makes it easier for them to monitor improvement and to link fluctuations in their mood with events in their relationships. In addition, the therapist helps adolescents to develop new social skills, including perspective-taking, to facilitate the identification of new solutions to problems, and skills for negotiating differences in relationship expectations. Lastly, the treatment has been modified to address special issues that arise in the treatment of adolescents specifically, such as school refusal, physical or sexual abuse, suicidality, and involvement of a child protective service agency.

A second necessary adaptation for the treatment of adolescents is the addition of a parent/guardian component to the treatment protocol. While IPT-A is largely an individual treatment, a parent or guardian is primarily involved to support the adolescent's engagement in treatment. In some cases, parents are directly involved in the work of the treatment. The optimal goal is to involve the parent in all three phases of treatment although the IPT-A allows for parent involvement in treatment to be flexible. At a minimum, however, the therapist ensures parental involvement in the initial phase of treatment. At this time, parents receive education about their teen's depressive disorder, ideas about how parents can be involved in treatment, and input on how they can support the adolescent's engagement in treatment. The parent may also be involved in the middle phase to work on specific relationship strategies determined by the identified problem area. During the middle phase, parents may attend a dyadic session to provide opportunities to practice learned skills with helpful coaching from the therapist or they may have their own session with the therapist to receive additional support and psychoeducation about adolescent depression and the IPT-A treatment model. Lastly, it is desirable for the parent or guardian to attend a final session to review the adolescent's progress in treatment, ways to identify signs of relapse or recurrence, strategies for managing potential recurrence, and future treatment needs (Mufson, Dorta, et al., 2004). Nonattendance is strongly discouraged but is sometimes necessary depending on the family's circumstances.

IPT-A is designed to be a once-a-week psychotherapy delivered over the course of 12 weeks; however, the session frequency can be increased or decreased as necessary in the event of a crisis situation or during a summer vacation. If a therapist is concerned about an adolescent's stability, it is possible to add extra sessions so the adolescent can be seen more frequently than once a week or extend weekly treatment beyond 12 weeks. The crucial element, however, is keeping the treatment time-limited and not open-ended. The therapist and the adolescent must clearly discuss and agree to the revised treatment contract.

Similar to IPT, a course of IPT-A is divided into three phases: initial, middle, and termination. Throughout treatment, each session may begin casually by asking how the past week has been, giving the adolescent a chance to report on her week and to provide the therapist with a snapshot of her mood. This is followed by a review of depression symptoms including suicidality and the adolescent rating her mood using the 1 to 10 scale (10 = most depressed). Best and worst ratings in mood are linked to the accompanying interpersonal events. Symptom review and mood monitoring are followed by tasks specific to the adolescent's current phase of treatment.

Initial Phase (Sessions 1–4)

IPT-A treatment is best initiated after the completion of a diagnostic evaluation to obtain information on current symptoms; previous diagnoses; and family, developmental, medical, social, and academic functioning (Mufson, Dorta, et al., 2004). Nonetheless, the therapist should do his or her own thorough review of symptoms in the first session—both to confirm the diagnosis and to use the review as the basis to educate the adolescent and family about the syndrome of depression.

Psychoeducation about Depression

Educating the adolescent and parent about the nature of depression, its associated symptoms and impact on functioning is very important since many families do not realize that the observed behaviors are part of a medical illness. Parent involvement in this phase of treatment is important. Specifically, parents often do not realize that irritability, decline in academic performance and the accompanying difficulties with concentration, motivation, and fatigue may be a function of the depression and not simply bad behavior by their teen. *Putting depression in the context of a medical illness removes the blame from the adolescent for the negative behaviors and places it on the depression.* It also provides an opportunity to discuss the variety of approaches for treating depression and express optimism that depressive symptoms will improve with treatment.

As part of the educational component, the IPT-A therapist explains to the adolescent and parent the idea of the *limited sick role* in a depression illness. The limited sick role refers to the idea that, since depression is a medical illness, it affects functioning in a similar way to other medical illnesses like pneumonia. When a person is sick, it is difficult to for her to complete regular activities as competently as when she is healthy. Furthermore, being sick decreases one's motivation to do regular activities and to fulfill one's responsibilities. However, giving in to those feelings of low motivation and fatigue and avoiding routine activities and responsibilities can actually make one's depression worse. For example, missing school and neglecting responsibilities at home may cause additional distress for adolescents as they may fall behind in their schoolwork and have increased conflict with family members in the home environment. Thus the therapist explains that the goal of the limited sick role is to encourage the adolescent to engage in as many of her usual activities as possible while being aware that her level of performance may be worse than when she is healthy. The therapist also explains that this is time limited, and that her motivation and performance in activities will improve as the depression improves. This is a very important concept for the parents to understand so that they can be supportive of their adolescent's current struggle with depression and encourage efforts to engage in routine activities without criticizing the quality of their teen's performance and outcomes.

Another aspect of psychoeducation is outlining the main principals and structure of IPT-A to the adolescent and family. The therapist explains that the underlying premise for IPT-A is that depression occurs within an interpersonal context and there is a reciprocal effect between our mood and the quality of our relationships. How we feel impacts our relationships, and problems in our relationships affect our mood, regardless of what initially caused the depression. With this in mind, the therapist focuses the treatment on identifying the relationship(s) most closely linked to the depression and then teaches communication and interpersonal problem-solving skills to improve the adolescent's relationships. Increased support and less conflict in significant relationships often lead to a reduction in the teen's depressive symptoms.

Conduct the Interpersonal Inventory

The main therapist task for the initial phase of treatment is to conduct the interpersonal inventory. The interpersonal inventory refers to an exploration of the adolescent's significant relationships to identify the interpersonal issues that are most closely related to her depression. To help in identifying the significant relationships, the therapist uses a closeness circle to visually depict the relationships and the adolescent's perception of attachment to the significant people included. A closeness circle is a series of four concentric circles that resembles a bull's-eye. The adolescent's name is placed in the innermost circle and the names of the people in the adolescent's life are placed in the outer circles according to the perceived closeness of their relationship, with those to whom the adolescent feels closest in the innermost circles. The therapist should help the adolescent understand that one can feel close to a person even if there is conflict. Once completed, the therapist asks the adolescent to identify four or five people on the circle who have the greatest impact on her mood (both positive and negative) and thus are most important to discuss. As part of the clinical inquiry about each relationship, the therapist should obtain information about the frequency and quality of the interactions, the expectations for the relationship, what the teen enjoys about the relationship, what about the relationship may be contributing to her low mood, and changes the adolescent would like to make in the relationship (Mufson, Pollack Dorta, Moreau, & Weissman, 2004).

Identify the Interpersonal Problem Area(s)

The interpersonal inventory culminates in the therapist's identification of an interpersonal problem area that will be the focus of the remainder of treatment. As part of the problem area formulation, the therapist links the depressive symptoms to interpersonal themes or relationship patterns revealed during the inventory. In a collaborative discussion with the adolescent, the therapist identifies common themes or problems in the adolescent's relationships and selects one of four interpersonal problem areas to be the focus of treatment:

- grief due to death,
- interpersonal role disputes,

- interpersonal role transitions, or
- interpersonal deficits.

Generally, one main interpersonal problem area is identified; however, it is possible also to identify a secondary and related problem area.

Grief

Grief is identified as the problem area when an adolescent reports that current mood symptoms are associated with the death of a loved one. It is important to note that the adolescent's loss could be recent and part of a normal grief reaction or it could be a past loss that is having an impact on current functioning due to a delayed or chronic grief reaction. The therapist's goal is either to help the adolescent experience a normal mourning process or to facilitate resolution of a delayed grief reaction. Integral to both of these goals is helping the adolescent to improve and/or develop other relationships that can provide the social and emotional support that has been missing since the death of this significant person in the adolescent's life (Mufson, Pollack Dorta, et al., 2004).

Interpersonal role disputes

An interpersonal role dispute refers to the conflict that arises in a relationship when the adolescent has different expectations for the relationship with an important person in her life. The conflict often centers on differing views regarding autonomy, sexuality, family responsibility, and values. In IPT-A, interpersonal role dispute is selected as the problem area when the adolescent's depression is most closely linked to conflictual interactions surrounding parents/peers differing views on the adolescent's role within a significant relationship. The avoidance of conflict in the relationships, characterized by social withdrawal and lack of communication, is another form of interpersonal role disputes wherein communication about the conflict is at an impasse. The therapist identifies skills that would help the adolescent to resolve the dispute and to cope with any limitations that cannot be addressed by modifying their expectations for the relationship (Mufson, Pollack Dorta, et al., 2004).

Interpersonal role transitions

An interpersonal role transition occurs when there is a change in an individual's life circumstances or routine that requires her to alter her behavior to adapt to a new role. With adolescents, role transitions may be biologically determined (transitioning into puberty) or a result of social and cultural practices (transitioning from middle school to high school). In addition, adolescents may experience unexpected changes that require them to take on new social roles, such as a change in family structure due to parents' separation or divorce. These situations often result in some distress, as the adolescent may miss the old, preferred role. When a role transition is unexpected or undesired or requires a new skill set, an adolescent may develop symptoms of depression in response to feeling psychologically or emotionally unprepared for the new challenges presented by the role transition. Feelings of depression and its associated symptoms of irritability and low motivation may in turn decrease the adolescent's ability to successfully negotiate a role transition. The goal of IPT-A in working with adolescents struggling with a transition is to help them mourn the loss of the old role, identify skills that would be helpful in the new role, and develop these skills through role-playing within the session and practice outside of the session (Mufson, Pollack Dorta, et al., 2004).

Interpersonal deficits

Interpersonal deficits refer to underdeveloped social and communication skills that impair the adolescent's ability to have positive relationships. While many depressed adolescents suffer from deficits in certain types of communication and social skills, they still maintain a network of social relationships. However, some depressed adolescents are unable to maintain their social support network for various reasons and have few close relationships. The interpersonal deficits problem area refers to the social isolation and loneliness experienced by many adolescents who are suffering from depression. The social isolation can be a result of the depression, can be helping to maintain the depression, or could be a trigger for the depression. Deficits may include difficulty initiating or maintaining relationships, verbally expressing one's feelings or needs effectively, or effectively eliciting information from others to establish constructive communication. Adolescents who report a paucity of relationships as the root of their depression (visually depicted by few people on their closeness circle) and report a pattern of struggles with maintaining strong relationships are those adolescents whose problem area would be identified as interpersonal deficits. The goal of treatment is to help these teens to improve or develop the interpersonal skills needed to have more satisfying relationships and reduce social isolation (Mufson, Pollack Dorta, et al., 2004).

Treatment Contract

After coming to a consensus on the identified problem area, the adolescent and therapist make a verbal treatment contract regarding each person's responsibilities in treatment and the practical details of the treatment. The therapist explains to the adolescent that it is her responsibility to bring in relevant information about relationships and interactions that occur each week so they can examine them and identify ways to improve the adolescent's relationships. While the therapist is predominantly working with the adolescent alone, the therapist reminds the adolescent that there may be times when it would be helpful for a parent to join the session to address certain interpersonal interactions related to the identified problem area. The therapist and adolescent decide together if and when the parent will be included in future sessions and, if so, discuss how to share important aspects about treatment without jeopardizing the adolescent's confidentiality. (See Chapter 4 for a more detailed discussion of confidentiality when involving parents in their child's treatment.) Lastly, the therapist reminds the adolescent of the importance of regular and on-time session attendance so that they can make the most progress possible in treatment.

Middle Phase (Sessions 5–9)

During the middle phase of treatment, the therapist and adolescent begin to work directly on the identified interpersonal problem area(s). The main tasks of this phase are to further elucidate the interpersonal challenges, identify effective strategies for managing the problem, practice more effective communication strategies within the sessions, and promote implementation of these strategies in interactions outside of the sessions. While some of the therapeutic techniques used during this phase of treatment are more frequently used with a specific problem area(s), most of them are used across problem areas. When beginning to practice the strategies, it is recommended that the IPT-A therapist apply them to an interpersonal issue that is relatively straightforward and has a high likelihood of success for the adolescent. This successful experience instills the hope that the teen will have successful outcomes in the future and the belief that developing these skills will facilitate changes in her relationships and subsequently improve her mood.

General Techniques

Encouragement of affect and linkage with interpersonal events

Throughout all three phases of treatment, the therapist works to encourage the adolescent's effective expression of affect and to increase awareness of what types of interpersonal events and relationships are linked to positive emotions and which are more closely linked to negative emotions. The goal is to help the adolescent better understand how emotions can impact relationships and how the quality of a relationship can affect mood. Some adolescents struggle to link their intense emotions to a particular event and others struggle to talk about their feelings. Helping adolescents to link interpersonal events with their mood allows for a deeper examination of the impact of relationships on the adolescent's feeling states.

Communication analysis

Communication analysis (CA) refers to the close examination of a conversation, communication, or argument that is linked to increased depressive symptoms. The goal of CA is to identify places where the adolescent could have expressed her feelings to another person differently which in turn might have led to a different outcome and a different emotional experience in the adolescent. Communication analysis is used to explore the teen's patterns of interacting with others and to identify problematic communication styles. Once identified, the IPT-A therapist helps the adolescent learn more effective communication skills that may assist the adolescent in having more satisfying relationships. When conducting a CA, the therapist asks the adolescent to describe a recent interpersonal event in great detail, almost as though watching the interaction on video. The therapist facilitates the CA by asking the adolescent questions, such as "How did the discussion start?", "When and where did it take place?", "What exactly did you say?", "What did the other person say back?", "Then what happened?", "How did that make you feel?", "How do you think it made the other person feel?", "Is that the outcome you wanted?" This process enables the therapist to illustrate for the teen the impact of her specific words on others, the feelings that arise during the interactions, and the messages she conveys verbally and nonverbally. This is followed by a discussion of how the adolescent might conduct the interaction differently, which could result in a better emotional experience. Specific communication skills, outlined in the Teen Tips, are taught to help adolescents communicate more effectively (Mufson, Pollack Dorta, et al., 2004). Teen tips include

1. *Aim for the right timing* to have a conversation when both parties will be receptive and *strike while the iron is cold,* which means have the conversation when one is not angry and more likely to say something unhelpful;
2. *Give to get,* which refers to starting a conversation with a statement expressing empathy and validation by acknowledging the other person's perspective in the situation;
3. *I statements* to start a conversation and directly communicate one's own feelings about a situation ("I feel sad or upset when . . .") to avoid blaming the other person;
4. *Have a few solutions in mind,* which emphasizes the importance of compromise and considering several options to resolve a conflict; and
5. *Don't give up* after one attempt to interact differently since changing interpersonal patterns take time and repeated efforts achieve lasting change.

Decision analysis

Decision analysis refers to steps in problem-solving similar to techniques that are used in other models of therapy, but here the focus is on applying problem solving techniques to interpersonal issues. The therapist teaches the adolescent to identify a specific problem that may be causing the negative mood, generate a list of possible solutions to the problem, evaluate the pros and cons of each solution, and select one solution to implement. The therapist and teen then practice a conversation in which the adolescent presents the solution to the other person in the relationship and then negotiates an agreement on the solution. A decision analysis may arise out of a communication analysis, which often identifies an issue that needs to be resolved through discussion. Once the adolescent has tried to implement the solution, the therapist and adolescent evaluate the outcome and determine if an alternative strategy or a different approach is needed.

Role-playing

Role-playing is a crucial technique in IPT-A because it promotes the practice and acquisition of both communication and interpersonal problem-solving skills needed to improve the adolescent's relationships. This requires the therapist to go beyond just a discussion of what the conversation might sound like to actually acting out the different roles with the adolescent. Playing both roles in the interaction may help the teen gain a better understanding of the other person's perspective and gives the therapist an expanded understanding of the adolescent's experience of the other person. It is important that the therapist and the teen explore both positive and negative outcomes of the interaction to make certain the adolescent feels prepared to implement these communication or problem-solving strategies on her own.

Adult Studies

There is strong empirical support for the efficacy of IPT in treating depression in adults (van Hees, Rotter, Ellermann, & Evers, 2013). Meta-analyses of randomized trials of psychotherapy for depression conclude that IPT works as well as other psychotherapies for treating major depression (Cuijpers et al., 2011; Cuijpers, van Straten, van Oppen, & Andersson, 2008; Jakobsen, Hansen, Simonsen, Simonsen, & Gluud, 2012). There is also good evidence that IPT can be beneficial in preventing recurrent episodes of depression in adults who have recovered from depression (Frank et al., 1990, 2007). IPT also has been shown to be an effective treatment in combination with pharmacotherapy (Cuijpers, van Straten, Warmerdam, & Andersson, 2009). A recent meta-analysis of IPT for mental health problems similarly concluded that IPT is effective in the acute treatment of depression (Cuijpers, Donker, Weissman, Ravitz, & Cristea, 2016). This strong evidence base was the foundation for adapting IPT for adolescents with depression and studying its efficacy.

Adolescent Studies

Since the initial adaptation IPT-A in 1991, there has been a growing body of evidence for its use in treating adolescents with depression. Efficacy and effectiveness studies have been conducted by several distinct research groups demonstrating that IPT-A is more efficacious than treatment as usual (TAU), clinical monitoring, and waitlist, and as efficacious as cognitive-behavioral therapy (CBT; Mufson, Dorta, et al., 2004; Mufson, Weissman, Moreau, & Garfinkel, 1999; O'Shea, Spence, & Donovan, 2015; Rossello & Bernal, 1999; Rossello, Bernal, & Rivera-Medina, 2008). In our initial efficacy study (Mufson et al., 1999) treatment with 12-weeks of individual IPT-A was compared to clinical monitoring (a maximum of two 30-minute meetings with a supportive therapist each month) in a randomized clinical trial of 48 clinic-referred adolescents who met criteria for major depressive disorder. The adolescents were largely female, Hispanic, and of low socioeconomic status. Adolescents who received IPT-A had significantly higher rates (75%) of recovery at week 12 (Hamilton Rating Scale for Depression [HRSD] < 6) than the control condition (46%) with average effect size of 0.54. Scores on both the Beck Depression Inventory and HRSD were lower at week 12 (after controlling for baselines scores) for IPT-A compared to the clinical monitoring. In addition, adolescents who received IPT-A reported significantly greater improvement in social functioning at week 12 while controlling for baseline scores than those in the control condition. The adolescents who received IPT-A also reported greater improvement in Positive Problem-solving Orientation and Rational Problem-solving scales on the Interpersonal Problem-solving Inventory than those in the clinical monitoring group at week 12, while no differences were found on the other subscales.

Another research group in Puerto Rico also has conducted studies of IPT with adolescents who are depressed, using their own adaptation of the original IPT manual (Klerman, Weissman, Rounsaville, & Chevron, 1984). In their efficacy study (Rossello & Bernal, 1999), 71 adolescents with depression (54% female, 12–17 years) were randomly assigned to three conditions: 12 weeks of IPT, 12 weeks of CBT, or waitlist. Both IPT and CBT were superior to waitlist in the reduction of depressive symptoms measured by the Children's Depression Inventory (CDI). Based on the CDI scores, the effect size of IPT compared to waitlist was 0.73, and 0.43 for CBT compared to waitlist. Using a score of ≤ 17 on the CDI, 82% of those who received IPT and 59% of those who received CBT returned to "functional" status at week 12. Adolescents who received IPT evidenced significant improvement on self-esteem and social adaptation compared to those in the waitlist group, unlike adolescents who received CBT who were not significantly different from the waitlist group in these outcomes. There were no significant differences between CBT and IPT at three-month follow up. Rossello and colleagues (2008) conducted an additional efficacy study of IPT-A, comparing group IPT-A with individual IPT-A, individual CBT, and group CBT. One hundred twelve adolescents with depression (12–18 years, 55% female; 100% Hispanic) were randomized to one of the four treatment conditions and received 12 weeks of treatment. Individual therapy consisted of once-a-week sessions for one hour, and group therapy met once per week for two hours. Adolescents reported significant decreases in depressive symptoms in each of the four conditions. Looking at the treatment approaches across both individual and group modalities, analyses of clinical significance suggested that 62% of the participants in CBT and 57% in IPT were functioning in the nonclinical range of depression at posttreatment. The results suggested that there was little difference in overall efficacy between group and individual treatment formats within treatment approaches (Rossello et al., 2008).

Clinical studies on IPT-A also have been conducted by a group of researchers in Australia. In a study comparing individual IPT-A with a group IPT-A format among 39 adolescents (85% female, 13–19 years) who were diagnosed with major depressive disorder (O'Shea et al., 2015), adolescents in both IPT-A conditions reported significant decreases in depressive and anxious symptoms and increases in overall functioning that were maintained at the 12-month follow-up. Those adolescents who showed greater decreases in depressive symptoms were identified as also showing greater increases in social skills and greater improvement in quality of parent–child relationships and attachment style compared to those adolescents who did not report as much improvement in depressive symptoms (O'Shea et al., 2015). These findings provide preliminary evidence for changes in interpersonal functioning as the mechanism for change in depressive symptoms, although research with larger samples is needed to more formally examine potential mediating relationships.

Mufson, Dorta, and colleagues (2004) completed an effectiveness study of IPT-A as delivered by non-research therapists in a community setting. In this study, treatment with IPT-A was compared to TAU in school-based mental health clinics for adolescents with depression to examine whether IPT-A could be equally as beneficial when delivered in a school-based clinic setting. In this study, 64 adolescents (84% female, 71% Hispanic, 12–18 years) who met study inclusion criteria (HRSD score of > 10, Children's Global Assessment Scale [C-GAS] score of ≤ 65, and a diagnosis of adjustment disorder with depressed mood, depression disorder not otherwise specified, major depression, or dysthymia) were enrolled. They were randomized to IPT-A (12 sessions over a 12- to 16-week period) delivered by school-based clinic mental health clinicians (N = 7) trained and supervised in IPT-A by treatment experts or TAU delivered by school-based clinic mental health counselors ($N = 6$) providing individual supportive psychotherapy. At week 12, adolescents in IPT-A reported significantly greater decreases in depressive symptoms than those in TAU with an average effect size of 0.50 for IPT-A over TAU. Fifty percent of those in IPT-A and 34% of those in TAU met the HRSD recovery criteria of ≤ 6. Results in global and social functioning were consistent: Adolescents in IPT-A experienced significantly greater overall improvement in functioning as measured by the C-GAS and the Social Adjustment Scale–Self-report than those in TAU at week 12. IPT-A was more effective compared to TAU in older (15–18 years) and more severely depressed adolescents. Adolescents with depression and comorbid anxiety had a better post-treatment outcomes when receiving IPT-A than TAU (Young, Mufson, & Davies, 2006) as did adolescents with high levels of parent–adolescent conflict (Gunlicks-Stoessel, Mufson, Jekal, & Turner, 2010). While those in IPT-A received more therapy hours than those in TAU, a difference in treatment dose was not responsible for the significant differences in depression outcome among the two conditions (Mufson, Dorta, et al., 2004).

This study provided the first evidence that IPT-A could be disseminated to community settings. It highlighted the ability to effectively teach IPT-A to school social workers using a fairly low-intensity training program (i.e., reading the IPT-A manual, one day of didactics, and weekly supervision). IPT-A has been adapted as a preventive intervention for adolescents at risk for depression to be delivered in the school setting as well (Young et al., 2016).

Summary

Although there are fewer studies of IPT-A than CBT for treating adolescents with depression, the IPT-A studies have resulted in moderate to moderately large effect sizes, ranging from .50 to .73, demonstrating its effectiveness in improving depression and overall functioning compared to clinical monitoring, waitlist, and TAU (Mufson, Dorta, et al., 2004; Mufson et al., 1999; Rossello & Bernal, 1999; Rossello et al., 2008; Spence, O'Shea, & Donovan, 2016). The IPT-A effect sizes are comparable to other empirically supported treatments for depression in adolescents, such as CBT, with the exception of one CBT treatment that involved parents (Weisz, McCarty, & Valeri, 2006). The evidence base would be strengthened by additional studies conducted with larger, more ethnically and gender-diverse populations, with long-term follow-up to assess the durability of the effects of IPT-A, as well as studies that examine the use of medication in combination with IPT-A and that enable examination of mediators and moderators of outcomes.

CHAPTER 3 Developmental Adaptations for FB-IPT for Depressed Preadolescents

Family-based interpersonal psychotherapy for depressed preadolescents (FB-IPT) is a promising psychosocial treatment for preadolescent depression developed as part of a research program on preadolescent depression (Dietz, Mufson, Irvine, & Brent, 2008; Dietz, Weinberg, Brent, & Mufson, 2015). FB-IPT is conceptually rooted in an interpersonal model of depression (Klerman et al., 1984; Mufson, Pollack Dorta, Moreau, & Weissman, 2004) and in developmental research on the antecedents of depression in youth. FB-IPT focuses on improving two domains of interpersonal impairment in depressed preadolescents—parent–child conflict and peer impairment—as a means to decrease preadolescents' depressive symptoms. We focus on improving communication and problem-solving skills in the parent–child relationship (the primary context for children's social and emotional development) to model effective interpersonal behavior with peers and to improve the quality of the parent–child relationship. The belief is that strong interpersonal skills and supportive relationships with family members and friends may buffer preadolescents from the effects of stress that may trigger depressive symptoms.

Developmental Modifications

FB-IPT includes several developmental modifications for 7 to 12-year-olds:

1. increased parental involvement and structured dyadic sessions,
2. an increased focus on developmental transitions,
3. visual representations of the mood ratings and communication analysis, and
4. an increased focus on comorbid anxiety.

Increased Parental Involvement and Structured Dyadic Sessions

FB-IPT actively involves parents in both conjoint and dyadic sessions with preadolescents during the different phases of treatment. For the initial phase of treatment (Sessions 1–5), therapists meet individually with the preadolescent (20 minutes) and then meet with the parent (20 minutes). Individual meetings with parents address psychoeducation about preadolescent depression, challenges in parenting their depressed preadolescent, and appropriate expectations for their child's behavior and performance at this time. Parental depression, marital conflict, and other concerns parents wish to share with the therapist are also discussed in these sessions; parents seeking their own psychiatric treatment are provided with referrals.

In FB-IPT, the limited sick role is a primary theme for conjoint sessions with parents during the initial phase of treatment (Sessions 1–5). As explained in Chapter 2, the goal of the limited sick role is to put the blame for the preadolescent's problems in functioning and behavior on depression, a medical illness. At the same time, the therapist encourages the parents to support the preadolescent in trying to engage in as many of his normal activities as possible with expectations that his performance in these activities may be less than his best. The expanded limited sick role focuses on the challenges in parenting a depressed preadolescent and is personalized to the specific struggles within a parent–child dyad. The limited sick role consists of ongoing psychoeducation with parents; direction for parents struggling with their expectations for their depressed preadolescent's performance across contexts; and parenting strategies for responding to their child's increased irritability, anergia, and/or social withdrawal. We have developed a complementary set of Parent Tips to guide parents to interact with their depressed preadolescents in ways that reduce negative emotionality and parent–child escalation (see Appendix D: Parent Tips and Box 3.1: Description of Parent Tips).

During the middle phase of FB-IPT (Sessions 6–11), therapists meet individually with the preadolescent (20 minutes) and then invite the parent to join the session (20 minutes). Introducing and role-playing communication skills and problem-solving strategies is a central feature in the middle phase of treatment. As noted in Chapter 2, IPT-A outlines several skills, known as "Teen Tips," that increase effective communication

BOX 3.1 Description of Parent Tips

- "Strike While the Iron's Cold": This tip reminds parents that it is better to approach the preadolescent with a request or to have a discussion when the parent is not experiencing strong negative emotions, such as anger. Trying to communicate with the preteen when parents' emotions are "hot" often leads to conflict or saying things that they later regret. In this case, keeping one's "cool" and then having a conversation is a better strategy.
- "Consider the Intention, Not the Outcome": This tip reminds parents to adhere to reasonable expectations for the depressed preadolescent's performance in school, at home, and in other activities, as outlined in the limited sick role. This parenting tip allows parents to focus more on the effort made by the preadolescent to adhere to his essential daily routine than on the outcome.
- "Kind and Firm (Find the Balance)": This tip reminds parents that preteens need both empathy and structure in order to recover from depression. Kindness and support from parents allow preadolescents to explore their feelings and attempt to use new communications skills at home. Structure and setting clear expectations about the essential activities in which they need to participate can help preadolescents maintain daily routines despite their depression. This parenting tip also allows you to help parents make modifications in their reactions to the depressed preteen in order to find the right balance of support and structure.
- "Put on Your Own Oxygen Mask First": This tip reminds parents that they need to attend to their own self-care and mental health needs in order to support their depressed preadolescent. This parenting tip allows you to talk with parents about how they are coping with their preadolescent's diagnosis and impairment across contexts. For parents who are also struggling with mental health issues, it provides an opportunity to talk about pursuing treatment for themselves in order to better support their preteen.

of emotion in depressed adolescents. For FB-IPT, these tips have been streamlined and simplified for use with preadolescents who often present with less sophisticated abstract reasoning and perspective taking skills (see Appendix E: Tween Tips and Box 3.2: Description of Tween Tips).

The Tween Tips often are presented as directives for effective communication in interactions with parents and peers ("Use Good Timing" or "Make 'I Feel' Statements"). Similarly, aspects of problem-solving have been expanded into more specific guidelines for how preadolescents can use compromise ("Meet in the Middle") or negotiation ("Let's Make a

BOX 3.2 Description of Tween Tips

- "Use Good Timing": This tip reminds preadolescents that picking the right time to have a conversation or make a request of a parent or peer is important in determining how successful that communication will be. Approaching someone who is busy, stressed, angry, or distracted often results in negative outcomes. Similarly, the preadolescent is less likely to be effective in his communication when he is angry, agitated, or distressed. Timing is everything!
- "Give to Get": This tip reminds preadolescents of the importance of expressing an understanding of another's perspective or concerns on an issue before expressing their own. By demonstrating that they understand their parent or peers, preadolescents increase the likelihood that others will be open to hearing their perspective or request.
- "Make 'I Feel' Statements": This tip reminds preadolescents to directly communicate their feelings about situations or interactions with another person. In this way, the preadolescent helps others understand his emotional state or concerns and may help with problem-solving. By talking about and taking responsibility for their own feelings, preadolescents are less likely to experience conflict with a parent or peer.
- "Have a Few Solutions in Mind": This tip reminds preadolescents to identify problems and possible solutions when they approach parents or peers with concerns. We identify two strategies that may be helpful for this age group to consider when coming up with solutions to problems:
- "Meet in the Middle": This strategy reminds preadolescents that some problems can be resolved with compromise, wherein each person gives a little of what the other wants, resulting in a solution that is satisfactory to both.
- "Let's Make a Deal": This strategy reminds preteens to negotiate as a way to resolve a dispute by offering to do something that would help a parent or peer be able or willing to reciprocate.

Deal"). Interactions using communication and problem-solving skills are scripted and role-played during individual meetings with preadolescents. Parents learn the same skills as their children in dyadic meetings, with the therapist assisting parents in practicing different Tween Tips in role-plays with their preadolescents.

In the termination phase (Sessions 12–14), therapists meet individually with preadolescents (20 minutes) and then with the parent–child dyad (20 minutes) to consolidate skills, discuss prevention strategies, and discuss when to seek treatment if depression recurs.

Increased Focus on Developmental Transitions

One of the identified problem areas in IPT-A concerns role transitions, the process by which adolescents recognize how changes in circumstances (i.e., move to new school, parental divorce/remarriage, blended family) necessitate changes in behavior in order to meet new challenges and responsibilities that come with the new role. Inherent to IPT is the understanding that physical processes, such as puberty and pregnancy, and developmental transitions, such as graduation from high school/ college and retirement, also present role transitions that may contribute to an increase in depressive symptoms. When identifying a problem area and discussing the onset of depression in preadolescents, FB-IPT therapists often highlight the stress associated with the developmental period of preadolescence—moving from childhood into adolescence. Common role transitions seen in preadolescents include the experience of moving from elementary to middle school and the beginning of physical changes associated with puberty.

Preadolescents also experience changes in peer relationships. During this time, preadolescents become increasingly autonomous in establishing friendships, which become more selective and based on shared interests and intimacy, as opposed to proximity. Preadolescents' peer relationships become increasingly important to them, and there are increased expectations for more skilled behavior in friendships. Bullying peaks during this period, and the consequences of peer rejection and exclusion are particularly difficult for preadolescents (Lereya, Copeland, Costello, & Wolke, 2015). Acceptance by friends becomes increasingly important for preadolescents' emotional well-being, and often they need to learn more mature interpersonal skills for communicating their feelings and managing conflict. Despite being increasingly autonomous in their school activities and with peers, preadolescents remain firmly embedded in their families and require parents' permission for most things they wish to do. A preadolescent's struggle with emerging independence and dependence on parents often results in increased conflict with family members.

FB-IPT therapists emphasize that learning new and more effective strategies for communicating and problem-solving can improve preadolescents' experience of developmental transitions, such as entering middle school or coping with more complex friendships. In highlighting these changes, FB-IPT allows for the possibility that both preadolescents *and* parents need a new set of strategies and behaviors to navigate successfully the new challenges inherent in the preadolescent period.

Visual Presentation of Mood Rating Scale, Communication Analysis, and Communication Skills

FB-IPT relies heavily on visual materials to help preadolescents at different cognitive levels to synthesize and integrate different types of information (event information, affective responses, perspective taking) for later problem-solving. Preadolescents learn to track changes in their mood using a "mood thermometer," which is a 1 to 10 rating scale anchored at three points with emotional faces or "emojis" (see Appendix A). Communication analysis (see Chapter 2) is mapped out on paper to help depressed preadolescents identify events in recent interactions and their affective consequences (see the Depression Circle in Appendix F). Communication skills (see the Tween Tips in Appendix E) are presented sequentially in the middle phase of treatment, accompanied by visual reminders of these communication strategies for rehearsal outside of therapy sessions.

Focus on Comorbid Anxiety

FB-IPT is also rooted in an understanding of the phenomenology of preadolescent depression, specifically, that comorbid anxiety disorders separation or social anxiety disorders in particular, are associated with early-onset depression. Some preadolescents have temperaments that predispose them to anxiety disorders that manifest in social or interpersonal contexts, such as social phobia and separation anxiety, and usually involve avoidance of anxiety–producing interpersonal situations. Other preadolescents experience anxiety that is secondary to the social withdrawal and anhedonia that often accompanies depression. Interpersonal avoidance is a common feature among depressed preadolescents with comorbid anxiety. When preadolescents stop socializing, their friendships suffer and it becomes increasingly difficult to approach and make new friends. Interpersonal avoidance also can stem from co-occurring anxiety associated with the identified problem area. Losses, transitions, and conflict can produce anxiety in preadolescents who are more affected by changes and/or distress in family environments. In addition, preadolescents with interpersonal deficits frequently experience anxiety in social contexts.

FB-IPT seeks to increase preadolescents' social interaction with peers by teaching them new communication and problem-solving skills for initiating conversations and handling conflict, and encouraging them to practice these strategies with peers outside of sessions in interpersonal experiments. Like in an experiment, preadolescents initiate a previously rehearsed social interaction with a peer in order to determine whether the identified skill or strategy is helpful in producing a positive social outcome. While engaging in interpersonal experiments and practicing interpersonal approach strategies aim to reduce preadolescents' depressive symptoms and social isolation, these strategies also decrease preadolescents' anxiety about initiating interactions with peers. With increased practice, preadolescents develop confidence and experience less discomfort in approaching friends. With improved communication skills, depressed preteens may experience positive social interactions and subsequently may demonstrate increased interpersonal approach behaviors. With increased confidence and renewed motivation for social engagement, depressed preadolescents may be more likely to expand their friend groups and social networks. Successful social contacts further improve depressed preadolescents' mood and may decrease their avoidance of interpersonal situations in the future.

During the initial phase of FB-IPT, therapists discuss with families how comorbid anxiety may exacerbate social isolation in depressed preadolescents, particularly in their peer relationships. First, therapists work with parents to reduce preadolescents' interpersonal avoidance through the expanded limited sick role. Preadolescents are encouraged to remain involved in essential routines, such as school and extracurricular activities, even if at a lower level of engagement than prior to the depression. Many parents struggle with pushing anxious preteens to engage in social interactions. Parents are encouraged to reinforce their children for maintaining these routines and to support them when re-engaging with these activities causes distress.

During the middle phase of treatment, therapists introduce interpersonal approach strategies to increase social interactions for depressed preadolescents. These focus on strategies for increasing preadolescents' initiation of interpersonal experiences with peers. Therapists help the preadolescent to identify peers who he could approach or social activities that he could participate in. In sessions, the preadolescent rehearses communication skills for initiating conversations or interactions with peers, and he enlists his parents' assistance to support his increased engagement with peers outside of school. At the same time, therapists work with the parents to encourage the preteen to engage in interpersonal experiments, wherein he implements the approach strategies that he has rehearsed in sessions. The goal is to have preadolescents attempt to initiate approach strategies with peers as practiced in session and then to assess the outcomes and effects of these engagement efforts on their mood.

FB-IPT Treatment Techniques and Mechanisms of Action

Putative mechanisms of change by which IPT reduces symptoms of depression are through increasing interpersonal skills, enhancing social support, and decreasing interpersonal stress (Lipsitz & Markowitz, 2013). As outlined in Boxes 3.3 and 3.4, FB-IPT treatment techniques target risk factors for interpersonal impairment at the child, parent–child dyad, and parent level to decrease parent–child conflict (see Box 3.3) and peer impairment (see Box 3.4).

BOX 3.3 FB-IPT Treatment Techniques and Mechanisms of Action: Decreasing Parent–Child Conflict

- Preadolescent Treatment Targets
  - Emotion labeling/directly communicating emotion
  - Perspective taking
- Dyadic Treatment Targets
  - Problem-solving
  - Increased exposure to positive interactions with parents
- Parent Treatment Targets
  - Decreasing parental criticism/increasing parental support

BOX 3.4 FB-IPT Treatment Techniques and Mechanisms of Action: Decreasing Peer Impairment

- Preadolescent Treatment Targets
  - Role-play and communication skills for approaching peers
  - Increasing initiation with peers
- Parent Treatment Targets
  - School attendance
  - Parent-facilitated opportunities for peer interactions

Decreasing Parent–Child Conflict

Preadolescent Treatment Targets

Emotion labeling/directly communicating emotion

FB-IPT therapists encourage preadolescents to identify their emotions in response to interpersonal events and to role-play the direct communication of feelings ("Make 'I Feel' Statements") as a way to reduce distress and de-escalate conflict with parents or peers. FB-IPT therapists also structure role-plays during which parents and preadolescents practice directly communicating emotions in response to a past event or upcoming situation.

Perspective taking

FB-IPT therapists coach preadolescents to deconstruct aspects of difficult or unsatisfying interactions with parents and peers through a depression circle, which is a concrete representation of a communication analysis (see Appendix F for an example of a depression circle). Therapists help preadolescents re-assess the interaction and identify ways to improve communication or decrease conflict by communicating an understanding of the other's perspective before making a request or expressing a contrary opinion ("Give to Get"). Therapists engage with the preadolescent in a role-play a recent parent–child conflict, providing a supportive and safe environment for the preadolescent to rehearse these new communication skills.

Dyadic Treatment Targets

Problem-solving

During parent–child meetings, FB-IPT therapists and preadolescents share with parents a recent interpersonal event mapped out in a depression circle. Both the parents and preadolescents engage in interpersonal problem-solving during the session, using compromise and negotiation techniques, such as "Meet in the Middle" and "Let's Make a Deal."

Increased exposure to positive interactions with parents

In addition to dyadic role-play and problem-solving in session, preadolescents and parents are given assignments to rehearse communication skills at home in nonconflict situations. Exercises include making appointments to talk with each other, using " 'I Feel' Statements," and demonstrating an understanding of the other's perspective on an issue. Therapists encourage preadolescents and parents to practice these communication skills at home as another way to consolidate skill development and increase the frequency of positive parent-child interactions.

Parent Treatment Targets

Decreasing parental criticism/increasing parental support

FB-IPT therapists coach parents to decrease their criticism of depressed preadolescents by providing psychoeducation about depression, reminding the parent about the preadolescent's limited sick role, and reinforcing use of the Parent Tips that focus on positive communication ("Kind and Firm [Find the Balance]") and praising efforts by the preadolescent to improve his functioning ("Consider the Intention, Not the Outcome").

Decreasing Peer Impairment

Preadolescent Treatment Targets

Role-play and communication skills for approaching peers

During individual and dyadic meetings, FB-IPT therapists and preadolescents role-play approaching peers and initiating social interactions. Therapists provide preteens both procedural knowledge about initiating communication with peers and strategies to decrease fear of social evaluation. Role-playing a range of scenarios with the preadolescent is integral to mastering the communication skills that are taught in FB-IPT. Therapists also enlist parents' participation in role-plays for initiating with peers and encourage them to rehearse with their preadolescents at home (see Chapter 6).

Increasing initiation with peers

FB-IPT therapists engage in problem-solving with preadolescents about ways to increase their interactions with peers. Preadolescents identify potential peers and agree upon a type of approach behavior they will attempt in the upcoming week. Therapists rehearse and script out different communication skills for approaching peers and inform parents of their child's interpersonal experiment in the upcoming week.

Parent Treatment Targets

School attendance

In establishing the limited sick role, FB-IPT therapists and parents identify specific routines preadolescents need to maintain despite being depressed. For most families, preadolescents' school attendance is strongly encouraged. Therapists help parents identify institutional supports in schools to support their preteen's regular school attendance, and coach parents about requesting academic accommodations for their child, if necessary. Therapists engage parents in an on-going conversation about reasonable expectations for preadolescents' school performance at different phases of treatment.

Parent-facilitated peer interactions

During dyadic sessions, parents and preadolescents engage in problem-solving to increase the depressed preadolescent's social interactions with peers. In comparison to adolescents, parents play a bigger role in orchestrating preadolescents' activities with peers. Parents are encouraged to provide opportunities for peer interaction and/or to facilitate peer activities that are acceptable to the preadolescent, in situations where he is unwilling or unable to initiate with peers himself.

Considerations for Conducting FB-IPT with Younger Age Groups

FB-IPT was conceptualized as a treatment for children younger than 12 years of age who present with depression or significant depressive symptoms. Within this sample of preadolescent children, prevalence rates of major depressive disorder are relatively low (between 0.4% to 2.5%) but steadily increases with age. Hence, depressive disorders are less prevalent in the younger age range corresponding to middle childhood (ages 7–8) and more prevalent in the older age range of preadolescents (ages 9–12). While the techniques and strategies presented in FB-IPT have been developed and tested across the 7-12 age group, the majority of these preteens have fallen between the ages of 9 and 12.

As fewer children in the lower age range of preadolescents were included in our studies, the strategies and techniques described in FB-IPT may need to be presented with different degrees of structure and flexibility for this younger age group. The FB-IPT therapist must help children between the ages of 7 and 8 to maintain attention, engage with the tasks presented in each session, understand complex and abstract ideas, and translate communication skills and problem-solving strategies into language and concepts that are developmentally appropriate. For these reasons, dividing the sessions between individual meetings with younger children and parent/dyadic meetings is helpful as children can engage with tasks presented in each session for shorter periods. Younger children are usually able to understand the tasks presented in individual meetings during the initial phase of FB-IPT. Most can participate in constructing a mood thermometer and understand the concept of scaling. FB-IPT therapists may need to use a restricted range for younger children's mood thermometer (e.g., 3 points on the thermometer corresponding to pictures of a happy, neutral, and sad face) and allow young children to mark where their mood has been in the past week in reference to these points. The visual representation of the mood thermometer may be utilized more frequently in sessions with younger preadolescents in order to provide concrete reminders of the scale, and how changes in the child's mood are linked to different interpersonal events.

Many younger children can identify qualitative differences in relationships with family members and friends and can represent differences in these relationships on their closeness circle (see Appendix B). However, FB-IPT therapists will often need to assist younger children as they describe their relationships with significant family members and friends for the interpersonal inventory (see Appendix C). Therapists may need to be more directive in asking questions in order to help the young child provide a narrative of his relationships. In the middle phase of FB-IPT, therapists will be challenged to help younger children understand and utilize the different communication skills presented in sessions. For this reason, the Tween Tips are often presented sequentially rather than all together, and some communication skills are focused on more than others. In our experience, younger children are most adept at "Use Good Timing" and "Make 'I Feel' Statements," two communication skills that involve a more concrete understanding of relating well to a parent or peer. Younger children are often more easily engaged in role-playing than older preadolescents, as "pretending" may seem more age-appropriate to 7- and 8-year-olds. Younger children may struggle with the perspective taking required for communication skills that are more sophisticated, such as "Give to Get." Maintaining a degree of flexibility in presenting skills to younger children based on their understanding is essential to the success of conducting FB-PT with younger children. For example, "Give to Get" is often presented to preadolescents by encouraging them to begin by saying how they think their parent or friend is feeling about a situation ("Give") so that the other person is better able to listen to them ("Get").

Parental involvement is perhaps the most important aspect of FB-IPT that increases its developmental relevance to younger children. FB-IPT therapists may find themselves working more with parents of younger children, particularly in situations where children are ambivalent or having difficulties engaging in therapy. Even with younger children who are engaged in treatment, parental involvement is particularly important because younger preadolescents are less autonomous in their functioning and rely on parental structure, support, and demonstration of effective interpersonal skills. By involving parents in all aspects of FB-IPT, therapists can teach parents strategies for decreasing conflict and increasing support for their children. In the middle phase of FB-IPT, therapists can shift the timing of the sessions when working with younger preadolescents so that there is less time spent in individual meetings with the child and more time is allotted for dyadic meetings. In addition to modeling new communication skills and problem-solving strategies, parents can actively coach their young preadolescents in practicing these skills at home or with peers. Parents can also work closely with FB-IPT therapists to negotiate accommodations for young children who experience significant distress or impairment in school. Parents can facilitate an increase in their depressed child's social interactions by encouraging and arranging playdates or pleasurable activities for their child.

Summary

Adapted from IPT-A, FB-IPT is a promising psychosocial intervention for treating depression in preadolescents (ages 7–12). FB-IPT includes several developmental modifications in order to improve preadolescents' understanding of and participation in treatment. These include systematically involving a parent weekly in treatment, presenting treatment strategies visually, teaching communication skills in age-appropriate language, and experimenting with increasing the preadolescent's social interactions outside of sessions. FB-IPT identifies treatment targets for both preadolescents and parents and is easily modified to target younger children's (ages 7–8) cognitive and verbal abilities. Chapters 5 to 17 of this Therapist Guide describe in detail the steps for conducting FB-IPT with depressed preadolescents and their parents.

CHAPTER 4 Assessment of Preadolescent Depression

Conducting a thorough clinical assessment to obtain a thorough diagnostic picture and an understanding of relevant family and psychosocial issues is an essential step before initiating FB-IPT. In this chapter, we review strategies for assessing depression in preadolescents. Assessment relies heavily on clinical interviews with the preadolescent and her parent(s), with self-reported symptom measures completed by the preadolescent contributing additional information. Many preadolescents struggle with providing a comprehensive timeline of their symptom progression and some underestimate their functional impairment; therefore, parents play a large role in the clinical assessment of a depressed preadolescent. In addition to providing another perspective on mood and behavioral changes in the preadolescent, parents often provide a more detailed understanding of their child's functioning at home, in school, and with peers. Parental report expands the therapist's understanding of the family and social relationships, as well as psychosocial stressors that may coincide with the onset or exacerbation of the preadolescent's depressive symptoms.

The structure of the assessment mirrors the structure of FB-IPT sessions in interviewing preadolescents and their parents both individually and dyadically. First, meet with the preadolescent and parent together to outline the psychological assessment process. Next, meet with the child alone, then with the parent alone, and end the assessment by meeting again with the parent and child together. Although the majority of the assessment relies on information obtained from both preadolescent and parent, it can also be helpful to get collaborative information from the school or other family members. See Box 4.1 for an outline of the assessment process.

BOX 4.1 Assessment Outline

Meet with the Preadolescent and Parent Together

- Explain the process and clarify the goal of the assessment

Using Standardized Measures of Depression and Anxiety

The Clinical Interview

- Meet with the preadolescent alone
- Meet with the parent alone

Putting the Pieces Together

- Meet with the parent and preadolescent together to discuss diagnosis and treatment plan.

Meet with the Preadolescent and Parent Together

Meet briefly with both the child and parent initially to explain what will happen during the assessment and to ensure that the preadolescent has an understanding of the reason why she is here. Often preadolescents are unsure why exactly they are sitting in your office. Sometimes they may feel that they are in trouble, particularly if school administrators necessitated their referral. Clarifying early on, with the parent present, that the assessment is to find out why the preadolescent may be struggling with her mood or behavior will help relieve some anxiety for both the parent and the child.

For the preadolescent, understanding why she is in your office will also help her to provide more accurate and helpful information. Begin by introducing yourself to the parent and preadolescent. We recommend starting by asking the preadolescent why she thinks she is here today. Many preadolescents will say, "I don't know." You can offer a simple explanation (i.e., *"I've talked briefly with your mom and heard you've been having some trouble in school. It's my understanding that we want to find out more about why that might be happening"*). Ask the preadolescent if it's okay to ask for her parent's perspective about why she is here today. By asking for permission, you begin to build trust with the preadolescent as well as model respectful behavior for the parent. At this point, it is completely reasonable for the parent to elaborate on the reason for the assessment. Check in with the preadolescent to determine if she understands her parent's explanation and if she agrees with her parent's concerns—and, if not, aspects where she disagrees. You want to make sure that the preadolescent understands that she is not in trouble and that this appointment is to help her.

It is also important to discuss the limits of confidentiality at the beginning of the evaluation so the preadolescent is not surprised if you need to breach confidentiality to discuss safety with a parent. You can say something like,

> *What you talk about here is private and it's my job to keep what you say confidential. There are times that the law says I need to tell someone what you tell me—if I have concerns that you are at risk of harming yourself or someone else or if someone is hurting you. However, I won't do that without speaking with you first about it. Does that make sense?*

Wrap up this section by explaining the structure of the assessment.

> *Now I'm going to meet with each of you individually to get more information and then we will all meet together and talk about a plan going forward. It's not uncommon to need more than one meeting to get a complete picture of what is going on, so don't worry if we don't get to everything today.*

If a preadolescent is having a hard time describing the events leading up to the assessment, you can help by asking questions that allow her to construct a narrative (e.g., "*How have things been for you for the past month? It's my understanding that you've been struggling at school*"). See Therapist Tips 4.1 for a summary of the initial meeting with the therapist, parent(s), and preadolescent.

Therapist Tips 4.1

Start with the preadolescent and parent:

- Ask for the preadolescent's understanding of why she is here today.
- Ask the preadolescent for permission to have the parent to share his or her perspective.
- Ensure that the preadolescent has an understanding of why she is here.
- Discuss limits of confidentiality.

- Set agenda for assessment. ("*Now I'm going to meet individually with you, then you'll have a break and I'll meet with your mom, and then we will all come together and make a plan. Sound okay?*")

Throughout Chapters 4 to 18 of this Therapist Guide we include vignettes, which are sample discussions between a child (or parent) and the FB-IPT therapist, illustrating the use of a FB-IPT technique or skill.

THERAPIST: Oliver, can you tell me your understanding of why Mom brought you to my office today?

OLIVER: I'm not really sure. I think it had something to do with the picture I drew at school a few weeks ago.

THERAPIST: Can you tell me about the picture?

OLIVER: Well, I drew a picture of me being dead and then my teacher saw it and she called my parents and they got really worried about me and so they made an appointment for me to come here.

THERAPIST: What specifically were they worried about?

OLIVER: They were worried that I might do something to hurt myself because I drew that picture.

THERAPIST: Were they right to be worried?

OLIVER: No, I don't think I was actually going to hurt myself. . .but I guess I haven't been feeling very happy lately.

THERAPIST: (reflective listening and clarifying) So your parents were worried that you might hurt yourself, but you think they were also worried that you haven't seemed like yourself lately?

OLIVER: Yes, I guess so. We didn't really talk about why I was coming here. I was a little worried that I was in trouble.

THERAPIST: A lot of kids who come here aren't quite sure why their parents are bringing them to my office. This is a new experience for you so it makes sense that you're a little unsure. It's my sense that your parents did get really worried when Mr. Logue told them about the picture you drew in class, and they began to think that maybe some of the other things that have been different lately (like not being able to sleep as much, having some trouble with friends) were part of something bigger. As a psychologist, it's my job to hear your perspective and try to figure out what symptoms you are having and what they mean. Do you have any other questions?

OLIVER: Well, I still don't know if I need to be here, but I think I understand a little better now.

Using Standardized Measures of Depression and Anxiety

Depending on your clinical setting, you may or may not be administering standardized measures; however, self-report measures are a good way to assess for a wide range of preadolescents' symptoms and behaviors and to monitor symptom improvement across treatment. A comprehensive assessment of preadolescent depression involves gathering information across informants (preadolescent, parents, teachers) using a variety of methods. A combination of clinical interviews and standardized self-report measures provides the best overall picture of symptoms and impairment, and facilitate an understanding of the presenting problem. We often find that depressed preadolescents are slow to warm up to the clinical interview, and those with social anxiety are particularly hesitant to self-disclose to a stranger. Because of their age, preadolescents may have difficulties answering open-ended questions about their mood, behavior, and functioning in clinical interviews. Therefore, we typically ask both preadolescents and their parents to complete several self-report measures. See Table 4.1 for a list of measures.

The Clinical Interview

Meet with Preadolescent Alone

We encourage therapists to start the clinical interview with preadolescents by obtaining basic demographic information and a general sense of the preadolescent's activities and family and peer relationships. This

Table 4.1. Assessment Measures of Preadolescent Depression and Anxiety

Tool	Administration Type	# Items	Time to Complete	Age	Response	Availability
Children's Depression Inventory-2 (CDI-2)	Self-report Parent Youth Teacher	28	5–15 minutes	7–17	0 to 2 Likert scale	Purchase[a]
Mood and Feelings Questionnaire (MFQ)	Self-report Parent Youth	13	5–10 minutes	8–16	Three ranked responses	Free[b]
Screen for Childhood Anxiety Related Emotional Disorders (SCARED)	Self-report Parent Youth	41	10 minutes	8–18	Three ranked responses	Free[c]
Children's Depression Rating Scale–Revised (CDRS-R)	Semi-structured Parent Youth Teacher	17	15–20 minutes	6–12	1 to 5 or 1 to 7 scale	Purchase[d]
Columbia–Suicide Severity Rating Scale (C-SSRS)	Clinical interview	Varies based on answers	5–10 minutes	7–11 and 12 +	Interview	Free[e]

Note. CDI-2: Maria Kovacs, 2004; MFQ: Adrian Angold, Costello, Messer, & Pickles, 1995; SCARED: Boris Birmaher, Khetarpal, Cully, Brent, & McKenzie, 2003a; CDRS-R: Poznanski, Freeman, & Mokros, 1985; C-SSRS: Posner et al., 2011; Posner, Melvin, Stanley, Oquendo, & Gould, 2007.

[a]http://www.mhs.com/product.aspx?gr=edu&id=overview&prod=cdi2. [b]http://devepi.duhs.duke.edu/mfq.html. [c]http:// www.pediatricbipolar.pitt.edu/content.asp?id=2333. [d]http://www.wpspublish.com/store/p/2703/childrens-depression-rating-scale-revised-cdrs-r. [e]http://cssrs.columbia.edu/the-columbia-scale-c-ssrs/cssrs-for-communities-and-healthcare/ #filter=.general-use.english.

information about typical activities, friends, and general likes/dislikes gives you topics to follow up on when asking preadolescents about recent changes in activities and relationships (e.g., *"You said you like soccer. Has your interest in playing soccer changed over the past month?"*). Beginning with these questions facilitate rapport-building and allows the preadolescent to become more comfortable talking with you. See Therapist Tips 4.2 for questions that can help you learn more about the preadolescent's home life, school experiences, friends, and interests while building rapport.

Therapist Tips 4.2

Questions to help build rapport and learn more about the preadolescent's life:

- Questions about home:
  - *Who lives at home with you?*
  - *How long have you lived in your current home?*
  - *Do you share a room?*
  - *What do you like to do when you're home?*
  - *Who do you like to spend time with?*
  - *How do you get along with brother/sisters?*
  - *How do you get along with parents?*
  - When the preadolescent's parents are divorced, it is important to get a sense of the custody arrangement, and how often the child sees each parent, if there are stepparents or siblings, and the child's overall satisfaction with the current arrangement.
- Questions about school:
  - *What school do you attend?*
  - *What grade are you in?*
  - *Did you ever skip or repeat a grade?*
  - *How long have you attended your school?*
  - *What do you like about school?*
  - *What do you dislike about school?*
  - *How often are you absent from school?*
  - *What sort of grades do you get in school?*
  - *Are you happy with your grades?*
  - *Are your parents' happy with your grades? Tell me more.*
  - *Do you get any extra help in school?*

- Questions about friends:
  - *Do you have friends at school, at home? Tell me about them.*
  - *Who do you like to spend time with?*
  - *How often do you see your friends?*
  - *Do you feel like you have enough friends or do you sometimes wish you had more?*
  - *Do you feel uncomfortable making new friends?*
  - *Have you had any problems with your friends recently?*
  - *Is there anyone who has been bothering you at school?*
  - *Have you ever been bullied? How did you handle it?*
- Questions about interests:
  - *What sorts of things (movies, shows, books, music, video games, sports, activities) do you enjoy?*
  - *What sorts of activities do you do for fun?*
  - *How often do you do these things?*
  - *Who do you like to do these things with?*

Assessing Depressive Symptoms

In our studies of FB-IPT we used the Children's Depression Rating Scale–Revised with the preadolescent and parent to assess for depression symptoms. This measure is not always available, so you may be assessing depressive and other symptoms primarily via clinical interview. You want to get a thorough understanding of the preadolescent's symptoms, onset and duration of symptoms, and any potential triggering events that coincide with the onset of symptoms.

Depressed or irritable mood

Sad mood is a hallmark symptom of depression. Depressed preadolescents, in contrast to adults, often present with irritable mood rather than sad mood. You can ask:

> *Have you noticed a change in your mood in the past two weeks? Have you been more sad than usual? More cranky? Do small things seem to bother you more than usual?*

Loss of interest or pleasure in activities

Anhedonia is another core feature of depression. In our experience, preadolescents often use the word "bored" to describe anhedonia. Once you have established activities that the preadolescent normally enjoys, you can follow up on her interest in those activities in the past two weeks. You can ask:

> *Have you felt interested in doing __________ over the past two weeks? Has soccer practice been fun? Have you felt bored a lot of the time? Are you feeling less interested in or less motivated to do these activities?*

Difficulties with sleep

Difficulty falling asleep and/or staying asleep is common in depression. You can ask:

> *Have you noticed that it has been more difficult to fall asleep over the past two weeks? Have you been waking up during the night and having trouble falling back to sleep? Is it easier to fall asleep with a parent than by yourself? How long has that been going on? Do you wake up earlier than you need to in the morning? Are you taking naps during the day?*

Fatigue or low energy

Change in energy level is a symptom of depression. Preadolescents with depression may endorse a decrease in their energy level. You can ask:

> *Have you noticed that you feel more tired than usual? Is it harder to get up for school or to participate in activities? Does it take a lot more effort to get out of bed or to do things you normally like to do? Do you feel tired even when you get a good night's sleep?*

Changes in appetite

Increased or decreased appetite, accompanied by weight gain or weight loss, is a symptom of depression. Weight gain may be hard to gauge in preadolescents who may be going through a growth spurt, so it is important to ask about changes in eating. You may ask:

Do you feel a lot hungrier than usual or a lot less hungry? Have your parents or friends commented that you don't seem to be eating much or that you're eating a lot more than usual?

Concentration difficulties

Trouble concentrating or sustaining attention is a common symptom of depression. It is also a common symptom of other mental health problems such as attention deficit hyperactivity disorder and anxiety disorders. Therefore, if the preadolescent endorses problems with concentration, it is important to establish the onset of the concentration difficulties. You may ask:

Are you having trouble paying attention in class? Are you having trouble paying attention when you are doing your homework? Can you concentrate on books or other activities? Is trouble concentrating a new problem or has this been something you have had trouble with for a long time?

Feelings of guilt or low self-worth (blame)

Excessive feelings of guilt or low self-worth are common in depression. Ask, *"Do you feel guilty for things that might not really be your fault?"* Sometimes depressed preadolescents feel inappropriately guilty for family conflict or stressors. If you are aware of particular stressors in the child's life, you can ask about guilt explicitly (i.e., *"Do you ever feel like it's your fault that your parents got divorced? Tell me more about that"*).

Assessing Non-suicidal Self-injury

Non-suicidal self-injury (NSSI) is defined as intentional self-harm which is not accompanied by the intent to die. This can be difficult to assess in adults, and it is more complicated in younger children who may not have the language to explain their motives for engaging in this type of behavior. There is limited research on rates of NSSI in children younger than 12, but two studies have identified rates of 4% to 8% in school-aged children and young adolescents between 11 and 14 years old (Barrocas, Hankin, Young, & Abela, 2012; Hankin & Abela, 2011). There is limited data on prevalence rates of NSSI among preadolescents, but several studies examining NSSI in adolescents found that 5.1% to 24% of adolescents who self-injure report initiating NSSI before age 11 (Whitlock, Eckenrode, & Silverman, 2006). NSSI can range from low severity (pinching, scratching oneself with nails) to high severity (cutting or burning oneself). Although NSSI may be less severe among preadolescents, it is still important to ask about intentional self-injury and to use language that is developmentally appropriate. See Box 4.2 for a list of sample questions that assess for the presence and severity of NSSI in preadolescents.

BOX 4.2 Assessment of NSSI

Presence of NSSI in preadolescents:

- *Have you ever hurt yourself on purpose when you were feeling sad or upset?*
- *Do you ever pick or scratch your skin?*
- *Do you ever hit yourself?*
- *Do you ever pull your hair?*
- *Do you ever bang your head against the wall?*
- *Do you ever cut yourself?*
- *Do you ever bleed or have bruises from these times when you hurt yourself?*

When asking these questions, remember to clarify whether there was any intent to die. "*When you were ____________________, what were you thinking or feeling? Did you want to die when you were ____________________?*"

Assessing for Suicidality

It is important to assess for suicidality during the initial assessment and in subsequent therapy sessions. It is a myth that asking about suicide will increase the likelihood that a person will engage in suicidal behavior. One of the challenges when assessing suicidality in younger children is determining the preadolescent's developmental understanding of death. Does she understand the finality of death? Does she still have magical thinking that death is somehow reversible? In order to obtain a thorough assessment of a preadolescent's suicidality, you need to understand her conception of death. You can begin by asking the preadolescent about thoughts of death and dying (i.e., morbid ideation). For example: *"Do you ever have thoughts about dying or being dead? What does death mean to you? Do you think it is like being asleep or it is more permanent?"*

Once you establish the child's understanding of death in general, you will want to assess for the presence of suicidal ideation. Ask, *"Are you having thoughts that it would be better if you were dead? Have you ever had thoughts about ending your own life?"* You will want to differentiate between passive thoughts of death and active thoughts of killing oneself. You will also want to find out how often the preadolescent is having these thoughts, how long they last, and what helps them go away. You will want to ask about method, plan, and intent to act on the plan.

At the initial evaluation, you will want to assess if the preadolescent has ever made a suicidal gesture or suicide attempt (i.e., *"Have you ever done anything to kill yourself?"*). You will want to find out if she stopped on her own or if the gesture/attempt was interrupted. Another important developmental consideration when assessing for suicidal intent among preadolescents is their understanding of lethality (i.e., they may think that they can kill themselves by stuffing their face into a pillow or by holding their breath). To get a more accurate sense of the preadolescent's suicidal intent, you will want to ask, *"How likely did you think it was that you would die from doing _________?"* (Posner et al., 2007).

There is some support for using standardized screening measures to assess suicide risk in youth. One option is the Columbia Suicide Severity Rating Scale, which has been validated, is available for youth ages 7 to 11 years and 12 years and up and is free and relatively fast to use (Posner et al., 2007, 2011). See Box 4.3 for sample questions to help assess for suicidality in preadolescents.

BOX 4.3 Assessment of Suicidality in Preadolescents

Presence of suicidality in preadolescents:

- *Do you have any thoughts about death or dying? Tell me about them.* (Assess preadolescent's understanding of death.)
- *Are you having thoughts that it would be better if you were dead?*
- *Have you ever had thoughts about ending your own life?*
- *How often are you having these thoughts?*
- *Do they last a long time?*
- *Are you able to distract yourself when you have these thoughts?*
- *Were you thinking about _______ for a long time or did these thoughts just come to you suddenly?*
- *Have you ever thought about specific ways to hurt or kill yourself? Can you tell me a little more?*
- *Have you ever done anything to hurt or kill yourself?*
- If yes, assess for the preadolescent's sense of lethality: *How likely did you think it was that you would die by ____________________?*
- *What keeps you from acting on these thoughts?* (Assess for protective factors.)

Assessing for Comorbid Anxiety

Comorbid anxiety is common among preadolescents with depression. It is important to assess for different anxiety disorders and to determine if the anxiety predates the depressive symptoms. The Screen for Childhood Anxiety Related Emotional Disorders (Birmaher, Khetarpal, Cully, Brent, & McKenzie, 2003) is a free, relatively quick self-report measure that can help shape the questions you ask about the preadolescent's history of anxiety and current anxiety symptoms. (i.e., *"Tell me more about the time when you had trouble sleeping by yourself"* or *"Can you tell me a little more about what happens when you are lying in bed and can't fall asleep?"*). You also want to determine if the anxiety or depression started first and which symptoms are most distressing to the preadolescent.

Generalized anxiety

To assess for generalized anxiety, you can ask:

> *Do you have a lot of worries? What are the things you worry about? Do you worry about how well you do things? Do you have trouble concentrating at school because of these worries? Do you worry about talking in class or playing a sport? Do you worry about going to school? Do you worry about getting good grades or about getting along with the other kids? Do you worry about other kids liking you?*

These questions will help you differentiate between generalized anxiety and other types of anxiety disorders.

Social anxiety

To assess for social anxiety, you can ask:

> *Do you worry about what other people think about you? Do you have trouble talking in class? Is it hard for you to meet new people? Are you worried about being embarrassed in front of other people? Do you worry about saying the wrong thing or saying something stupid? Is it hard for you to use the bathroom at school or in other public places? Tell me more about it.*

Separation anxiety

To assess for separation anxiety, you can ask:

> *Do you worry about being away from your family? Do you have hard time sleeping by yourself? Do you go on sleepovers to other kids' houses? Is it hard to leave your parents to go to school every day? Do you worry about bad things happening to you or to people you love? Do you worry about being kidnapped or worry about people in your family getting sick? Do you have nightmares?*

Obsessions/compulsions

To assess for obsessions/compulsions, you can ask:

> *Do you ever worry about something bad happening if you don't do things a certain way? Do you worry about germs or getting sick? Do scary thoughts pop into your head? Do you ever feel like you have to check things over and over (like if the door is locked)? Do you ever wash your hands over and over? Do you take really long showers and worry if you are asked to shower faster? Do you repeat things over and over until they are just right? Do you need to arrange things in your room a certain way?*

Assess whether the preadolescent's anxiety increases if unable to do these behaviors.

Somatic symptoms

Anxious preadolescents may experience a range of somatic symptoms. To assess for these, you can ask:

> *How often do you get stomachaches or headaches? Tell me about them. Do they seem to come out of the blue or do they happen at specific times? Do you ever notice times when your heart beats really fast? Do you ever feel shaky, sweaty, or dizzy? Do you frequently go to the nurse's office at your school?*

Contraindications for Use of FB-IPT

Having a good understanding of the preadolescent's current anxiety symptoms will help you determine if FB-IPT is the best treatment for her. FB-IPT is not a first-line treatment for primary anxiety disorders in the absence of depressive symptoms. Moreover, FB-IPT is contraindicated for preadolescents with active posttraumatic stress disorder or obsessive-compulsive disorder (OCD) symptoms. You will want to refer the preadolescent to trauma-specific or OCD treatment, with the option to return for FB-IPT if the depressive symptoms are still present at the conclusion of that treatment. See Chapter 14 for more information on treating depressed preadolescents with comorbid anxiety disorders.

Meet with the Parent Alone

Meeting with the parent alone will help you get a better sense of parent awareness of the onset of depression in the preadolescent and the effect of the preadolescent's depression on the family. In addition to asking the parent about specific symptoms of depression and anxiety in their child, you also want to gain a more thorough understanding of family circumstances and any family history of depression and anxiety. This is a time to expand upon the information you have already received from the preadolescent as well as to get the "back story" about family circumstances that the child may not be aware of or willing to share. Since preadolescents often have difficulty giving an accurate report of the onset of symptoms, you will want to clarify when the parent observed that the preadolescent's mood and behavior began to change. See Therapist Tips 4.3 for sample questions.

Therapist Tips 4.3

Questions for meeting with the parent alone:

- Questions about depression/anxiety:
  - You will want to ask the parent questions about the preadolescent's depression and anxiety similar to the ones that you asked the preadolescent earlier to get the parent's sense of the preadolescent's symptoms.
  - You will want to establish the onset of symptoms: *Tell me more about when you noticed that something seemed different about your daughter?*
  - Pay attention to the parent's feelings toward the preadolescent. Is the parent concerned about the preadolescent? Frustrated with the preadolescent? Why does the parent think these symptoms have emerged?
- Questions about home:
  - *Who are the members of your family? Tell me about them.*
  - *How has everyone been getting along in your family? Is that a change?*
  - *Are there any family circumstances that you think could be affecting your child's mood?*
  - When the preadolescent's parents are divorced, it is important to get a sense of the custody agreement, how often the child sees each parent, if there are stepparents or siblings, and the parent's overall satisfaction with the current arrangement.

- Questions about school:
  - *How is your daughter doing in school? Has she always struggled in school or is this a change?*
  - *What type of feedback have you gotten from her teachers?*
  - *Does your daughter like going to school?*
  - *Does your daughter have an Individualized Education Plan (IEP)?*
- Questions about friends:
  - *Does your daughter have friends? Tell me about your daughter's friends.*
  - *Do you feel like she has enough friends?*
  - *Is she uncomfortable making new friends?*
  - *Has she had problems with her friends recently?*
  - *Has she ever experienced bullying? How did she handle it? How did you handle it?*
  - *How often does she get together with friends? Does she initiate play dates on her own or do you organize them for her?*
- Questions about interests:
  - *What sorts of things does your daughter like to do for fun? Has she been doing these things lately?*
  - *What do you like to do together?*
  - *How often do you do these things?*

Parental Psychopathology

It is important to talk explicitly with the parent about his or her own mental health history, specifically addressing any prior episodes of mental illness, treatment history, and the impact of such illness on the parent–child relationship ("*Do you have a history of anxiety or depression?*"). Ask about the impact a parent's psychiatric illness has had on the parent, the impact it has had on the family, and the impact on the parent–child relationship. Assess for past and current substance use to evaluate the role that potential substance use has played in the parent–child relationship. Be sure to ask these questions in a sensitive way, as many parents struggle with guilt that their illness has affected their child. If you need more time to do a thorough interview, remember that you can expand upon this conversation by meeting again individually with the parent during the initial phase of treatment.

Putting the Pieces Together: Meet with the Parent and Preadolescent Together to Discuss Diagnosis and Treatment Plan

At the conclusion of the assessment, bring the child and parent back into the room to give them your diagnostic impression and to make an initial treatment plan. Depending on your clinical setting, you may only have an hour allotted for an initial evaluation so you may need to another session to complete the clinical assessment. Your diagnostic impression will be a synthesis of information gathered via any self-report measures, preadolescent report, and parent report. Keep in mind that parents and preadolescents are often exhausted at this point in the assessment, so try to keep things as simple as possible. See Therapist Tips 4.4 for a summary of putting the pieces together.

Therapist Tips 4.4

Putting the pieces together:

- Keep it simple—the preadolescent and parent are probably emotionally drained at this point in the assessment.
- Present a working diagnosis.
- Discuss treatment options: therapy, medication, higher level of care.
  - If you think the preadolescent needs a higher level of care, you can say, *"Based on the symptoms Holly is having, I think she may need more support than weekly therapy. She is having trouble leaving the house, she has been losing weight, and she is thinking about being dead, which suggests that a different treatment might be needed. I would like you to think about having an evaluation with a psychiatrist to discuss medication in addition to talk therapy. Holly, I'd also like to set up more frequent appointments so that we can keep an eye on your symptoms."*
- Develop a safety plan if there is suicidality.
- Ask if the parent and child have questions and if they are in agreement with the treatment plan.

You will present the parent and preadolescent with a working diagnosis for the symptoms the child is having, present treatment options, review a safety plan if the preadolescent reports suicidal ideation, and set up a follow-up appointment or refer them for other treatment as needed.

Developing a Suicide Safety Plan

For preadolescents without suicidality, you will not develop a safety plan, but you will give the parent instructions for what to do if they feel their child's symptoms have worsened and need to be seen urgently. Provide them with a phone number for a local 24/7 crisis hotline or the national suicide prevention lifeline phone number (1-800-273-TALK) and the address of a local emergency room so that they have these resources on hand if their child's symptoms worsen.

Research on safety planning has been historically mixed, but there has been recent support for the use of the Safety Plan Intervention (SPI) developed by Stanley and Brown (Stanley & Biggs, 2014; Stanley & Brown, 2012) in adults. The SPI has been identified as a best practice by the Suicide Prevention Resource Center/American Foundation for Suicide Prevention Best Practices Registry for Suicide Prevention (www.sprc.org). The studies looking at the SPI in youth are still ongoing, but it is anecdotally thought to be beneficial and is currently being used in many clinical settings. SPI involves six steps to help the individual identify:

1. warning signs or triggers,
2. internal coping strategies,
3. social situations and people to help with distraction,
4. people to ask for help,
5. professionals to contact during a crisis, and
6. ways to make the environment safe (i.e., removing guns or pills).

The SPI has been adapted into two different mobile applications, Safety Plan and MY3—Support Network, which you can access in iTunes or Google Play for free.

With preadolescents, parents will be an essential part of suicide safety planning. Sometimes parents of younger children are resistant to the idea that suicidality exists in younger children, so provide psychoeducation to help parents understand that suicidality does occur in children, especially in the context of depression. Parents may also benefit from psychoeducation that asking about suicide does not make a preadolescent suicidal. Parents need information and a plan for handling disclosure of suicidal ideation by their preadolescents (i.e., observation and monitoring, calling a crisis service, bringing the preadolescent to a local emergency department for evaluation).

With a preadolescent with more active suicidality, the safety plan will be more comprehensive and will include many more activities and steps to help ensure safety. Safety planning with preadolescents at the initial assessment is different than with adolescents or even with preadolescents later in treatment because there is wide variability in a preadolescent's ability to use internal coping mechanisms. Some preadolescents may be able to use distraction or engage in self-soothing activities on their own before talking to an adult, but many may be unable to do that. At the initial evaluation, the main goal of safety planning is to help the preadolescent communicate her thoughts of self-harm to an adult, most likely a parent.

If the suicidal ideation persists, instruct the preadolescent to communicate her thoughts to a trusted adult (i.e., parent or teacher), and assess her ability to do so. You may also want to recommend that the parents explicitly ask the child about suicidal ideation at designated check-ins. Once the parents have been told about the suicidality, they can monitor the preadolescent's safety and help decide when it may be necessary to seek additional services. Engaging in designated distraction or self-soothing activities together is appropriate for preadolescents who are experiencing thoughts of death or nonemergent thoughts of self-harm. You will identify these activities with the preadolescent, and they may include reading, watching funny videos on YouTube, relaxation strategies, seeking out social interactions, or listening to music. If there are more emergent safety concerns, the parent should contact you and reach out to community services for immediate evaluation.

Sharing the safety plan in a discussion with both the preadolescent and parent together takes place at the end of the initial evaluation. This collaborative process sets the stage for other collaborations between you, the parent, and the preadolescent that are essential to the process of conducting FB-IPT. See Chapter 18 for more on working with suicidal preadolescents.

THERAPIST: Hi, Mark, Annie. I know it's been a long morning and thank you both for answering all of my questions and talking so openly about what's it's been like for you both since Annie started feeling depressed. Now that we're all together, I want to let you know my impressions and my recommendation for treatment. It's my sense that Annie is struggling with depression, which is a medical illness. Based on our discussion and the forms you completed, it sounds like Annie has been feeling more sad and irritable, crying more frequently, isn't as hungry as usual, is having trouble sleeping, is feeling guilty about some things that aren't really her fault, is not feeling motivated, and is feeling tired a lot of the time. Annie, these are all symptoms of depression.

DAD: Yeah, at first I just thought it was the adjustment to all of the changes that have been going on. Feeling like the house was more empty . . .. needing to make new friends at the new school, but when we got into that fight two weeks ago and you said you wanted to die, well, something clicked and made me realize something more serious was going on.

ANNIE: I'm sorry. I didn't mean to cause a problem for you.

DAD: No, Annie. I'm sorry I didn't realize sooner how badly you've been feeling.

THERAPIST: Well, I'm glad Annie is here now, and I want to talk about treatment options. I think it's reasonable given Annie's symptoms to start with weekly talk therapy and see how she responds. There's a particular talk therapy that I think might be a good fit. It will involve weekly, 60-minute appointments where I will meet with you together and separately for approximately 14 sessions. If Annie symptoms don't change after four weeks of therapy, we can talk about meeting with a psychiatrist to discuss medication options to go with the therapy to best treat the depression.

DAD: That sounds okay.

ANNIE: I don't know if I want to do this.

DAD: Annie, it's not really a choice.

THERAPIST: Annie, I know therapy may seem scary. We'll talk more about what therapy is and how it can be helpful to you, but first, one thing I want to follow up on is the feeling of wanting to die. When you told your dad how you were feeling, which was a very brave thing to do, he got pretty scared and brought you to the pediatrician who then referred you to me. Feeling like you don't want to be alive or that you want to do something to hurt or kill yourself is scary and can really make the people who love you worried. These types of thoughts are a symptom of depression – one that can be very scary – and a symptom we take seriously.

ANNIE: But I don't feel like that anymore.

DAD: I don't know about that, Annie—remember the other day when you were really upset and you went into your room? When I asked what was going on and if you were okay, you said something like it would've been better if you'd never been born?

ANNIE: Dad! I was just mad.

THERAPIST: Annie, when you talk about not wishing you are alive it's hard for adults to know if you're just mad. As we begin working together, we are going to be learning new ways to share your feelings and solve problems. Even though you haven't been feeling this way more recently, I want to set up a plan in case you start feeling this way again.

DAD: I definitely want there to be a plan.

ANNIE: Okay, fine.

THERAPIST: Annie, when kids your age start wishing they aren't alive or having thoughts about wanting to hurt themselves, it's important for you to tell a grown-up you trust so that you don't have to handle those scary thoughts and feelings all by yourself.

ANNIE: But you and Mom will just freak out.

DAD: What do you mean? I'm not freaking out.

ANNIE: Yeah, but if we were at home and I told you I wanted to die, Mom would start crying and you would start fighting about what to do and it would be a big deal.

DAD: Well, it scares me. It is a big deal.

THERAPIST: I think there's truth to what both of you are saying. Parents typically feel really scared when their kids are having thoughts about hurting themselves, and a lot of times kids don't want to tell their parents because they are afraid of upsetting them. I think it's important for your parents to know how you're feeling so they can help you cope with having these feelings and they'll have more information so that they don't need to nag you or take you to the hospital if that's not really necessary. Does that make sense?

DAD: Makes sense to me. I would be so much more relieved to know that you *would* tell me if you were having suicidal thoughts, Annie. Then I wouldn't have to worry every time you look really upset.

THERAPIST: And one of the things we will do is talk about how you would want your parents to react.

ANNIE: Okay, maybe you could just stay calm and not fight. I think that would help me calm down too.

DAD: I think Mom and I can work on that, especially if I know you would really tell me if you were thinking about hurting yourself.

THERAPIST: So, Annie, if Mom and Dad can work on staying calm, do you think you'd be able to tell your mom or dad if you start having the thought that you want to die again?

ANNIE: Right, and my mom won't cry.

DAD: I'll talk to Mom about that, but I can work on staying calm too.

THERAPIST: Then Annie can tell you guys what's going on and you can do something comforting like hang out together, listen to music, cook something, or watch a TV show—something to distract her from her thoughts.

DAD: Okay, I can do that.

THERAPIST: Okay, good. Now if Annie ever had specific thoughts about hurting herself, has made a plan to hurt herself, or has actually done something to hurt herself or you were worried that she wouldn't be able to keep herself safe—Dad, that's a time that you would need to take Annie to the hospital or call the 24/7 crisis hotline number that your pediatrician gave you earlier.

DAD: Okay, that makes sense.

THERAPIST: Does that sound okay to you Annie?

ANNIE: Yeah.

Summary

During the initial assessment, you met with the preadolescent and parent to explain why the preadolescent is being evaluated, explained the format of the initial meeting, and discussed the limits of confidentiality. You met with the preadolescent individually and assessed her symptoms of depression, anxiety, NSSI, and suicidality to get an understanding of her symptom severity and overall functioning. You also explored her interests, general relationships with friends and family, and school functioning to begin to develop an understanding of the interpersonal context of her depressive symptoms. You met with the parent individually to get his or her perspective on the child's symptoms and to gather more information about relevant family circumstances that may be affecting the preadolescent's mood. This helps to round out your picture about what's going on in the family system. You also inquired about the parent's own history of depression or other psychiatric illnesses, to consider if and how that may be affecting the preadolescent and the potential impact on treatment planning. Finally, you met with the preadolescent and parent together to give them your diagnostic impressions and develop a treatment and safety plan integrating information from the clinical interview and self-report or semi-structured standardized measures. You concluded the session by briefly introducing the family to the format of FB-IPT and why you think this treatment is a good fit (see Therapist Tips 4.5 for concerns regarding completing the initial assessment). Congratulations, you have done all of this while building rapport with the preadolescent and parent and modeling the dyadic approach to treatment that you will use in FB-IPT!

Therapist Tips 4.5

What if I can't get through all of the steps in the initial assessment in one appointment?

Don't be concerned if you're unable to get to all of the information discussed in this chapter. You are free to conduct the initial assessment in more than a single session. In the first meeting, make sure to review safety issues with the preadolescent and use your best clinical judgment to get the most important information using the time that you have. There will be time to ask more detailed and specific questions during the initial phase of treatment.

PART TWO

Initial Phase of FB-IPT

CHAPTER 5 Session 1: Introducing FB-IPT and the Mood Thermometer

During the initial phase of FB-IPT, you will build upon information obtained from the preadolescent and parent during the assessment to introduce the treatment model and define treatment course. The two broad tasks involved in this phase of FB-IPT include (a) obtaining a detailed exploration of the ways disruptions in interpersonal relationships with family members and/or peers have contributed to or currently maintain the preadolescent's depressive symptoms and (b) identifying one of four problem areas that will provide the framework for introducing specific strategies to reduce the preadolescent's depressive symptoms. FB-IPT applies the four interpersonal problem areas outlined in the adult and adolescent IPT treatment models:

- Grief
- Role transitions
- Role disputes
- Interpersonal deficits

See Chapter 2 for an overview of these problem areas and Chapter 9 for a detailed description of how each problem area more specifically relates to preadolescent depression.

The FB-IPT treatment model utilizes a series of activities presented in Sessions 1 to 4 to gather information necessary to inform an interpersonal formulation of the preadolescent's depression and to present a problem area to the preadolescent and parent in Session 5 (see Chapter 9). Sessions 2 to 4 of FB-IPT are structured to allow time for a short check-in with both the preadolescent and parent, followed by an individual meeting with the preadolescent and an individual meeting with the parent. In Sessions 1 and 2, the check-in with the preadolescent and parent allows an opportunity to provide psychoeducation about depression, present the treatment model, and introduce the limited sick role. As in IPT-A, individual meetings with the preadolescent during Sessions 1 to 4 include the following activities: (a) introducing a mood rating scale (e.g., the mood thermometer), (b) constructing the preadolescent's closeness circle, and (c) conducting the interpersonal inventory. FB-IPT also outlines a set of activities specific to working with the preadolescent's parent, who will be participating in all sessions. In order to help the parent understand the limited sick role and structure parental expectations of the depressed preadolescent accordingly, you will initiate a series of discussions with the parent to identify his or her biggest parenting challenge and to assess the changes in his or her relationship with the preadolescent since depression onset. A set of Parent Tips (see Appendix D) outline suggestions for addressing common parenting challenges associated with depressed preadolescents and are introduced to parents to help them personalize the limited sick role as it pertains to their child. Lastly, these individual meetings with the parent also allow you to explore the possibility of untreated parental depression and the degree to which this may complicate the parent–child relationship and the parent's ability to help support the preadolescent. These discussions can facilitate the process of referring the parent for individual treatment for depression as another strategy for improving stressful family relationships that may contribute to the preadolescent's depressive symptoms.

Session 5 (Chapter 9) culminates in presenting the interpersonal formulation to the preadolescent and his parent, thus identifying the problem area that will provide the framework for skill development during the middle phase of FB-IPT. In this session, you will meet with the preadolescent and parent together and then meet with the preadolescent individually to determine his understanding of the information presented and to address any remaining concerns or questions he did not feel comfortable bringing up in the presence of his parent. Session 5 provides specific suggestions for developing the interpersonal formulation prior to meeting with the child and parent, as well as examples for establishing the treatment contract and identifying goals for the middle phase of treatment (Sessions 6–11).

Clinical vignettes are used throughout Chapters 4 to 18 to illustrate different treatment principles and techniques of FB-IPT. Some vignettes will involve repeated cases to give you a sense of continuity across the initial, middle, and termination phases of treatment. In this chapter we briefly introduce three preadolescents who have recurring vignettes. All of these cases are composites of actual clients who were treated as part of the FB-IPT efficacy trial (Dietz et al., 2015). The names of clients used in these case vignettes are fictional, and no identifying information has been provided.

Case Introductions

- Maya, age 12, was referred to a child and adolescent outpatient clinic for depression after several months of declining school performance, high levels of irritability at home and at school, and disclosing to her teacher that she sometimes thought about killing herself.
- Oliver, age 9, was evaluated for depression after doing some drawings in school that depicted a person hanging from a gallows with the caption, "This is me." His parents and school officials were concerned with the drawings given that Oliver had become increasingly withdrawn at school and had appeared sad for the past two months.
- Jessica, age 10, was brought to the ER of a local children's hospital after impulsively swallowing four Tylenol gel caps. Although she vehemently insisted that her intention was not to die, Jessica did relate her actions to her desire to escape the consequences of bringing home a "bad" report card. Her father, the primary custodian, reported that Jessica had been more isolative and down since moving from her mother's house to live with him, his wife, and her younger step-sister, and transferring to a new school two months prior to this event.

Goals for FB-IPT Session 1

- Review symptoms with preadolescent
- Construct mood thermometer
- Psychoeducation about depression
- Brief introduction to FB-IPT

Materials

- 1–3 pages of blank paper
- Mood thermometer (Appendix A)
- Markers, pens

Structure for FB-IPT Session 1

- Check-in with preadolescent and parent together (10 minutes)
- Meet alone with preadolescent (15 minutes)
- Meet with preadolescent and parent (25 minutes)

Preadolescent and Parent Together

This is the first meeting with the preadolescent and parent after completing the initial assessment. Begin by outlining the structure and aims of the first session of FB-IPT (e.g., "*We're going to start off today's meeting all together so I can get a sense of how the past week has been for Oliver. Then Oliver and I will have some time to talk one-on-one and work on his mood thermometer. We'll bring Mom back for the last part of the session. I'd like to talk to you both about family based interpersonal psychotherapy, or FB-IPT, and give you a better understanding about what we'll be working on in the first five weeks of treatment. Then we'll wrap up and plan for our next meeting.*")

Check-in with Preadolescent

One of the advantages of beginning the session with a brief meeting with the dyad is that you can identify any problems or difficulties within the family since the initial clinical assessment and address these issues within the FB-IPT session. During this meeting, begin by asking the preadolescent for an update about his mood and functioning in the past week using open-ended questions, such as, "*Tell me about how you have been feeling in the last week?*" or "*Tell me about how things have been going for you since we last met?*" Follow up with some more directive questions regarding the preadolescent's mood and depressive symptoms identified during the assessment. Be aware that it is common for younger preadolescents to want their parents to speak for them when a parent is present.

Check-in with Parent

Next, address the parent after requesting permission from the preadolescent (e.g., "*Maya, with your permission, I'd like to ask your mom about how she thinks things went in the past week*") and then pose similar questions about the preadolescent's mood and functioning. There are two primary benefits of having the parent report in front of the child:

1. Parents may be more forthcoming with identifying problems that arose since the assessment than depressed preadolescents, who may not remember specific incidents or who may wish to avoid rehashing past difficulties.
2. The process of parental involvement in therapy is more transparent for the preadolescent.

During parent report of the child's depressive symptoms, attend to differences between the preadolescent's and the parent's perspective and how each identifies the presenting problem. Observe the level of support, tension, and/or negotiation between the dyad. Suggestions for obtaining important information from both the preadolescent and parent during the check-in are listed next. In addition, Therapist Tips 5.1 provides guidance for common scenarios you may encounter while checking in with both the preadolescent and parent.

- Be patient and encourage any attempt by the preadolescent to describe his depressive symptoms or the circumstances related to worsening symptoms in the past week.
- Minimize interruptions from the parent when the preadolescent is checking in. It may be helpful to remind parents that they will also have an opportunity to share their impression and concerns about their child.
- Observe the preadolescent's reaction to parental report of his mood and other depressive symptoms, as well as other information the parent may share during check-ins. Often preadolescents will

disagree with their parents' assessments (e.g., "*No, I didn't*") or try to explain themselves (e.g., "*That was only because I was tired*"). These observations can inform later psychoeducation with parents or identification of problem areas.

- Preadolescents commonly minimize their symptoms in the first treatment session (e.g., "*I was feeling sad last week but am better now*") to avoid revisiting information disclosed in the initial psychiatric evaluation. Validate the preadolescent's improved mood. Ask questions about things that were different in the past week that could have been associated with the preadolescent's improved mood.
- Address any ambivalence about continuing therapy given the preadolescent's improvement since assessment. It is common for preadolescents to endorse relief and feel hopeful after their initial assessment. Many preadolescents experience an increase in social support from parents. Encourage the preadolescent and parent to continue with treatment as a learning experience to figure out what types of events or situations were connected with the preadolescent's recent depressive symptoms and as an opportunity to learn different strategies for handling similar situations in the future.

Therapist Tips 5.1

What happens if the preadolescent doesn't like to talk in front of his parent?

Don't panic! Many preadolescents do not like to disclose information about their mood and depressive symptoms in front of their parents, some for fear of upsetting their parent or having a negative consequence such as too much parental oversight. However, it is better to have the preadolescent report on his mood with his parent present. Many preadolescents will comply with this request and gladly hand their parents the opportunity to share their observations. Keep in mind that you will be working with the preadolescent toward being more open with his parents in later FB-IPT sessions, when you rehearse communication skills and engage in dyadic problem-solving. At this early point, you can start slowly with reticent preadolescents.

What should I do if the parent is talking too much?

This is something to monitor. Parents who talk too much often may feel like you are not hearing their concerns, or they may be seeking your support and validation. Redirection is often necessary (e.g., "*I hate to interrupt you because the concerns you're sharing are important. However, I am mindful of the time and would like to transition to my one-on-one meeting with Maya so there's enough time for the three of us to go over her treatment plan. Would that be okay with you?*"). Another strategy is to reassure parents that they will have time in upcoming sessions to share their concerns in detail during one-on-one meetings with you (e.g., "*After today, I promise that you and I will have some individual time to discuss these concerns at greater length*").

Preadolescent Alone with Therapist

Review Preadolescent's Depressive Symptoms in the Past Week

After the parent has left the room, follow up with the preadolescent on his depressive symptoms or other significant events that have occurred in the past week. It is often a good time to ask the preadolescent about how he felt coming in for therapy today—as a means to gauge his degree of comfort with the process. Reassure the preadolescent that he is doing a good job and that you hope to help him feel comfortable in your meetings.

Introduce and Construct the Mood Thermometer

The primary goal of Session 1 with the preadolescent is to construct the mood thermometer. Introduce the child to the mood rating scale, using a number on a scale from 1 to 10 to describe the intensity of his depressed mood. Explain that just as when the preadolescent goes to his pediatrician and gets his temperature taken, the first part of every FB-IPT session will start out with the mood thermometer to get a general idea of how he was feeling during a given time period (e.g., in the last week, in the past day, right now). You and the preadolescent will construct the mood thermometer (see an example in Appendix A), to serve as a concrete reminder of the higher numbers representing more intense feelings of sadness or irritability. The number 1 on the scale represents no feelings of sadness or anger, or the happiest the child can ever remember feeling. The number 10 on the scale is an anchor point for the most intense feelings of sadness or depression. It is important to remember that this mood rating scale does not account for duration of time that the feeling lasted. (See Therapist Tips 5.2 for alternative scaling for constructing the mood thermometer.)

> **Therapist Tips 5.2**
> Use the mood thermometer rating scale in the direction that makes the most sense to the preadolescent. To use the scale in the reverse direction (mood rating of 10 being equivalent to a happy, positive mood and mood rating of 1 being linked to strong feelings of sadness/irritability), avoid the thermometer analogy and make it a visual mood rating scale instead.

Ask the preadolescent to provide examples of times in his life when his mood was at different points along the continuum. Start anchoring events/experiences to the highest (10) and lowest (1) points on the mood thermometer and then focus on corresponding experiences for neutral mood (5). Then see if the preadolescent can identify experiences where his mood was less extreme but in the positive range (ratings of 2, 3, 4) and less extreme but in the negative range (9, 8, 7). This activity is typically fun for the preadolescent and provides information that can inform a later problem area or provide hypotheses to explore in his interpersonal inventory. See Box 5.1 for ways to present the mood thermometer to younger preadolescents ages 7 to 9.

THERAPIST: Sometimes it's hard to describe to other people how we are feeling. When someone says that he is feeling sad, I can understand what it's like to be sad, but I don't know how strong that feeling is for the person who I'm talking with—people can be a little sad, moderately sad, or very sad. In order for me to understand how you are feeling, Oliver, we're going to start every one of our meetings with you taking your mood temperature.

OLIVER: What's that?

THERAPIST: I am going to explain it to you. If you go to the doctor's office when you have a cold, the first thing the nurse will do is to take your temperature to make sure you don't have a fever. The nurse will put a thermometer in your mouth that beeps when it's done reading your body's temperature. I'm a feelings doctor, so we will use this paper mood thermometer to get an idea of how hot or cool your feelings have been in the past week, or the past day, or right now. This is how it works: the numbers on the thermometer represent the strength of a feeling, with lower numbers representing less strong feelings of sadness or anger and higher numbers representing stronger feelings of depression. Can you think of a time when your mood was a 10? Tell me about that.

BOX 5.1 Developmental Tips

With younger preadolescents (7- to 9-year-olds) make sure they understand the concept of scaling. You can provide examples using simple scales (e.g., *"How sad were you feeling today? A little, a medium, a lot?"*) or use an abbreviated version of the mood thermometer with three faces indicating positive (1), neutral (5), and negative (10) mood states.

You may wish to provide scenarios for younger children to link different interpersonal events to changes in their mood using the 3 anchors on the mood thermometer:

- *So let's do an example: If you won a free trip to Universal Studios/Disneyland, what would your mood thermometer read?*
- *If you flunked a test in school, what would your mood thermometer read?*
- *How are you feeling right now?*
- *How did you feel when you walked into this room for the first time?*

After constructing the mood thermometer, begin to wrap up with the preadolescent in order to transition for having the parent join the session. It is helpful to praise the effort of the preadolescent and provide some explanation of how the mood thermometer will be used going forward (e.g., "*From now on, I'll be asking you to rate your mood on the mood thermometer when we talk about different situations at home and at school. Then we can see if there are any patterns to changes in your mood*"). You can also ask the preadolescent whether he would like to share his mood thermometer with his parent, but reassure him that he does not have to share his mood thermometer if he is not comfortable doing so.

Inform the preadolescent that you will be inviting his parent back into the room and that the discussion will shift to the treatment plan.

Preadolescent and Parent with Therapist

Psychoeducation about Preadolescent Depression

Provide basic information about depression to help preadolescents and parents understand changes in the preadolescent's mood and behavior. Present depression as an illness that includes a cluster of symptoms and difficulties similar to what the preadolescent or parent has previously described. This provides them with the same foundation of knowledge about the illness that helps avoid assigning blame for the preadolescent's depression. It is helpful to label the depressive symptoms as clues that *depression* is the problem, rather than the preadolescent. Reiterate that depression can negatively affect a preadolescent's relationship with his family members and friends and that the accompanying irritability, social withdrawal, lethargy, and anhedonia are not purposeful, nor can they be turned off by the preadolescent like a light switch. Similarly, inform parents that they are not to blame for changes in their child's mood and behavior that are part of the depression and that they will be key allies in the preadolescent's treatment. See Therapist Tips 5.3 for suggestions of relevant information to convey to families about depression in preteens.

Therapist Tips 5.3

What sort of information should I provide preteens and parents about depression?

Although it is important to provide information about depression in preadolescents to families, it is far better to be concise and present ideas clearly and in language that is easily understood. Keep in mind your goal—to define depression as a treatable medical illness.

Here are some suggestions for key points to cover:

- Depression can affect children although it is often misunderstood because symptoms may manifest differently than in adults.
- Up to 3% of children experience depression prior to adolescence.

- Depression is thought to be caused by both a genetic or biological predisposition and life stress associated with loss, changes in routine, and/or problems in relationships.
- There are different ways of treating depression (other therapies, medication), and the good news is that most preadolescents get better.
- The preadolescent can be referred for adjunctive treatments, such as medication, if the preadolescent's depression does not improve.

Rationale for FB-IPT

Next, describe FB-IPT and its rationale for treating depression by improving relationships, particularly those in the family and with friends. Explain that although there are many different causes of depression, we know that our relationships with others affect the way that we feel and that depression has a negative effect on our relationships. Thus treatment will focus on improving relationships in the hope that this will lead the preadolescent to feel better. Make explicit the role of parent involvement in the depressed preadolescent's treatment. Talk about the role of the parent as an essential part of therapy (i.e., helping the parent and preadolescent to feel more as if they are on the same team).

MOM: So, I just wanted to get some more information about FB-IPT and why we're taking this approach to treat oliver's depression.

THERAPIST: I'm so glad you're asking about this, Joan. FB-IPT was developed to fill a gap in treating depression in younger kids. In general, depression in adults and older kids can be treated effectively with talk therapy, medications, or both. Doctors haven't had as much luck with the medications used to treat depression in younger kids and there just isn't a lot of research studying what types of talk therapy are effective in treating depressed preadolescents.

MOM: Well, I know I've taken antidepressants to treat my depression, but I wasn't crazy about putting Oliver on medication while he's still so young.

THERAPIST: I completely understand that. A lot of parents are uncomfortable using medication as the first line of treatment with younger kids. I think it makes sense to try therapy first. We'll be monitoring Oliver closely to make sure he's improving.

MOM: Okay, that sounds good.

THERAPIST: Although FB-IPT is a new treatment for preadolescent depression, it's based on interpersonal psychotherapy (IPT), a psychological treatment that has been shown to be effective in caring for depression in adults and adolescents. IPT is a type of talk therapy that relates depression to difficulties in personal relationships due to loss, conflict, or transitions in life circumstances. FB-IPT therapists help preteens understand the link between interpersonal relationships and depression and to learn better communication and problem-solving skills to improve their relationships. One of the differences between IPT used with older kids and adults and FB-IPT is that parents regularly participate in their preadolescents' FB-IPT sessions.

MOM: That is one of things I like about this treatment. I want to know what he's doing in therapy.

THERAPIST: We think it makes sense for you to be involved in Oliver's therapy so that you help coach him on some of the skills at home. Also, you've been talking about how much you two have been fighting, so having you involved in the sessions will help you both feel like you're on the same team instead of working against each other.

MOM: I hope so.

Summary

In the first session of FB-IPT, you have introduced the mood thermometer, a strategy to help preadolescents communicate changes in their mood that can allow them to link their depression to different interpersonal events with family members and friends. You provided the preadolescent and parent with a framework for understanding depression as a medical illness and an understanding of how FB-IPT will focus on treating depression. You will introduce the limited sick role in Session 2 and build upon this theme in subsequent FB-IPT sessions with parents to help them better support their depressed preadolescent in the initial phase of treatment. See Therapist Tips 5.4 for common concerns about completing the goals of Session 1 in a single session.

Therapist Tips 5.4

What happens if I don't get through everything I needed to in the first session?

Balancing your introduction of FB-IPT with the preadolescent's *and* the parents needs to be heard during the first few sessions of treatment is often challenging. Be assured that you can pick up with any information you were not able to address in your next session of FB-IPT, even if it means pushing the goals identified for subsequent sessions forward. The initial phase of FB-IPT is longer than the initial phase of IPT-A or IPT for adults because session are divided between the preteen and the parent. It is common for FB-IPT therapists to feel that they are falling behind in meeting session goals when working with depressed preadolescents with complicated psychosocial histories (e.g., divorced or blended families, shared custody situations, grandparents as co-parents).

CHAPTER 6 Session 2: Completing the Closeness Circle and Identifying Parenting Challenges

Goals for FB-IPT Session 2

- Review preadolescent depressive symptoms and significant events in past week
- Introduce the limited sick role
- Construct the closeness circle with preadolescent
- Discuss with parents their most challenging aspect of parenting a depressed preadolescent and the limited sick role

Materials

- 1–3 pages of blank paper
- Closeness circle (Appendix B)
- Stickers or adhesive tabs that you and the preadolescent can write on

Structure for FB-IPT Session 2

- Check-in with preadolescent and parent (10 minutes)
- Meet with preadolescent (20 minutes)
- Meet with parent (20 minutes)

Preadolescent and Parent with Therapist

Begin by reviewing the structure of the session for the preadolescent and parent (e.g., "*We're going to start off all together so I can get a sense of how the past week has been for Maya. Then Maya and I will have some time to talk about how she's been feeling. Then Mom, you will switch places with Maya so we can talk as well*").

Mood Check-in with Preadolescent

Ask about the preadolescent's mood in the past week and have her rate her average mood on the mood thermometer. Begin to explore connections between the preadolescent's mood and interpersonal events (e.g., "*Tell me about what was going on when you felt most depressed in the past week*"). Ask questions about fluctuations in mood (e.g., "*Was there a time in the last week when you were feeling better than a(n)* _________ (her average mood rating on the mood thermometer)*? What was going on at that time?*").

Mood Check-in with Parent

Then ask the parent to report on the preadolescent's mood and behavior in the past week.

THERAPIST: Hi, Jessica and Dad. It's nice to see both of you. Tell me how you've been feeling since we last met.

JESSICA: Okay, I guess.

THERAPIST: Do you remember the mood thermometer?

JESSICA: Yeah, I think so. The lower numbers are better, right?

THERAPIST: Exactly. Can you tell me what your mood is on the mood thermometer right now?

JESSICA: Probably about a 3. I had a good day at school.

THERAPIST: I'm glad to hear today was a good day. Were there times when your mood was worse than that?

JESSICA: Yeah, on Wednesday. I got my report card and I found out I'm really not doing well in a lot of classes and then I got in a big fight with Dad about it.

THERAPIST: That sounds like a rough night. What would you say your mood was then?

JESSICA: Probably about a 9 or a 10.

THERAPIST: Jessica, when you and I meet alone together later today, I think it will be important to talk more about Wednesday night. Would it be okay if I ask Dad to share his impressions of how the week was for you?

JESSICA: Okay.

THERAPIST: Dad, how you think Jessica's been feeling in the past week?

FATHER: Well, I think Jessica's pretty much right on, although I think she had a couple of really good days before getting her report card back on Wednesday. She was really upset that night.

THERAPIST: Thanks for sharing your impressions, Dad. Jessica, it sounds like the past few days have been stressful and I'm sorry to hear about your report card. Maybe you and I can talk more about it when we meet one-on-one.

Introduce the Limited Sick Role

The limited sick role is a way to establish a common understanding of participation in daily activities and performance expectations for the preadolescent's general functioning now that she has been diagnosed with depression. Because the preadolescent is suffering from depression, it may be difficult for her to participate in daily activities—such as going to school, doing homework, playing sports, or engaging in extracurricular activities—at the same level as before she was depressed. The limited sick role validates the preadolescent's experience of depression as impairing. It gives the preadolescent and her parents permission to lower their expectations of the preadolescent's level of performance in daily activities. At the same time, the limited sick role emphasizes that keeping a routine and participating in essential activities is necessary for improving the preadolescent's depression (see Therapist Tips 6.1). Keeping busy helps the preadolescent to feel less depressed, and when she is feeling less depressed, it is likely that she will have more motivation and energy to engage in routine activities at a higher level.

Therapist Tips 6.1

Remember the two aspects of the limited sick role: (a) expectations commensurate with the preadolescent's symptoms and (b) increased effort to maintain essential responsibilities or routines. For many depressed preadolescents this might translate into:

- Attending school on a daily basis but having a modified class schedule.
- Agreeing to complete as much of a homework assignment as possible, even if the preadolescent cannot complete all of it.
- Not taking on new activities but continuing to attend extracurricular activities.
- Continuing to honor responsibilities at home (e.g., taking out the trash, feeding the pet, making the bed) with the expectations that these tasks can be completed at a "good enough" level.
- Discussing with parents which responsibilities at home can be taken off the table for now to avoid arguments.

Based on information gleaned during the assessment and the first FB-IPT session, have a plan about which aspect(s) of the limited sick role are most relevant to the current level of functioning of the preadolescent. For example, many depressed preadolescents avoid going to school because they lack motivation (anhedonia) or are lethargic. In these cases, the limited sick role would highlight the need for regular school attendance and participating in activities at home (e.g., chores or homework) as much as possible as a means to reduce depressive symptoms. Other depressed preadolescents maintain school routines, responsibilities at home, and extracurricular activities but notice that the quality of their performance is worse than usual. In these cases, the limited sick role can validate the struggles of continuing routines when feeling depressed and provide an explanation for the child's impaired or diminished performance. Focus more on adjusting the preadolescent's and parent's expectations for performance and provide hope that, once the depression improves, so will the child's performance on schoolwork and in other activities. Lastly, many depressed preadolescents feel burdened by too many extracurricular activities that take away from homework and relaxing time. Often, they worry that their parents will not support the option of reducing these extra activities. The limited sick role can help frame a discussion of reducing the preadolescent's participation in non-essential, less enjoyable activities. See Therapist Tips 6.2 for suggestions on extending discussion of the limited sick role when meeting separately with the preadolescent and the parent in subsequent meetings.

Therapist Tips 6.2

- The aim of introducing the limited sick role at the check-in is to allow both the preadolescent and her parent time to think about what aspects each would need to work on (i.e, maintaining routines, adjusting expectations, reducing non-essential activities).
- In the individual meetings during today's session, you will have time to talk about the aspects of the limited sick role as it applies to the preadolescent and how it applies to parents' behavior. Validate the parent's wishes to extend the conversation about how the limited sick role could be applied to the preadolescent, but table this conversation for later in the session.

THERAPIST: I understand that things have been stressful between the two of you, Maya and Michelle. It seems like Maya has been feeling sad and angry and has not been able to figure out how to handle difficult situations at school and at home with her sister. She has also been more tired than usual and has been having a hard time getting out of bed in the morning. (Continue with examples of depressive symptoms.) Does that seem right?

MAYA: (nodding)

MOM: Yes.

THERAPIST: Again, these are symptoms of depression—not deliberate bad behavior by Maya. A person who has the flu can't help sneezing or having a fever or a sore throat. Depression is a "mood flu," and a preadolescent with depression often can't help feeling irritable and sad, wanting to spend time alone, having trouble falling asleep or getting up in the morning, and having trouble concentrating on schoolwork. This sort of behavior is not part of Maya's personality, and when her depression is treated successfully, she will return to feeling and behaving more like herself.

MOM: So should she just stay at home and rest until the depression runs its course like the flu?

THERAPIST: So this is where treatment for the mood flu is different from the cold flu. It is important for Maya to participate in her normal routine as much as possible. Withdrawing from her daily activities is likely to make the depression stronger, rather than letting it run its course. Sticking to her normal routine may be tough for Maya because she is suffering from depression, and she may not feel like participating in daily activities, such as school, church group, or basketball. However, this will get easier and easier once she starts feeling better. The way we go forward is with this type of understanding: Mom, I'm going to ask you to encourage Maya's involvement in her normal activities and support her efforts to do so when she's depressed and it's hard for her. Also I want you to support her performance in these activities even if it is not as good as it was before she began to feel depressed.

MOM: Okay.

THERAPIST: Maya, we understand that you are not feeling well and may struggle with doing all the things you normally do. You're not on your "A-game." Mom and I are asking you to do the best you can right now, even if it's not the best you've done in the past. We know you are depressed and do not expect you to perform at a level in school or on the basketball court like you do when you are feeling good. What do you think?

Preadolescent Alone with Therapist

Review Preadolescent's Depressive Symptoms in the Past Week

See FB-IPT Session 1.

Revisit Limited Sick Role with Preadolescent

Follow-up on this topic by asking the preadolescent about ways that her depressive symptoms continue to interfere with her daily routine. It may be helpful to ask the preadolescent to share with you what her routine was like before she was feeling depressed and what her routine is now. Fold a sheet of paper in half length-wise, labeling one side "Before Depression" and the other side "Now." This is a good exercise to see the effects of the preadolescent's depression on her current functioning. Ask the preadolescent about what activities she has trouble with, has withdrawn from, or is not enjoying. Inquire about why these activities are difficult or less enjoyable: Are there issues or problems with these activities that are contributing to the preadolescent's depression, or is the depression negatively affecting her experience of these activities? Assess whether the preadolescent's daily routine and participation in activities is reasonable or overwhelming given her symptom severity.

It may be helpful to ask preadolescents to rank the activities they deem to be the most important and to describe their rationale for their rankings. Use their ranking of activities to ask about reducing participation in nonessential activities that take away from the emotional resources needed for activities that are more important. Explore any resistance by the preadolescent to increase participation in certain activities or to reduce participation in others. It may also be informative to ask if she thinks her parent would rank the importance of these activities in a similar manner (e.g., "*How do you think your mother would rank these activities?*"). This brief exchange may inform your understanding of nonreciprocal expectations in the parent–child relationship which may contribute to conflict.

After identifying the most important aspects of her routine, talk with the preadolescent about how remaining active has a positive effect on alleviating her depressive symptoms. Ask the preadolescent to consider what she could do in the upcoming week to (a) participate in important activities or (b) increase her participation in activities that she enjoys (e.g., "*activities that re-charge your battery*"). The following are some issues to keep in mind when discussing the limited sick role and the importance of maintaining daily routines with depressed preadolescents. Therapist Tips 6.3 provides specific information for approaching the issue of regular school attendance with depressed preteens.

- Many depressed preadolescents (especially those with comorbid anxiety) are ambivalent about getting back to their daily routine. Help them discuss any mixed feelings about the limited sick role, particularly about resuming daily routines. Validate their experience of the limited sick role as difficult, and reassure them that these tasks will feel easier over time and as their symptoms improve.

- Remember that parents need to scaffold much of the preadolescents' participation in daily routines (e.g., insisting they go to school). Preadolescents will often participate if their parents do not let them avoid activities.

> **Therapist Tips 6.3**
> It is important to prioritize school attendance over participation in other activities, even if the preadolescent reports a high level of difficulty with attending school.
> - Based on the ranking of activities, ask the preadolescent about reducing or suspending certain activities in order to prioritize school attendance.
> - Engage her in a discussion of how she feels about frequently missing school or how that affects her ability to be engaged with friends.
> - Explore the effect of missing school on the preadolescent's anxiety (e.g., falling behind in work, missing instruction that may make tests harder, having to explain to well-meaning teachers and peers why she is missing class).
> - Suggest the possibility of increasing school attendance as a way of reducing distress and difficulties related to frequent absences.
> - Assess the preadolescent's degree of distress with her current school performance and her expectations for herself.
> - Define expectations for the preadolescent's school performance on tests or papers that are commensurate with her degree of symptom severity (e.g., "*You would not expect yourself to run a marathon with a broken leg/sprained ankle, so you can't expect yourself to be getting the grades you got when you were feeling well when you are feeling depressed right now*").

Introduce the Closeness Circle

A closeness circle is a visual diagram that allows you and the preadolescent to map out and display the level of perceived intimacy in different relationships. First, present a diagram of five concentric circles and ask the preadolescent to place her name in the innermost circle. (See

Appendix B for a blank closeness circle and an example of a completed closeness circle for Maya.) Explain that you will be constructing a relationship map of important people in the preadolescent's life. Each person's name will be written on a sticker, and the preadolescent will place each sticker on the closeness circle. The physical placement of each sticker in relation to the center circle (e.g., the preadolescent) will represent the degree of closeness the preteen experiences in that relationship:

1. Help the preadolescent write a list of relationships to include in her closeness circle.
2. After identifying these relationships, begin constructing the closeness circle by having the preadolescent (or you) write each person's name (from the list) on a sticker.
3. Then work with the preadolescent to place all of the stickers on the circles, with those placed closest to the child's circle indicating closer relationships compared to those placed furthest from the center circle.
4. Ask the preadolescent if there is any person not already mentioned who has a significant impact on her life but to whom she does not feel close. These relationships should also be represented on the closeness circle. For example, you can suggest putting noncustodial parents, step-parents or step-siblings, and/or a parent's significant other on the list for inclusion on the closeness circle, if the preadolescent is willing.

Box 6.1 provides suggestions for completing the closeness circle with younger children (ages 7–9).

THERAPIST: Maya, I thought we would spend some time today talking about the important people in your life. You've already mentioned several people, and I'd like us to start off by making a list of names. Who should we put on the list?

MAYA: I guess my family.

THERAPIST: That's a good place to start. I'll make a heading for Family Members, and you tell me who to write down.

MAYA: My mom, my sister Bri, my grandma . . .

THERAPIST: Anyone else?

MAYA: I don't know. Maybe my Aunt Denise and my cousins? They live out of state and I don't see them too much, though.

THERAPIST: Let's put them on the list. What about your dad?

BOX 6.1 Developmental Tips

The most important aspect of the closeness circle is helping the preadolescent to understand degrees of closeness in relationships. Younger children (ages 7–9) may have more difficulty understanding the subjectivity of feeling closer to some individuals and less close to others.

- Explain the degree of closeness each circle represents. In other words, the inner circle is reserved for people to whom the preadolescent feels closest, and the next circle is for people to whom she feels closeness but at a medium amount (less than those in the innermost circle). The outermost circle is for people who are important in the preadolescent's life but with whom there is more emotional distance and perhaps more conflict.
- Many younger children in this age group have a more concrete understanding of closeness and equate the outer circles of their relationship map as a place for individuals whom they dislike. Emphasize to the preadolescent that it is perfectly normal to feel close to family/friends and still have times when she feels angry or upset at those individuals.
- Some preadolescents dislike the idea of rating their closeness to different friends and family members. Reassure them that this exercise is to help you have better sense of how their relationships with important people are different, not to make judgments about the people in their lives.
- Remind preadolescents that they do not have to share this information with their parents. However some preadolescents like to go over their closeness circles with their parents because it sometimes helps them talk about difficulty relationships with family members or with friends.

MAYA: I guess.

THERAPIST: Okay. What about relationships with friends or non-family members?

MAYA: Mariah, Julia, and Ashley . . .

THERAPIST: Got it. Are those your friends at school?

MAYA: Yes.

THERAPIST: Anyone else?

MAYA: No, I think that's it.

THERAPIST: Sounds good. We can always add someone to your list we may have overlooked.

THERAPIST: Here's a sheet of paper with circles within circles—the middle circle is where we'll place your name. We're going to use these stickers to make a diagram of how close you feel to these important people in your life and how they may affect your mood. People who you feel closest to will go close to your circle in the first ring, people who you feel less close to will go in the middle rings, and people that you don't feel very close to or don't always get along with will go in the outer rings.

MAYA: Can I put more than one person in each of the rings?

THERAPIST: Absolutely . . . some people will go in the same circle because you feel similarly close to them.

MAYA: Are you going to show this to my mom?

THERAPIST: That is entirely up to you. Some kids like to go over their closeness circles with their parent because it sometimes helps them to talk about relationships in their family that are hard for them.

MAYA: I don't know what I want to do.

THERAPIST: That's fine. We'll hold off showing her until you decide.

MAYA: Okay.

THERAPIST: Who would you like to put on the closeness circle first?

MAYA: I'll start with my mother (placing sticker in second circle from the middle).

THERAPIST: Can you tell me about what makes you put your mom there?

MAYA: Because we are really close, but I can't always tell her stuff that's going on with me because she gets really stressed out and yells.

THERAPIST: Gotcha. Who would you like to place on the circle next?

MAYA: I guess my dad (placing sticker in outermost circle).

THERAPIST: He's pretty far out there. Can you tell me a little about why you put your dad there?

MAYA: He lives far away with his girlfriend and their new baby. I don't get to see him that much.

Continue this line of questioning until all of the stickers with identified people have been placed onto the closeness circle. (See Therapist Tips 6.4 for thoughts about including pets on the closeness circle.) Once completed, explain to the preadolescent how you will use the closeness circle in the next two sessions in conducting the interpersonal inventory, a more detailed discussion of all aspects of the identified significant relationships.

Therapist Tips 6.4
Can the preadolescent put her pet on the closeness circle?
We have had many preadolescents who have asked about placing family pets on their closeness circles. While we allow this, we don't want to devote large chunks of time to discussing a preteen's pets at the expense of talking about family members and friends during the upcoming interpersonal inventory.

THERAPIST: Over the next few sessions, we're going to talk about your relationships with these people a lot more. We're going to discuss the positive and negative aspects of these relationships, who you feel comfortable with and who you don't feel comfortable talking to, and things you'd like to change in your relationships with the people who are most important to you. We're also going to figure out how your depression (and anxiety or behavior problems) has affected these relationships and ways to help you have the type of relationship you want to have with people in your life.

Parent Alone with Therapist

The primary goals of an individual meeting with the parent are to identify the challenges parents experience in daily interactions with their depressed preadolescent and to help parents begin to conceptualize their preadolescent's depressive symptoms and behavior within the framework of the limited sick role.

Discuss Parents' Experiences in Parenting the Depressed Preadolescent

You may find it helpful to initiate a discussion with parents about what it has been like for them to learn that their preadolescent is depressed. It is common for parents to be anxious and sometimes defensive about bringing their preadolescent into therapy as they may fear being blamed for the preadolescent's depression or judged as bad parents by the preadolescent's therapist. They may be angry that their preadolescent cannot snap out of it and may minimize the preadolescent's symptoms if they have difficulties accepting the diagnosis of depression.

Often parents will attribute difficult behavior, such as increased irritability, low energy and motivation, or decreasing school performance, to their preadolescent being willful, argumentative, lazy, or selfish instead of these being symptoms of depression. Your job is to help parents understand that the mood and behavior changes they have observed in their child are part of an illness called depression. This type of psychoeducation is very specific to the depressive symptoms the preadolescent in question exhibits and can lead to the discussion about what it is like to parent this depressed child.

Clarify the Parents' Biggest Challenge in Parenting the Depressed Preadolescent

THERAPIST: Hi, Michele. I like to spend some time in the first four weeks of treatment meeting alone with parents so we can speak openly about what has been going on with your child. Can you share with me what it has been like for you and your family?

MOM: I am at the end of my rope. I have been a wreck since her teacher called me up and told me what Maya said in class ["Sometimes I want to kill myself when my Mom yells at me"]. I don't want to yell, but everything is a battle with her now. It started about a month after school started. Maya wasn't doing her homework, but when I'd check in with her about it she would tell me that she did it in school or on the bus. When I got a call from her teacher about missing homework, I was furious and maybe I overdid the yelling.

THERAPIST: Can you tell me a little about why you were furious?

MOM: Mostly because she lied to me. Maya has always been a kid who keeps to herself, but we have always been able to talk with each other. I do not understand why she didn't even talk to me if she needed help with her homework or she was having a hard time finishing assignments. I really hate having to hear about what is going on with my kid from a stranger.

THERAPIST: What was her mood like during this time?

MOM: It seemed like she was either cranky or crying . . . kind of like she still is. She's always irritating her younger sister, Brianna—it gets to the point that I can't have the two of them in the same room by themselves. So, I'm in the kitchen trying to make dinner and Bri is screaming, "Mom! Maya took my game! Mom! Maya hit me!" Then I yell at Maya and she starts crying and telling me how I never take her side and how it's not fair that I'm yelling at her. I don't want to yell at Maya but she just can't seem to leave her sister alone.

THERAPIST: How do you feel when the whole incident is over?

MOM: Awful . . . I felt so guilty when I found out that my yelling makes her want to kill herself. I don't want to come down on Maya all the time, but she makes a lot of her own problems.

THERAPIST: It's a hard position for parents—preadolescents who are depressed are oftentimes pretty irritable and the people in their families often feel the effects the most. A lot of time this sort of behavior frustrates parents and that makes the kids feel worse . . . it's a perfect example.

Identify the Biggest Challenge in Parenting the Depressed Preadolescent

THERAPIST: Right now, what would you say is the biggest parenting challenge you're having with Maya?

MOM: The biggest fight with Maya is about getting out of bed in the morning. It takes her about 45 minutes to wake up and get out of bed! Nothing works—until I'm screaming at the top of my lungs and she's upset. I'm late for my job practically every day and I'm always afraid that I'm going to be fired.

THERAPIST: Any idea as to why Maya has a hard time getting up in the morning?

MOM: No. I mean, Maya's never been a morning person but she really has to drag herself out of bed now. She goes to sleep at a reasonable time and gets about eight hours of sleep a night.

THERAPIST: Not an easy situation, but one that is pretty consistent with a diagnosis of depression. Depressed kids sometimes sleep a lot and have low energy. Sometimes parents get upset because they think their children are dragging around on purpose or are just being oppositional. Right now, I think we need to have a working assumption that Maya's sleepiness and difficulty starting her day is related to her depression.

Expand upon the Limited Sick Role to Help with Parenting a Depressed Preadolescent

The limited sick role provides a springboard for parents in managing the preadolescent's frustrating behavior (i.e., not doing homework, not getting out of bed) in a constructive manner that validates the preadolescent's struggles with depression (see Therapist Tips 6.5 for suggestions for presenting the limited sick role to parents). It also introduces a target for FB-IPT that helps preadolescents and parents feel as if they working on the same goal (on the same team) instead of working at opposite purposes.

THERAPIST: This is where the limited sick role may be helpful. Like we spoke about with Maya earlier, we understand that it's hard for her to get up in the morning because of her depression, and we're shifting our expectations so that she can take a back seat with extracurricular activities and even schoolwork, but there are still things that she needs to do. Getting up and going to school is one of those things.

MOM: Yeah, but I'm a single parent—I need my job! I feel like Maya's behavior is making my stress level go through the roof.

THERAPIST: No doubt that you need to keep your job, feel less stressed, and change the morning routine so that everyone can get out of the house. We can certainly make this an early focus of therapy.

> **Therapist Tips 6.5**
> Know your A-game:
> In sports, "bringing your A-game" or "being on your A-game" means that you put your full effort into your play so nothing is holding you back at performing your personal best. We often use this language to discuss the limited sick role with depressed preadolescents and their parents. Depression interferes with the preadolescent being on her A-game at school, with friends, or at home. Despite not being on their A-game, preadolescents must continue to "play" or participate in their routines.

MOM: So how do I get her out of bed in the mornings?

THERAPIST: If there was only an easy answer! Let's do some problem-solving. Walk me through a typical morning.

MOM: I wake up at 6 AM and wake up Maya for the first time. She groans and then I let her sleep for another half-hour. Then I wake her up at 6:30, and she still wants to sleep. I finish getting myself and the other kids ready and then it's 6:45. Maya's not up yet. I go into her room and scream at her, because she has to get to the bus at 7:15. Then she's mad at me, can't find clean clothes (because she never puts them in the hamper), and then can't find her backpack. She usually can't even eat breakfast because it's a mad rush to get out of the door in time. If she misses the bus, I have to wait around for the younger kids' bus to come and then drive her to school. By that time, I'm about 20 minutes late for work.

THERAPIST: How are both you and Maya feeling at that point, regardless of whether or not she makes the bus?

MOM: Well, I'm feeling lousy because I just spent like an hour yelling at my daughter. Maya probably feels mad at me because of the yelling and because she's not enjoying school anyway.

THERAPIST: It sounds like a terrible way to start the day, even if you both make it to school and work on time.

MOM: (nods)

THERAPIST: Look, Michelle. I know we're not going to solve this issue in 20 minutes, but I agree that this is a problem for both you and Maya, and this seems to contribute to a lot of the stress at home. What sorts of things have you tried to help the morning routine run smoother?

MOM: Everything. Waking her up later, giving her time to get up, giving her an alarm clock . . . (trails off)

THERAPIST: Okay. Here's a possibility to consider: because she's struggling with depression, Maya is probably going to need more support and structure in order to get up in the morning. Remember, with the limited sick role, right now she's depressed and not on her A-game. Getting up in the morning has never been her thing even when she wasn't depressed, right?

MOM: True.

THERAPIST: You can't drag Maya out of bed in the morning, but you can help to make sure she's getting enough sleep. How about having her go to bed at an earlier time?

MOM: Oh, boy. She'll love that.

THERAPIST: Well, why don't we talk with her about it? If she's feeling so tired in the mornings, an earlier bedtime may help her get more sleep.

MOM: I'm not sure how that will go over . . .

THERAPIST: Okay – what about helping her with the organizational stuff so the morning isn't spent running around looking for clean clothes and backpacks? Could you help her lay out her clothes the night before school and pack up her things (e.g., coat and shoes by the door)?

MOM: Well, don't you think Maya should be able to do that herself? I mean, she is in middle school.

THERAPIST: Is this something Maya was pretty good about doing herself before her depression?

MOM: I know being organized was hard for her, but not to this degree. I just don't want her to get used to me helping her and then not ever learn to do these things on her own.

THERAPIST: I think it's okay to assume that the depression is making things like keeping track of her clothes and school stuff harder for Maya and she needs some help with organizing her things for school right now. The limited sick role allows you to help Maya with these things now because she's struggling with energy, concentration, and motivation. The goal would be for her to do these things on her own once she's feeling better. Ultimately, we'd both like her to be able to do these things on her own, but right now getting up and getting to school on time is enough.

Summary

In the second session of FB-IPT you have outlined the structure for the remainder of the initial phase of treatment (e.g., the check-in, time with the preadolescent, and time with the parent). The preadolescent has learned how the mood thermometer will be used during check-in and has received further clarification of how her mood is associated with different interpersonal events. You have completed the closeness circle with the preadolescent, and you are ready to start conducting the interpersonal inventory in the next session. Importantly, you are also working with the preadolescent's parent to identify a challenging aspect of parenting his or her depressed child where the limited sick role can be applied. The framework has been set to introduce the parent's interpersonal inventory—a discussion of the parent's relationship history with the preadolescent—to be conducted in the next session. See Therapist Tips 6.6 for concerns about completing goals outlined for Session 2.

Therapist Tips 6.6

I did not get as far as I wanted to with the parent in Session 2. Our time ended, and I only covered the most challenging aspect of parenting.

Remember that you are just beginning to make links between preadolescent depression and challenging behaviors when talking with parents. This is really the first step toward expanding upon the limited sick role. In the next session, you will follow-up on the theme of helping parents address these challenging behaviors and making active suggestions about parenting strategies that can be effective.

CHAPTER 7 Session 3: Conducting the Interpersonal Inventory

Goals for FB-IPT Session 3

- Review preadolescent depressive symptoms and significant events in past week
- Begin the interpersonal inventory with preadolescent
- Conduct the interpersonal inventory with parent

Materials

- 1–3 pages of blank paper
- Markers, pens

Structure for FB-IPT Session 3

- Check-in with preadolescent and parent (10 minutes)
- Meet with preadolescent (20 minutes)
- Meet with parent (20 minutes)

Preadolescent and Parent with Therapist

Mood Check-in with Preadolescent

In addition to the mood check, ask the preadolescent to update you about his daily functioning as contracted through the limited sick role.

Mood Check-in with Parent

After inviting the parent to give her impressions of the preadolescent's past week, ask the parent to report on any positive change in his child's mood or behavior that he has noticed in the past week. This question allows the parent to make a positive report about the preadolescent. It also allows you the opportunity to assess the parent's ability to focus on positive aspects of the preadolescent and the effect of positive parental feedback on the preadolescent's mood. Ask the parent follow-up questions to highlight his reaction to any reported improvement in the preadolescent's mood: "*How did you feel seeing [preadolescent] in a better mood?*" "*Tell me about why it was so important to see [preadolescent] looking like her old self?*" or "*How does it feel to see [preadolescent's] mood improving?*" The following are some additional suggestions for checking-in with the preadolescent's parent:

- Encourage the parent to make links between the preadolescent's positive mood and interpersonal events most likely to occur in the family context (e.g., "*Tell me what was going on at the time [preadolescent's] mood was brighter than usual?*").
- In situations where a parent is unable to identify an antecedent for change in the preadolescent's mood or behavior, directly ask about the quality of the parent–child relationship: "*How have things been going between the two of you?*"

Preadolescent Alone with Therapist

Review Preadolescent's Depressive Symptoms in the Past Week

See FB-IPT Session 1.

Begin the Interpersonal Inventory

The interpersonal inventory is a clinical interview about the preadolescent's significant relationships identified on the closeness circle. With open-ended questions from you, the preadolescent talks about strengths and difficulties in these relationships, as well as patterns of communicating feelings and solving problems. You then help the preadolescent make connections between the felt closeness in these relationships and his depressive symptoms.

Use the preadolescent's closeness circle and guide him in identifying three or four important relationships to discuss in greater detail. (See Therapist Tips 7.1 for a discussion of identifying relationships to explore in the interpersonal inventory.) Let him pick the first person who he would like to describe. Then, using open-ended questions, begin to ask about this relationship using questions outlined in Interpersonal Psychotherapy for Depressed Adolescents (IPT-A; see Appendix C: Questions to Guide the Interpersonal Inventory [Mufson, Pollack Dorta, Moreau, & Weissman, 2004]). Ask close-ended questions to gather more specific information about the quality of the preadolescent's relationship with the identified person. See Box 7.1 for suggestions for conducting the interpersonal inventory with younger preadolescents (ages 7–9).

Be sure to address three broad areas for each identified relationship:

1. the positive aspects of the relationship (e.g., shared activities, situations when the preteen perceives high levels of support),
2. the negative aspects of the relationship (e.g., conflict, disagreements, situations when the preteen perceives low levels of support), and
3. what changes (if any) the preadolescent would like to see in the relationship that could improve his mood.

Continue to make links between the preadolescent's mood and interpersonal relationships. Pay careful attention to common themes or patterns regarding the preadolescent's perception or behavior in relationships, which can inform the interpersonal problem area formulation. The information obtained during the preadolescent's interpersonal inventory is used to augment your understanding of the following questions:

- How do positive aspects/negative aspects of relationships affect the preadolescent's mood?
- Were there any changes in each of these relationships that corresponded to the onset or exacerbation of the preadolescent's depressive symptoms?
- How has the preadolescent's depression or experience of recent stressors related to the onset of depression affected his relationships?

BOX 7.1 Developmental Tips

Younger preadolescents may find it difficult to respond to nonspecific, open-ended questions about their relationships with family members and friends.

- Be prepared to follow open-ended questions with more specific inquiries.

Preadolescents may seem reticent to disclose difficulties in relationships with parents, for fear of "telling on" them.

- Reassure preadolescents that you will not share information about the interpersonal inventory with their parents.

The interpersonal inventories of depressed preadolescents are sometimes less rich in detail and sometimes less complex than those of depressed adolescents. Here is our understanding of this developmental difference:

- Preadolescents tend to describe their relationships in more concrete ways (e.g., good vs. bad) than do adolescents, who often demonstrate more nuanced descriptions of their relationships.
- Preadolescents may have fewer close peer relationships than adolescents. Many preadolescent relationships with peers depend on proximity and convenience or on shared interests/activities. Due to their increased independence and autonomy, adolescents may have more friendships based on interpersonal intimacy.

Therapist Tips 7.1

Should I let the preadolescent pick the people to talk about for the interpersonal inventory?

It's generally a good idea to let the preadolescent pick the first few relationships he would like to discuss in further detail when beginning the interpersonal inventory. Usually preadolescents will pick individuals with whom they have more positive relationships, and this strategy of beginning the interpersonal inventory with less conflicted relationships is a good one. It allows the preadolescent time to ease into a more detailed discussion of his relationships and to get used to the types of open- and close-ended questions you will ask. If the preadolescent does not have a preference for who to begin discussing, ask him to choose someone from his inner circle or a relationship that he has identified as a close one.

What if the preadolescent doesn't pick the individuals I think are the most relevant?

In this case, you may need to initiate a shift in the individuals identified for discussion when completing the interpersonal inventory. An example of initiating this shift may be: "*I'm curious to hear about your relationships with people who are further out on your closeness circle. Can you tell me more about your relationship with ___________?*"

THERAPIST: Let's look at your closeness circle, Jessica. I'm interested in hearing more about the important people in your life and how your depression has affected your interactions with these folks. Who would you like to talk about first?

JESSICA: I don't know.

THERAPIST: How about starting with someone in your family.

JESSICA: Okay. I guess my father.

THERAPIST: Great. Can you tell me about your relationship with your dad?

JESSICA: It's okay, I guess.

THERAPIST: We've already talked a little about some of the ways you and your dad are different and how sometimes you two have a hard time agreeing on things like homework. I see that you placed him in the second circle – he's not in your inner circle.

JESSICA: Yeah. Things with Dad haven't been so good lately.

THERAPIST: Most relationships we have with important people have aspects that are good and aspects that are challenging, Jessica. Maybe you can start by telling me about the times that feel good in your relationship with your dad.

JESSICA: We hang out together.

THERAPIST: What sort of things do you do together?

JESSICA: We mostly just watch TV together.

Follow-up Questions 7.1

Examples of follow-up questions for Jessica

- What sorts of shows do you both like? Do you talk while you watch?
- How does watching TV with Dad affect your mood? Has depression/anxiety changed your wanting to hang out with Dad?
- Do you ever want to hang out with Dad and do other things? What sort of things? Have you talked to your dad about these ideas? What gets in the way of talking to Dad about doing those things?

THERAPIST: Everyone has disagreements, even with important people in their lives and even when there are good things in the relationship. What sort of things do you and Dad disagree about?

JESSICA: Probably going to bed at night.

THERAPIST: Tell me more about that?

JESSICA: Well, my dad wants me to be in bed by 8 o'clock just like Tali, my step-sister who is 7, and he won't let me watch the tv shows that I like.

THERAPIST: Okay. How do you feel about that?

JESSICA: I don't think it's fair.

Follow-up Questions 7.2

Examples of follow-up questions for Jessica

- Have you tried to talk with Dad about that? What keeps you from talking about it? What's it usually like when you try to talk with him about it?
- How does this issue affect your mood? Does the issue ever get resolved? How much does it affect your relationship with Dad? Does it make you feel closer to him? Why or why not?
- Have these disagreements changed since you started feeling depressed?

THERAPIST: Jessica, is there anything that you'd like to change in your relationship with Dad?

JESSICA: I don't know.

THERAPIST: Okay. If you had a magic wand and could change two things to make your relationship with Dad better, what would they be?

JESSICA: Um, first I'd wish that we won the Powerball so my dad won't have to work at a job that he doesn't like and we'd have enough money. Then I'd wish for Tali to go away.

Follow-up Questions 7.3

Examples of follow-up questions for Jessica

- Tell me more about [Wish 1]/[Wish 2].
- What sorts of things make you think Dad dislikes his job? What's it like for you knowing that he dislikes his job?
- Do you know when Dad's worried about money? How does that affect your mood? How do you think it affects his mood? If these things weren't stressful anymore, how would things be different?
- Tell me more about your step-sister Tali "going away." How long have you felt this way? How would things be different if Tali went away? Does Dad know how you feel about Tali? How do you think he'd respond?
- Do you think that this is an issue that is related to your depression? Has this wish gotten stronger since you began feeling depressed?

Therapist Tips 7.2 provides suggestions for guiding preadolescents who struggle with describing their relationships during the interpersonal inventory.

Therapist Tips 7.2

Help! My preadolescent client is uncharacteristically quiet during the interpersonal inventory despite identifying a "cast of thousands" on his closeness circle—I feel like I'm struggling to get more than one-word answers!

Should your preadolescent client struggle with the interpersonal inventory, reassure him about the challenge of the task (*"It can be hard trying to describe to someone else what our relationships with parents, siblings, or friends are like"*). Try to follow up on the information he does provide, even if it feels unimportant (see follow-up questions for vignette of Jessica). Lastly, readjust your expectations for the exercise. Sometimes the most important information gleaned from the preadolescent's interpersonal inventory is the paucity of close relationships.

Parent Alone with Therapist

Begin by explaining the purpose of the interpersonal inventory in IPT and how it is used to discuss how depression can affect important relationships in the depressed individual's life. In FB-IPT, you will interview the parents about the nature and quality of their relationship with their depressed preadolescent. Similar to conducting the interpersonal inventory with the depressed preadolescent, ask the parents a series of open-ended questions about positive and negative aspects of their relationship and things that they would like to change. The following are some suggestions for conducting the interpersonal inventory with parents:

- Assess the extent to which the preadolescent's depression has complicated the parent–child relationship and is related to the parent's earlier identification of the biggest challenge in parenting the depressed preadolescent. In this case, continue to discuss aspects of the limited sick role and engage with the parent to come up with a plan for addressing this problematic behavior.
- Determine whether long-standing difficulties have complicated the closeness or quality of the parent–child relationship prior to the preadolescent's depression. What sort of long-standing issues have contributed to difficulties between the parent and preadolescent before the onset of depression? You may want to follow up about issues that were identified during the assessment, such as the parent's mental health history, marital discord, special-needs siblings, or other stressful situations that may reduce parents' emotional availability to children, if they appear to be affecting the parent's relationship with the preadolescent.
- You may find that parents report close relationships with their preadolescents despite the onset of depression. Use the interpersonal inventory with the parent to gather information about the preadolescent's relationships with other family members or about conflicts between family members that may affect the

preadolescent. Ask about the quality of the parent's relationship with his or her spouse, as marital conflict is often a significant stressor for preadolescents. This issue may be particularly important in divorced or blended families, where conflict between parents may strongly contribute to the preadolescent's depressive symptoms.

- In situations where family relationships are close, supportive, and stable, use the interpersonal inventory to obtain the parental perspective on the preadolescent's relationships with peers. What are the preadolescent's peer relationships currently like? Have they been negatively affected by the onset of depression? Did the preadolescent experience difficulties in peer relationships prior to depression? What was the nature of these peer difficulties? Does social anxiety inhibit the preadolescent in peer interactions?

In this chapter we present two vignettes of the therapist meeting individually with Jessica's father that depict different ways to use the interpersonal inventory to gather additional information that can inform the problem area selection and formulation that will be presented to the preadolescent and the parent in Session 5. The first vignette with Jessica's father focuses on the effects of the preadolescent's depression on the parent–child relationship. The second vignette focuses on the relationship history between Jessica's divorced parents and how their difficulties with co-parenting may contribute to her depressive symptoms.

THERAPIST: I'd like to spend some time today talking about your relationship with Jessica and how things have changed since she has started feeling depressed.

DAD: Well, usually we have a good relationship. We have a lot of the same interests and we used to spend time doing things together, like riding bikes or going to the park. Since Jessie came to live with me full-time, we haven't done much of that and it feels like we fight all of the time now.

THERAPIST: What do you think changed?

DAD: Well, I think it's been hard for her to get used to living with me. She was living with her mom and I was taking her on the weekends until just a few months ago. At first, it seemed like she was doing well living with me and my new wife and her daughter, Tali. I mean, Jessie's known them for years and it's not like she hasn't been a part of our family.

THERAPIST: So at first it seemed like Jessica had an easy transition to living at your house full-time and seeing her mom on the weekends?

DAD: Yes. It was even better than I expected. Jessie seemed happy, and I thought maybe she was relieved to get away from all the chaos of living with her mom. It seemed like everything started going downhill in the beginning of the school year, and I guess that's when she starting feeling depressed. Yes, the fighting is probably related to her depression and my stress.

THERAPIST: What types of things do you fight about?

DAD: Oh, it seems like we manage to fight about everything. Bedtime, homework, all the things she wants me to buy her. It seems like I'll just tell her it's time to do homework and she explodes at me, saying that I'm always bossing her around and I don't understand her and she doesn't understand why I'm so mean.

THERAPIST: Have you tried to talk to Jessica about that?

Follow-up Questions 7.4

Examples of follow-up questions for Jessica's father

- What keeps you from talking about this with her?
- What is it like when you try to talk with her about it?
- How does it affect your mood?
- Does the issue ever get resolved?
- How much does it affect your relationship with Jessica?
- Does it make you closer to her? Why or why not?
- Have these disagreements changed since Jessica started feeling depressed?

THERAPIST: Can you give me some background about your relationship with Jessica's mother? I know you are divorced, but we really haven't had the opportunity to talk about that in any detail.

DAD: For the most part, I think we get along pretty well—better than we ever did when we were together. Well, we were really young when we had Jessie and split up when she was still a baby. I think she was almost two years old. Jessie has no memory of her mom and me ever being a couple. We have joint custody of Jessica, and before a few months ago, she split her time between the two of us. Jessica would usually spend three days at her Mom's house and two days at my house during the week, and we would alternate on weekends. Jessica's mom lives pretty close to her old school and works nights so she could take care of Jessie after school or if I was running late for pick up.

THERAPIST: How smoothly did this arrangement usually work out for you and Jessica's mom?

DAD: Usually it worked out pretty well, especially when I started my job and my schedule was changing a lot. There have been times when Jessica's mom got pretty mad at me when I would call her at the last minute to change plans, but I don't think Jessica knew about those arguments.

THERAPIST: How did Jessica do with this arrangement?

DAD: Pretty well, for the most part. Sometimes Jessie complained that she couldn't really make neighborhood friends because she didn't end up spending a lot of time in any one place. Because she's a worrier, Jessie would sometimes get freaked out when plans changed at the last minute and she's wasn't sure which parent she was going to be staying with.

THERAPIST: So why the recent change in Jessica's living situation?

DAD: Well, Jessie was going to be starting middle school and her mom lives in a pretty bad area. The schools are not very good, and there's lots of problems I don't want Jessica exposed to. If she lives with me, she can go to a much better school and get away from the chaos of living with her mom.

THERAPIST: What kind of chaos?

DAD: Jessica's mom is a mess. There's always a problem with her family and the new boyfriend. Lots of arguing among the adults. Jessie would end up taking care of her mom's boyfriend's kids most of the time. I'd get crazy hearing about it. Every time I talked to her mother, she'd deny that things were that bad for Jessie at her house and then would yell at Jessie for telling me her business.

THERAPIST: It sounds like there was a lot of tension between you and Jessica's mother. Do you think this tension between you and Jessica's mom affected Jessica and influenced her adjustment to living with you?

Summary

In the third session of FB-IPT you have oriented both the preadolescent and the parent to the structure of treatment and have made the mood thermometer a part of your common language in linking shifts in the preadolescent's mood with particular interpersonal events. You have begun conducting the interpersonal inventory with the preadolescent and will continue to do so in the next session. You also have obtained information from the parent about his relationship with his preadolescent as well as his perspective about the preadolescent's peer relationships. The information about the parent–child relationship provides a context for discussing the Parent Tips in the next session.

CHAPTER 8 Session 4: Introducing Parent Tips

Goals for FB-IPT Session 4

- Review preadolescent depressive symptoms and significant events in past week
- Complete the interpersonal inventory with preadolescent
- Introduce Parent Tips in the course of discussing the limited sick role with parents

Materials

- 1–3 pages of blank paper
- Markers, pens

Structure for FB-IPT Session 4

- Check-in with preadolescent and parent (10 minutes)
- Meet with preadolescent (20 minutes)
- Meet with parent (20 minutes)

Preadolescent and Parent with Therapist

Mood Check-in with Preadolescent

Refer to previous sessions. Seize upon opportunities to investigate the preadolescent's report of symptom improvement: Why does she think her mood or symptom(s) improved (e.g., nothing, luck, interactions with others)? Draw out aspects of the preadolescent's behavior that may have positively influenced a potential problem or situation. Did the preadolescent do anything different in the past week that might have positively affected her mood?

Mood Check-in with Parent

Check-in with the parent regarding the preadolescent's mood and behavior in the past week. Listen closely for any positive report from parents and highlight these with the preadolescent in the room by asking for more details (e.g., "*Jessica did her homework without a fight four out of five days last week? Tell me more about that. How did that affect your evening together? How did that make you feel?*").

Help the parent to identify ways that the preadolescent is making an effort or behaving differently to positively influence her mood and interpersonal situations (e.g., "*Why do you think Maya was able to get out of bed on time several days last week? Do you think she's trying harder to get out of bed on time? Do you think she's trying harder because she wants to please you or because she's trying to make the mornings less stressful? How does that make you feel?*").

Check-in with the preadolescent about the effect that parental praise/acknowledgement/validation has on her mood (e.g., "*Jessica, how does it feel to hear your dad saying what a great job you did last week?*"). Point out the positive relationship between parental praise and the preadolescent's mood.

Many therapists wonder about how to approach check-in with parents who have difficulty reporting any positive behavior in their preadolescents in the past week. This is a difficult situation and one that has the potential for decreasing the preadolescent's motivation to make changes or to persevere at school, at home, and with friends when she is not on her A-game. The following vignette is an example of how to illustrate for parents the effects of their negative and positive feedback on their child's mood and motivation to uphold aspects of the limited sick role.

THERAPIST: It's good to see you again, Maya. Tell me how things have been over the past week.

MAYA: Things have been okay. Everything has been fine.

MOM: That's not true at all! Maya still stays in her room all of the time and hasn't been doing any of her chores. She's also still picking on her little sister all of the time! I don't think anything is different.

THERAPIST: Maya, how do you feel about what Mom is saying?

MAYA: Kind of sad and mad I guess. I feel like she doesn't care how hard everything is for me right now.

THERAPIST: You are not really on your A-game right now because of the depression.

MAYA: Yeah.

THERAPIST: Makes sense. Do you think there's anything that's going better than it was when you first came into therapy?

MAYA: Well, I guess I've been doing my homework more and I got a B on my science test.

THERAPIST: Have you had to push yourself harder than usual to get your homework done and to get a B on your science test?

MAYA: Yes.

THERAPIST: Mom, how do you feel about what Maya is saying?

MOM: Maybe I'm being a little hard on her. I'm really proud that she got a B on her science test. I thought things would get better when she started therapy, but I feel like things are still pretty hard.

THERAPIST: I hear what you're saying, Mom. It sounds like both you and Maya wish Maya's depression could get better a lot faster. Is that right?

MOM: Yes.

MAYA: Yeah.

THERAPIST: Mom, you mentioned that Maya got a B on her science test and you are really proud of her. Have there been other things that went well or at least okay?

MOM: Well . . . on Saturday she did play nicely with her sister when her cousin was over.

THERAPIST: Maya, how are you feeling about what your mom is saying now?

MAYA: A little better, I guess.

THERAPIST: Does it help when Mom notices your effort or the things that you're doing well?

MAYA: Yes.

THERAPIST: Mom, maybe you and I can talk more today about how you can support Maya in her efforts to do well in school and get along with her sister.

Preadolescent Alone with Therapist

Review Preadolescent's Depressive Symptoms in the Past Week

See FB-IPT Session 1.

Interpersonal Inventory

Resume conducting the interpersonal inventory with the preadolescent. Continue discussing her significant relationships identified on the closeness circle. If the previous session focused on her relationships with family members, use the time in today's session to get a sense of relationships with friends. Ask about peer relationships in school and at home and explore any changes in them before and after depression onset. Explore the possibility of peer conflict and exclusion, bullying, and social isolation as possible antecedents for preadolescent-onset depression. See Box 8.1 for suggestions for inquiring about preadolescents' friendships and interactions with peers over social media.

THERAPIST: Hi, Jessica. Let's take a look at your closeness circle again. We talked about your dad, your mom, and your stepsister, Tali; can we talk a little about some of the friends you put on your closeness circle?

JESSICA: Yeah, okay. I guess we should talk about Sophie first.

THERAPIST: Can you tell me why you put her all the way on the edge of your circle?

JESSICA: Yeah, I hate her now. She was my best friend last year but then she started hanging out with a bunch of jerks and stopped talking to me.

BOX 8.1 Developmental Tips

Did you know that 10 is the average age that most children in the United States get their first cell phone? When conducting the interpersonal inventory, talk about the preadolescent's relationships with friends, in person and on-line. Explore their interactions with friends through social media, and how these on-line interactions may contribute to conflict and closeness in peer relationships.

- Does the preadolescent experience frequent distress when interacting with peers on social media?
- Are the preadolescent's online interactions with peers better or worse than her interactions with peers at school or in extracurricular activities?
- Does she present differently on social media than in person? How does this affect her perceptions of closeness in peer relationships?
- Does the preadolescent identify close relationships with cyber friends—peers who she interacts with through video game play or other on-line forums but has not met IRL (in real life)?
- What aspects of cyber friendships are better or easier for the preadolescent to navigate as compared to actual peer relationships?
- Does the preadolescent share information with her parents about these cyber relationships and other factors that could influence her online safety?

THERAPIST: Yikes. What happened?

JESSICA: Well, over the summer she went to a daycamp with some girls from my old school and they all got really close. They all got really into make-up and boys. My dad won't let me wear make-up and I'm really not into boys. I just felt really left out with them. Then I moved in with my dad and started going to a different school. We don't talk anymore. It's like she forgot I ever existed.

THERAPIST: Wow. I can understand why you've been so sad, Jessica. Moving away from your friends and starting a new school is hard enough, but it is also really painful when a friendship grows apart. Are there any kids you feel close to in your new school?

JESSICA: Well, Lily. She lives across the street from my dad so we hung out a few times in the summer. Sometimes we get together after school and on the weekends.

THERAPIST: What do you guys like to do together?

JESSICA: In the summer we rode our bikes. Now we just play video games or watch TV.

Follow-up Questions 8.1

Examples of follow-up questions for Jessica

- Tell me about the sorts of things you enjoyed doing with Sophie before she started daycamp.
- How often would the two of you spend time together?
- Tell me about a time that you felt close to her/trusted her/confided in her.
- Before she started daycamp, were there any aspects of your friendship with Sophie that bothered you/hurt your feelings/made you sad?
- Did you try to talk to Sophie about feeling left out? What did you say?
- What stopped you from talking to Sophie about feeling left out?
- Did you avoid Sophie after she got closer to these other friends? Did she avoid you?
- Do you think the change in your relationship with Sophie contributed to your depression?
- Do you think your depression stopped you from trying to spend time with Sophie?
- Can the relationship be repaired? How would you feel about that possibility?

After completing the interpersonal inventory with the preadolescent, begin integrating information about her significant relationships with the circumstances surrounding the onset of depression. These observations will assist you in identifying an interpersonal problem area and formulating a focus that will guide treatment in the middle phase of FB-IPT (see FB-IPT Session 5, covered in Chapter 9). Be cognizant of the possibility that the preadolescent may have very few close relationships despite identifying many individuals on her closeness circle. Determine possible antecedents for the few close relationships on the closeness circle. Many times difficulties establishing and maintaining close relationships with others are a function of the preadolescent's interpersonal deficits (e.g., temperament, poor social skills). At other times, the paucity of close relationships is a result of parental isolation, neighborhood (e.g., unsafe, urban neighborhood; rural communities with few close neighbors; neighborhood with few similar age kids), or few opportunities for the preadolescent to establish friendships.

Parent Alone with Therapist

Begin the meeting by summarizing and revisiting the difficulties previously identified by the parents in parenting their depressed preadolescent or in the parent–child relationship. Tell the parent that the goal of today's session is to make an action plan for improving parent–child interactions in regard to the preadolescent's behavior that the parent has defined as most challenging.

The first part of the action plan will involve talking about modifying the way in which one parents a depressed preadolescent as opposed to a nondepressed preadolescent. Educate the parents that it is normal to be unsure about how to respond to the depressed feelings and symptoms of their preadolescent. Many parents respond to depression-related changes in their preadolescent's mood and behavior by (a) holding fast to old rules that no longer work or (b) not providing structure or consequences for the preadolescent's behavior because of guilt or fears about making the depression worse. In keeping with the IPT framework, explain that there may be different ways to support a depressed preadolescent.

Normalize any feelings of guilt or blame that parents may feel and reassure them that the discussion of parenting in today's session is not an indication that they have caused their preteen's depression:

> *Many parents worry that others blame them for their child's depression. I am wondering if you have ever felt that way? I ask because in this session we're going to talk about changes in parenting that might make things easier between you and your preadolescent, but I don't want this discussion to be misunderstood.*

Encourage parents to share their feelings while reinforcing the idea that the causes of depression in preadolescents are multifaceted. Help parents focus on moving forward and not feeling guilty about their child's depression.

Give the parent a copy of the Parent Tips (see Appendix D), and suggest these strategies for handling some common struggles when parenting depressed preteens. Review each of the Parent Tips (see Chapter 3, Box 3.1: Description of Parent Tips) and talk with the parent about how each strategy could be helpful in daily interactions with the child. You may find that some of the tips are more relevant than others depending on the specific circumstances for each parent–child dyad. It is completely reasonable to match Parent Tips to the most challenging parenting situations previously identified or to identify those related to the preteen's limited sick role.

The Parent Tips help guide parent behavior in ways likely to minimize interpersonal stress and maximize support in the parent–child relationship during the initial phase of FB-IPT, before new communication skills and problem-solving strategies are introduced in the middle phase of treatment. Suggestions for implementing the Parent Tips are as follows:

1. Time-out on arguing: Depressed preadolescents are often irritable, and their irritability may trigger their parents to respond similarly. The goal is to have the parent respond in a way that does not heighten the likelihood that a conflict situation arises. Suggest ways in which the parent can avoid taking the preadolescent's irritability personally. Role-play strategies such as responding in a calm manner (e.g., "*Did something happen at school today? You seem angry and I'm worried that something is wrong*"), or "Strike While the Iron's Cold," a reminder to address the preadolescent's irritability when the parent is not angry.
2. Daily check-ins: Depressed preadolescents tend to isolate and may withdraw from family members. Parents often fluctuate between wanting to give their preadolescent space and closely monitoring their child's mood and behavior. Scheduling a daily check-in is a possible compromise: the parent approaches the preadolescent at a quiet time, perhaps in the evening, and asks how she is doing. The check-in may provide an opportunity for the parent and child to

talk at least one time per day without distraction. It may provide the parent with an opportunity to support the preadolescent (e.g., "*I know you are having a hard time and I just want you to know that I'm here,*" "*I wanted to let you know what a help you were to me today*") and demonstrate a focus on the "Intention and Not the Outcome" (e.g., "*I know that you're not feeling like yourself and I'm proud of how hard you're trying at school*").

3. Sharing pleasurable time: Parents can increase their support and monitoring of their depressed preadolescent by spending time doing something enjoyable with their child. This pleasurable time (approximately 20 minutes) should be something that fits into the family's normal routine and should not be something that requires extensive planning or expense. Work with the parents to generate ideas of possible shared time (e.g., taking a walk, watching a movie, cooking together, doing a puzzle, playing a card game) that can be adopted into daily schedules. Encourage parents to persist despite the preadolescent's low mood and lack of interest. The goal is to demonstrate support and activate the preadolescent.
4. Attention to self-care: In order to support their child, parents must be aware of their own mental health needs and the emotional strain of caring for a depressed preadolescent. Introduce the metaphor of "Put on Your Own Oxygen Mask First," and discuss whether the parent may benefit from having his own treatment. Offer to make a facilitated referral for individual therapy, but remember that depressed parents typically do not seek treatment for themselves (Swartz et al., 2008, 2016). While you must avoid conducting individual therapy with the parents, continue to engage them in a meaningful conversation about self-care: taking time for oneself, getting additional social support, and not taking on additional tasks at this time if possible (keeping expectations for themselves reasonable). Parents with psychiatric issues are often motivated to seek their own treatment after participating in their preadolescent's treatment and seeing their child improve.

THERAPIST: We've been rolling up our sleeves and trying to figure out ways to handle the morning routine, which you've said is the biggest parenting challenge with Maya right now.

MOM: Yes. Still not great, but it's getting better.

THERAPIST: What's helping?

MOM: I'm not sure, exactly. We're more consistent with setting Maya's alarm, and I'm having an easier time getting her to go to bed at night, I guess. It's not like we haven't tried these things before.

THERAPIST: Is there something different about how you and Maya are working together?

MOM: What do you mean?

THERAPIST: Well, do you think both of you are trying to make the morning routine better, like you're on the same team?

MOM: Definitely. I think Maya and I have been more tuned in with each other about why the mornings are so hard and that we don't want to make things worse by fighting with each other before we leave the house.

THERAPIST: I think you're right. I've seen you and Maya try really hard to make things in the morning go smoothly because you both care about each other. Also, having a morning without fighting may help you better support Maya as her depression improves.

MOM: (nods)

THERAPIST: (presenting paper) I'd like to take some time and talk about some helpful reminders for parenting depressed preteens. We call them Parent Tips.

MOM: (teasing) You've been holding out on me!

THERAPIST: (laughs) No magic wands or surprises here, believe me! Okay, take a look. The Parent Tips are suggestions for approaching a depressed preteen while you're keeping in mind the limited sick role—we have to encourage Maya to keep going to school even though it's hard for her and she's not on her A-game right now. Check out "Consider the Intention, Not the Outcome." Do you think that could help you relate to Maya when you get frustrated with her?

MOM: (reads) I guess . . . but what do I do with it?

THERAPIST: This is why we are a good team—I love how you get to the heart of the matter! First, this tip is really one that I ask parents to hold in their minds when they are getting frustrated with their depressed preteens: she's trying, she's struggling, this is hard. Many times, keeping this tip in mind is a good way to prevent an argument.

MOM: I can see that. I think I'm doing better at this than before we started therapy.

THERAPIST: I know you are. See, nothing so new. Here are my thoughts about taking it one step further: be clear in praising Maya for trying, regardless of the outcome. One way parents can do this consistently is to start a daily check-in with their kids and praise them for their efforts. You could use that time to tell Maya about the times during the day when you noticed how hard she's been trying even though she still feels pretty lousy. What do you think?

MOM: I can do that. I think Maya might start getting sick of me checking-in with her, though.

THERAPIST: Well, it doesn't have to be so formal like we check in during our sessions. What about 20-minutes of doing something fun with Maya that would allow you to talk with her?

MOM: Like what?

THERAPIST: Anything that you and Maya enjoy—I remember you said that she likes to go with you when you walk the dog and is your right hand in the kitchen when you cook.

Summary

By the end of the fourth session of FB-IPT, you have completed the interpersonal inventory with the preadolescent (see Therapist Tips 8.1, for a discussion of adding another session to the initial phase of FB-IPT for completing the interpersonal inventory). This information, along with the background information obtained in previous sessions from both the preadolescent and parent, will help you formulate the problem area and set the focus for the next phase of treatment. Your next goal is to organize this information and begin preparing the formulation you will present to the preadolescent and parent in the next session. (See Chapter 9 for suggestions to help identify and present one of the four problem areas.) Working with the parents, you have outlined some strategies for helping them interact and support their depressed preadolescent, and you have explained relevant Parent Tips. You will be able to follow up with the parent about implementing the Parent Tips in subsequent sessions.

Therapist Tips 8.1

Can I really complete the interpersonal inventory in just two sessions?

Yes, many preadolescents complete the interpersonal inventory in two sessions. Preadolescents, particularly those between the ages of 7 and 10, have fewer significant family and peer relationships than do adolescents. They also tend to provide less detail in their descriptions of these relationships, which is why the interpersonal inventory in FB-IPT focuses on three broad aspects of relationships: positive aspects, negative aspects, and wishes for improving these relationships. Information provided by the preadolescent in combination with parental report is often sufficient for identifying a problem area and formulating a treatment plan for the middle phase of FB-IPT.

However, some preadolescents, particularly those who are older and expansive in their descriptions of significant family and peer relationships, may require additional time to complete the interpersonal inventory. Should this be the case, add another session to the initial phase of FB-IPT to ensure you have adequately obtained information necessary to formulate a problem area(s) to focus on for the middle phase of FB-IPT.

CHAPTER 9 Session 5: Formulating the Problem Area

Goals for FB-IPT Session 5

- Review preadolescent depressive symptoms and significant events in past week
- Present problem area formulation to preadolescent and parent
- Discuss treatment contract with preadolescent and parent
- Identify goals for middle phase of FB-IPT with preadolescent

Materials

- 1–3 pages of blank paper
- Markers, pens

Structure for FB-IPT Session 5

- Check-in with preadolescent and parent (10 minutes)
- Meet with preadolescent and parent (20 minutes)
- Meet with preadolescent (20 minutes)

Preadolescent and Parent with Therapist

Mood Check-in with Preadolescent

See FB-IPT Session 2.

Problem Area Formulation

The treatment formulation consists of identifying a problem area and outlining some realistic goals for treatment, as well as outlining possible strategies that will be used to make treatment successful. It is important that you elicit feedback from both the preadolescent and the parent to make sure that the identified problem area makes sense to them and reflects the interpersonal events that may be related to the onset of the preteen's depression.

Do Your Homework

The formulation of the problem area (grief, role transition, role disputes, and interpersonal deficits) is a crucial element to the success of treatment and a unique feature of IPT. Prepare your formulation to present to the preadolescent and parent in advance of your meeting.

Create a Timeline of Important Interpersonal Events Prior to Depression Onset

Take the time to put all the information the preadolescent and parent have shared with you in chronological order. Link changes in the preadolescent's mood to these different events or to the preadolescent's experience of changes in his relationships with family members and peers. The following questions may help you target the problem area that best fits the circumstances surrounding the preadolescent's depression:

- Has there been a death of a family member, friend of the family, peer, or pet that the preadolescent has been grieving? (GRIEF)
- Has there been a death of a significant person causing the preadolescent's parent to grieve and be less emotionally available? (GRIEF)
- Have there been any changes to the preadolescent's living situation, school, or peer group associated with an external event? (TRANSITION)
- Have there been any significant changes in family or peer relationships? (TRANSITION)

- Has the preadolescent experienced his parent as being less available due to changes in the family, such as separation/divorce, birth/addition of a new sibling or step-sibling, parental job change, parental depression, or illness of a family member/ sibling? (TRANSITION)
- Has the preadolescent experienced any normative developmental transitions, such as going to middle school, taking on increased responsibilities at home, or experiencing puberty earlier than peers? (TRANSITION)
- Has there been an increase in conflict between the preadolescent and parents or other family members? (DISPUTES)
- Has the preadolescent experienced incidents of peer conflict or bullying? (DISPUTES)
- Is there conflict between parents or other family members that is distressing to the preadolescent? (DISPUTES)
- Does the preadolescent have long-standing challenges with peer relationships that are causing more distress at this age? (DEFICITS)
- Is the preadolescent lonely, isolated, or without peer relationships? (DEFICITS)

See Therapist Tips 9.1 for an expanded discussion of common questions about selecting and presenting an interpersonal problem area during this session.

Therapist Tips 9.1

What if there is more than one problem area that is relevant? The preadolescent I'm working with has just moved to another state with his family and has been having troubling fitting in with friends in his new school. He's been arguing with his parents and refusing to participate in family activities.

Often there is overlap between *role transitions* (e.g., family move to another state, starting a new school, establishing a new friend group) and *role disputes* (e.g., increased parent–child conflict). It is helpful to present both problem areas as part of the FB-IPT formulation and to choose a primary area to work toward resolving. In this case, reducing conflict with parents may provide increased social support to the preadolescent as he is transitioning to a new home, school, and peer group.

How do I present the problem area of interpersonal deficits in sensitive manner? My preadolescent client's poor response to frustration is making her adjustment to middle school hard. I think she behaves in ways that may be off-putting to peers.

Interpersonal deficits are common among depressed preadolescents. Instead of using the language of *interpersonal deficits,* try describing the issue as being one of having difficulty connecting with peers because of the depression, which may have made the preadolescent more irritable and less patient with others. The preadolescent has been more isolated and lonely, and now needs to put herself out there and initiate social interactions with peers. In the middle phase of FB-IPT, you will work with the preadolescent to learn and use different strategies for communicating and resolving frustration with peers.

What if no problem area truly captures the circumstances of the preteen's depression?

IPT maintains that there are many factors—biological, social, and cultural—that contribute to depression onset and that the four problem areas are not inclusive, causal mechanisms for all individuals experiencing depression. That said, the identification of a problem area serves to focus treatment and goals for the middle phase of FB-IPT. Many preadolescents have a family history of depression and experience depression onset because of strong genetic predisposition. *Role transitions* may be a problem area that is helpful in framing the onset of depression. Developmental transitions, such as becoming a preteen or starting middle school, can be stressful and many preadolescents need extra support and guidance during these times. For depressed preadolescents, teaching them adaptive communication and problem-solving strategies can help them to manage stress during these developmental transitions.

Present the treatment formulation to the preadolescent and parent together, in order to collaborate on the focus for the middle phase of treatment. See Therapist Tips 9.2 for suggestions for eliciting feedback from both the preadolescent and parent while presenting the treatment formulation and identifying a problem area.

THERAPIST: Maya, I've been mostly meeting with you and your mom individually, but now I thought that we could all meet together and get a plan for how the three of us will work together to help your depression get better. I've asked a lot of questions over the last few sessions and have gotten both of your perspectives on what sorts of things were going on right before you began showing symptoms of depression. Now we are going to try to put all the pieces together.

THERAPIST: Let me start: it seems like there have been many changes happening in a short amount of time, over the past few months. Maya, you started middle school. This was different from elementary school because you had to move between classes for the first time, be more independent in keeping track of your assignments, and adjust to a new group of kids. Because you tend to be a quiet girl, Maya, you might not have shared some of these stresses with the people closest to you – your mom and grandma. At the same time, Mom started a new job—her first real job after finishing her associate's degree. Mom, you and the kids have had to scramble in the mornings to get out of the house, juggle schedules with Grandma about who is putting the kids on the bus or picking them up, and so on.

THERAPIST: So, Maya, you're adjusting to a new school situation and Mom's adjusting to going to work, and everyone is trying to figure out what the normal routine is supposed to be. Here's the tough part: all of the stress at home is starting to affect the family. There is less down time for everyone to relax with each other, check in with each other, and have fun. You're both not tuned into each other because of all the stress from these changes. Maya, you're struggling at school but don't know how to talk to Mom about it. Mom, you're feeling frustrated with Maya because you don't understand that she's depressed. Maya, you continue to feel sad and angry because Mom doesn't understand how hard things are for you, and then you don't even want to try to ask her for help. That keeps the cycle going all over again.

Therapist Tips 9.2

Check in with preteen and parent frequently during presentation of the formulation:

- *Does this story sound right to you?*
- *Did I miss anything?*
- *Does it capture what was going on at the time Maya became depressed?*

Ask the preteen and parent to restate the formulation in their own words to make sure that there is no misunderstanding and everyone's on the same page:

- *Tell what you heard/took away from what I just said.*

Establishing Treatment Contract for Middle Phase of FB-IPT

Explain to the preadolescent and parent that resolving the identified problem area will involve them both talking about their feelings related to grief, transition, dispute, or interpersonal deficits and learning a variety of interpersonal skills such as

1. Understanding how each is feeling in different situations
2. Telling others when you feel stressed out
3. Figuring out another person's point of view
4. Compromising when there are different points of view on an issue
5. Initiating and maintaining new relationships

THERAPIST: Maya and Mom, I thought that we could clarify exactly what it is that we will be doing for the next part of treatment. Like we agreed, Maya's depression started around the same time as some big changes were happening in the family. It is our experience that as depressed preadolescents develop certain skills—such as understanding how they feel and communicating their feelings to others—they begin to feel better. We also think that as parents develop a better understanding of how family stressors or transitions affect their preadolescents' mood, they become better able to support their preteens by helping them find new ways to manage the stress or reduce conflict. The increased support preadolescents get from parents is another important part of helping them recover from depression. Over the next few weeks, we'll work together and try new ways for both of you to communicate better. We can also figure out how to handle some of the changes that came when Mom started her new job. Then we can find ways to make the new routines in the family less stressful so you both feel better about these new changes. What do you think? Do either of you have any questions right now?

Preadolescent and Therapist Alone

Check-in with Preadolescent about Problem Area

Use your time alone with the preadolescent to make sure that he understands the problem area or if there is any aspect of the problem area that he did not feel comfortable talking about in front of his parent.

Link Goals for Treatment with Problem Area

Some preadolescents are able to talk about aspects of family and peer relationships that are currently problematic but struggle to identify the changes that they can make to improve these situations. Given the identified problem area, begin talking with the preteen about changes that could help him feel better or happier. For example:

- *I think we've good a handle on how your depression got to where it is now, Maya. What do you think you, Mom, and I can do in our meetings to help things get better?*
- *I wonder if talking to Mom about how you feel would help your mood?*
- *Do you think things would be better if you and Mom could talk without arguing?*
- *Do you think meeting new friends would help you to feel happier?*

Summary

This session concludes the initial phase of FB-IPT. You've accomplished a lot in this session—presented the formulation of the problem area, elicited feedback from the preadolescent and parent, and made sure that the three of you are working from a common understanding of the preteen's depression and are on the same team. You also have introduced the treatment contract and clarified how the problem area will be addressed in the middle phase of FB-IPT. Most importantly, the session concludes with a discussion of using new communication skills and problem-solving strategies that will be introduced to both the preadolescent and the parent in ensuing sessions. Therapist Tips 9.3 addresses whether it is necessary to review the interpersonal formulation individually with the preteen's parent.

Therapist Tips 9.3

Why is there no planned individual meeting with the parent to go over the formulation/identified problem area?

In many cases, parents are able to piece together the proximal and distal interpersonal stressors that may have contributed to their child's depression before preteens do. This may be due to the preteen's limited understanding of family or external stressors or a narrow focus on symptom distress. Nevertheless, you may find that you have previously discussed the key issues comprising the problem area formulation during individual meetings with the parent in Sessions 2 through 4. For these reasons, it is often unnecessary to review the formulation with the parent individually. However, you can meet individually with the parent to discuss the formulation and any concerns the parent may have about the identified problem area.

PART THREE

Middle Phase of FB-IPT

CHAPTER 10 Session 6: Introducing the Tween Tips and "Use Good Timing"

During the middle phase of FB-IPT, you will use the identified problem area to further explore the ways disruptions in interpersonal relationships have contributed to or currently maintain the preadolescent's depressive symptoms. The overarching goals for working with a preadolescent experiencing one of the four problem areas are as follows:

- **If the identified problem area is grief**, your goal is to help the preadolescent express her feelings about the loss and its impact on her current mood. Guide the preadolescent to share with you detailed memories of the events and feelings surrounding the loss. Explore the effect of the loss on her existing relationships with family members and friends. Is the preadolescent more isolative? Does she perceive a reduction in social support from family members or friends?
- **If the preadolescent presents with role transitions**, identify behaviors/routines that would help her be able to better adjust to the new responsibilities in the new situation. What behaviors or routines could make the preadolescent's current situation more satisfying? What aspects of the old role (routines, activities) could be maintained in the new situation?
- **When working within the problem area of role disputes**, your goal is to help the preadolescent clarify her expectations for relationships with parents, family members, and friends. Often, preadolescents become stuck in role disputes when they feel parents and/or peers are not meeting their needs. What does the preadolescent want from her relationships with parents and/or peers? You will also work with preadolescents to understand how they currently communicate their needs within these relationships. Many preadolescents struggle to

communicate with others in constructive ways. How may their depressive symptoms contribute to conflict with parents and/or peers?

- **To help those preadolescents identified with the interpersonal deficits problem area**, your goal is to teach skills that will help them develop new relationships or expand their social support networks by increasing their social approach strategies, such as sitting down in the cafeteria with peers and initiating a conversation or learning how to join an ongoing conversation.

While the problem areas differ in focus, their resolution often involves an overlapping set of strategies, such as assisting the preadolescent to emotionally process her experience related to the problem area, communicate her needs more effectively, handle interpersonal conflict through negotiation and problem-solving, and initiate new relationships with peers. A set of Tween Tips (see Appendix E) identify specific communication skills and problem-solving strategies that you will introduce and rehearse with preadolescents and their parents during the middle phase of FB-IPT. In FB-IPT Sessions 6 through 11, we introduce the Tween Tips individually so that they can build upon each other sequentially. While we suggest introducing new communication or problem-solving techniques one at a time, you have flexibility in deciding which Tween Tip to present first.

During the middle phase of FB-IPT, sessions are divided between individual meetings with the preadolescent and dyadic meetings with the preadolescent and parent. Individual meetings with the preadolescent will consist of teaching and rehearsing interpersonal skills related to the identified problem area. During these sessions, you will engage in role-playing each skill with the preadolescent during individual meetings and then structure role-plays between the child and parent to rehearse new skills during dyadic meetings. The goal of the dyadic meetings with parents is to complement the focus on interpersonal skills and problem-solving with preadolescents. Dyadic role-plays will help to determine how the preadolescent and parent can practice each skill at home between sessions. Through parental involvement in the role-playing, the family can help support the preadolescent's experiments and practice between sessions.

Goals for FB-IPT Session 6

- Review preadolescent's depressive symptoms and mood thermometer
- Discuss significant events in the past week in relation to the identified problem area
- Begin discussion of communication skills ("Use Good Timing")
- Dyadic meeting to focus on rehearsing communication skills/problem-solving

Materials

- 1–3 pages of blank paper
- Markers, pens

Structure for FB-IPT Session 6

- Check-in with preadolescent and parent (10 minutes)
- Meet with preadolescent (20 minutes)
- Meet with preadolescent and parent (20 minutes)

Preadolescent and Parent with Therapist

Mood Check-in with Preadolescent and Parent

Just as in the initial phase, begin the session by meeting with both the preadolescent and parent together and outline the structure of the session for them. Be sure to note that the middle phase of FB-IPT has a structure different from that of the first five sessions, for example:

For the middle phase of FB-IPT, we're going to break up the session a little differently than we did in the initial phase. Today we're going to spend a little bit of time checking-in all together, then Mom, you will take a break in the waiting room outside so Maya and I can have some one-on-one time to talk. Then, we'll have Mom join us again so the three of us can work together.

Ask the preadolescent to rate her mood on the mood thermometer over the last week, and follow up with the parent's report of the preadolescent's mood and symptoms.

Preadolescent Alone with Therapist

Introduce Communication as a Focus

One of the goals of FB-IPT is to help preadolescents find better ways of communicating with important people in their lives. Begin by introducing the idea that there are different ways of approaching problems and handling disagreements. Explain that the way we choose to communicate in these situations can lead to good/not so good outcomes and affect how we feel about our relationship with the person with whom we are interacting.

Focus on the preadolescent's problem area (grief, transitions, disputes, deficits) and outline ways that previous styles of communication may have been problematic. The following vignette outlines a case example of a preadolescent having a role dispute with her father since moving in with him and starting a new school.

THERAPIST: Over the past five weeks, we've talked a lot about how fights with your dad have made you feel sad and angry. Now we're going to roll up our sleeves and help you and Dad talk to each other differently.

JESSICA: I don't want to talk to my Dad.

THERAPIST: Tell me more about that.

JESSICA: Just that my dad is always telling me that I didn't do something good enough or that I have to try harder.

THERAPIST: And that makes you feel . . .

JESSICA: Bad.

THERAPIST: That it doesn't matter how hard you try, he won't think it's okay?

JESSICA: Well, yeah – I guess.

THERAPIST: I'd like to help you and your dad feel like you're on the same team again—instead of being at odds with each other. I know that you are not the only one who needs to change and communicate better. That's why we're going to be having Dad meet with us, too. What I do know is that figuring out how to let your dad know how you are feeling, even when you might have different ideas, could help you feel better.

JESSICA: (shrugs)

THERAPIST: I know that you're not sure about this. It's new and it's okay to be unsure. I appreciate your willingness to try this.

Map Out Problematic Communication by Constructing a Depression Circle

It is helpful to make a visual flowchart of how communication between the preadolescent and another person happened in a particular situation. The depression circle (see Appendix F) is a map of a communication analysis used to assess patterns of problematic communication and to identify ways of improving the preadolescent's interactions with family members and peers.

- Start with identifying one social interaction—ask the preadolescent to tell you when and where the interaction took place, who was there, and how she was feeling right before the interaction. Refer back to the mood thermometer and ask the preadolescent to rate her mood.
- Then ask her to tell you about how the interaction started (e.g., "*Who spoke first? What did you/your dad say?*")
- Create a "text box" in the upper left of a piece of paper—write down what was said and who said it, and have the preadolescent rate her mood at that time.
- Ask the preadolescent about how she responded or how the other person replied to the first statement; write these words in another text box to the right of the first (move in a clockwise pattern) and have the preadolescent rate her mood.

- Continue this process of adding text boxes with the preadolescent's and other person's verbal exchanges with mood ratings, in a clockwise direction, until the interaction is complete.
- Use frequent prompts to help the preadolescent recall the specific exchanges in the interaction (e.g., "*What did you say next? What words did you use? How did your father respond? What did he say? Were those the exact words he used*?")

The following vignette illustrates a case example of a therapist and a preadolescent constructing a depression circle in session.

THERAPIST: You and Dad talked about getting into a big fight about your homework last week.

JESSICA: Yeah, I remember.

THERAPIST: Let's go through that argument and slow it down. We're going to map it out on this piece of paper. First, start out by telling me when it happened and where you were.

JESSICA: Well, we got home from school and I started to go outside to ride my bike. My dad said I had to do my homework. I told him I really needed a break, but he said I just had to do it.

THERAPIST: Okay, so who started talking first? Was it you or Dad?

JESSICA: My dad.

THERAPIST: What did he say?

JESSICA: That I had to do my homework.

THERAPIST: Try to remember the exact words he said if you can.

JESSICA: I think he said, "Is your homework done?"

THERAPIST: Let me write that down over here (in square). How were you feeling right before Dad said that?

JESSICA: Okay.

THERAPIST: What number would you give it on your mood thermometer?

JESSICA: About a 3.

THERAPIST: So you were feeling good. How did you feel when Dad said, "Is your homework done?"

JESSICA: Bad – a 6 on my mood thermometer. My friend Lily was already outside playing and it was getting late.

THERAPIST: So then what happened?

JESSICA: I got mad. I didn't want to do my homework then.

THERAPIST: Did you say something to your dad?

JESSICA: I think so.

THERAPIST: Do you remember what you said?

JESSICA: I said something like, "It's not fair. Lily is outside and I don't even have that much homework anyway."

THERAPIST: How were you feeling on your mood thermometer then?

JESSICA: Bad – about a 7.

THERAPIST: What did your dad say next?

JESSICA: I can't remember it all.

THERAPIST: Just give it a try . . . it doesn't have to be perfect, just what you can remember.

JESSICA: I think he said something like, "I knew it. How many times do I have to tell you that the rule is you do your homework as soon as you get home?"

THERAPIST: Let me write that down here . . . where were you on your mood thermometer?

JESSICA: 9.

THERAPIST: What did you say next?

JESSICA: I told him that I wanted to go back and live with my mom.

THERAPIST: (writing) Jessica, was your tone of voice the same as the one you're using when you're talking to me?

JESSICA: No. I yelled it at him.

THERAPIST: What happened next?

JESSICA: He started yelling at me and I ran up to my room. I tried to do my homework but I couldn't concentrate. I didn't even come down for dinner.

THERAPIST: So that fight really brought your mood down. Did you and your dad ever talk about the fight afterwards?

JESSICA: No. I saw him at breakfast the next morning and we were back to normal.

Follow-up Questions 10.1

Examples of follow-up probes for the depression circle:

- *Did your words come out the way you wanted them to?*
- *What were you really trying to say?*

- *Do you think your parent/friend understood what you meant when you used those words?*
- *How do you think your parent/friend felt when you said ________?*
- *Do you think your parent/friend knew why that was so important to you?*
- *Do you think you and your parent/friend were on different pages?*

After completing the depression circle, spend some time with the preadolescent assessing where the communication began to break down. Validate the preadolescent's work in helping you understand the situation better and ask about whether this exchange is typical in her relationship with the person involved. If the example involves the preadolescent's parent, ask her if she would be willing to share the depression circle with her parent. If the preadolescent refuses, spend some time assessing her worries about doing so (e.g., the parent would be mad, the parent would deny the incident, the preadolescent would be embarrassed). Ask the preadolescent if there would be any potential benefit to sharing the depression circle with her parent. Reassure the preadolescent that sharing the depression circle with her parent is her choice but that you think it may be helpful.

Introduce a New Communication Skill/Problem-Solving Technique

The Tween Tips outline several different communication skills and ways to approach problem-solving in relationships with parents and peers. Pick a skill to teach the preadolescent and parent that relates to the issue discussed within the framework of the problem area. Introduce skills individually (one at a time/one per session) to the preadolescent to make sure she understands the concept and has time to practice the skill.

In the scenario with Jessica and her father, "Use Good Timing" is a skill that can help preadolescents pick the right time to approach another person (e.g., talk to a parent or a friend about an important issue or initiate an activity). Provide psychoeducation about the keys to successful social interactions. Successful social interactions are often a result of good timing—when the conversation or exchange happens—as external circumstances and stressors can potentially interfere with someone paying attention, listening, and being open to engaging with the other person. Ask the preadolescent to come up with an example of when she had a bad interaction with a family member or peer because someone was tired/busy/stressed/preoccupied/angry at someone else or something else. Provide an example of a conflict the preadolescent has previously shared to illustrate the effect of approaching someone at a bad time and reinforce the connection between bad timing, bad outcomes, and bad mood.

THERAPIST: Let's look at what we have here and figure out what could have been different. Homework is definitely a hot-button issue for you and Dad. Were you ready to have that discussion with your dad right after you got home from school?

JESSICA: No. I wanted to play outside with Lily. Plus, I had just been at school all day and wanted a break.

THERAPIST: And your dad had just gotten home from work so he was probably tired too. Do you think talking about this at a different time could have made the interaction different?

JESSICA: I don't know – but how could we not talk about it right then when the fight was about when to do homework?

THERAPIST: That's a good point, Jessica. It's true that it might have been hard to avoid that fight right then, but since doing homework tends to be something you and your dad fight about, it seems like it's worth finding a way to discuss it. Do you think the conversation might go differently if you had it at a different time . . . let's say, after you had time to relax and unwind a bit and Dad had time to relax and unwind after work? How might that have changed the situation?

JESSICA: Maybe we'd both be less stressed?

THERAPIST: I think you're onto something. Why might being less stressed at the beginning make for a better conversation?

JESSICA: Because maybe you're less likely to snap at someone?

THERAPIST: You got it – you may be less likely to have a negative tone of voice, and you might be able to better choose your words. In this case, maybe you would have been able to talk to your dad instead of yelling at him.

JESSICA: Maybe – I think that made him really mad.

THERAPIST: So, here's the skill we're going to focus on today: "Use Good Timing." That means pick the right time to have a conversation. Having a conversation when you or Dad are stressed or angry often leads to saying something that someone later regrets or makes the conversation get worse. Jessica, you may be able to get your message across a little better to your dad if you choose a time when you're both calm.

JESSICA: Yeah, but he's the one that starts the conversation.

THERAPIST: True. How would you be able to ask Dad for a different time to have this conversation?

JESSICA: I'm not sure.

Introduce Role-playing

Role-play is an essential component in FB-IPT, as it provides the preadolescent with practice utilizing a new communication skill, problem-solving technique, or strategy for initiating social interactions with peers. Explain how role-playing works: you and the preadolescent will practice talking to each other like two characters in a television show/movie/play. First, you will work together to create a script—a set of sentences that the preadolescent can use to assess whether it is a good time to talk and, if not, how she can make an appointment to talk at a better time ("Use Good Timing").

Next, assign roles in the play. It is often better for the preadolescent to play the other person (e.g., parent, peer) and for you to deliver the preadolescent's lines the first time around. This allows you to model the tone and timing of the delivery, while having additional time for the preadolescent to get a feel for using this new communication skill. This distribution of roles often allows the preadolescent to respond to the script in the way she thinks the other person will respond. Depressed preadolescents often fear being challenged, dismissed, or rejected when they approach others. As an adult playing the role of the preadolescent, you can demonstrate appropriate ways to end the conversation and retreat. Together, you and the preadolescent can revise the script to anticipate negative responses and have a plan for curtailing an argument (e.g., "*This doesn't seem to be a good time to talk, I don't want to get into an argument*").

Finally, switch roles with the preadolescent so that she can rehearse the script as herself and you can assume the role of the other person. Validate the preadolescent's attempts at role-playing with the script, and respond appropriately to her queries (e.g., "*I can put my work aside if you'd like to talk,*" or "*Thanks for noticing I'm kind of busy right now. Can we talk after dinner?*"). Ask the preteen how it would feel to have a family member or peer respond in these ways.

Ask the preadolescent to practice again, and this time respond in a less agreeable manner (e.g., "*No*" or "*Does it seem like it's a good time for me to talk?*"), to allow the preadolescent to experience a response she worries will occur. Validate her handling of the situation and emotional experience (e.g., "*How would it feel if your dad really said that? Do you think you could respond in such a calm way?*"). These steps for role-playing are outlined in Therapist Tips 10.1.

Therapist Tips 10.1

Steps for role-playing:

- Explain you will practice speaking to each other like characters in a play or show.
- Identify the goals for the conversation.
- Create a script to use.
- Assign roles.
- Practice the conversation.
- Switch roles and practice again.
- Discuss the experience of the conversation and any changes needed.

Some preadolescents feel uncomfortable role-playing with their therapist during sessions. Some may feel silly, as if they are pretending, or may simply feel uncomfortable about getting their words just right. Having the preadolescent agree to role-play can be challenging but often becomes much easier once she practices a few times in sessions. Validate her hesitation to try something new, but encourage her to participate.

THERAPIST: Okay, maybe I can demonstrate an example of how to ask for a different time to have a conversation. Do you know what role-play means? (Silence) Role-playing is kind of like acting or putting on a short play. One person plays one part and the other person plays a different part. First, we can figure out who we want to play – for example, I could play you and you could play your dad. Then we could talk through a script, or the words, for how to use good timing to avoid a fight like the one we just talked about. We could practice the script, talk about it, and then switch parts—you play you, and I'll play your dad.

JESSICA: Do we have to do this? It sounds weird.

THERAPIST: It's different than what we've been doing for the past five weeks. It might feel uncomfortable at first, but role-playing really helps you practice how to say things and how to be prepared for when the other person answers the way we want him to answer and doesn't answer the way we want him to answer. Let's just give it a try.

Prepare Preadolescent for Dyadic Meeting

After role-playing with the preadolescent, prepare for the parent re-joining the session. Let the preadolescent know that when her parent comes into the meeting, you and she will teach the parent about the communication skill ("Use Good Timing," in this case). Next, you will help the parent role-playing this skill with the preadolescent and then assign practice for the upcoming week.

Preadolescent and Parent with Therapist

Introduce the Communication Skill to the Parent

When the parent joins the session, briefly outline for him the goals for the dyadic meeting (see previous discussion). Begin by telling him about the work that you and the preadolescent have done in the first half of the session and that, together, the three of you will be rolling up your sleeves and learning new ways of communicating and problem-solving.

Tell the parent that you and the preadolescent learned about a new communication skill today. Ask the preadolescent to name the skill (e.g., "Use Good Timing") and explain to her parent what it means. Often, preadolescents will need assistance in coming up with a simple definition, so be prepared to contribute to their response. If the preadolescent has agreed, share the depression circle with the parent, and discuss ways that "Use Good Timing" could help decrease conflict or miscommunication that may have occurred.

THERAPIST: Thanks for joining us, Dad. Jessica and I were talking more about specific problems associated with the move to a new school. One of the new communication techniques that we were talking about today is "Use Good Timing." I'm going to hand it over to Jessica to tell you a little bit more about it.

JESSICA: Basically, it's picking the right time to talk about something—not when you or the other person is stressed out or doing something else, like watching TV.

THERAPIST: Exactly. We tell parents to "Strike While the Iron's Cold" to remind them that trying to solve a problem when feelings are "hot" usually ends in disaster. "Use Good Timing" is a reminder to make sure you and the person who you need to talk to are calm and ready before beginning a conversation. Does that make sense?

Introduce Role-playing to the Parent

As you did with the preadolescent, define role-playing for the parent and the rationale for utilizing role-plays during FB-IPT. Enlist the preadolescent's help in telling the parent about how role-plays allow for rehearsal and refinement of new communication skills such as "Use Good Timing." Share the script you and the preadolescent constructed that demonstrates how to "Use Good Timing" in an interaction with another person. Ask the parent to role-play with you. Assign parts—the parent will play himself and you will play the preadolescent. After the role-play, check-in with the parent to see if the script is acceptable for the preadolescent to practice. If so, ask the preadolescent to role-play the script for "Use Good Timing" with her parent.

THERAPIST: One of the things I'd like you guys to do is to practice finding good times to talk about topics that might be hot topics or things you might disagree on. Let's just rehearse how you two can approach each other to make appointments—that way you'll have a basic script to use that you both will recognize. Jessica, why don't you start first?

JESSICA: I'll say something like, "Dad, I know you're busy right now, but can we figure out a time to talk later tonight?"

THERAPIST: What do you think, Dad?

After the role-play, ask the parent to come up with some examples where he could apply this skill in his interactions with the preadolescent (e.g., asking her to do a chore, following up about homework or a responsibility, checking-in with her about her day at school or plans for the evening). Ask the parent to role-play how he could "Use Good Timing" with his preadolescent, and ask the preadolescent to take on the role of herself.

THERAPIST: How might you approach Jessica?

DAD: Maybe I'd say, "Hey, Jess, can we talk about this later when I have a minute to catch my breath?"

THERAPIST: What do you think, Jessica?

JESSICA: I guess it's okay . . .

THERAPIST: (pause) but . . .

JESSICA: He just sounds like he wants me to go away.

THERAPIST: Dad, how could you make it clear to Jessica that you do not want to dismiss this conversation but want to have it later?

DAD: I could just say, "Jess, I'm not trying to avoid talking to you about this, I just want to be able to talk when I'm not making dinner."

THERAPIST: Jessica?

JESSICA: That sounds good.

Assign Practice at Home for the Upcoming Week

Suggest that the preadolescent and parent make some goals for practicing their new skill at home in the upcoming week. Provide a rationale for practicing at home. Talk about how rehearsing new communication skills may at first feel contrived but that over time it will become a more automatic and natural response to situations. Highlight that both the preadolescent and the parent will be asked to practice "Use Good Timing" in the upcoming week (see Therapist Tips 10.2 for suggestions on ways preteens and parents can practice "Use Good Timing" at home) and that they can remind each other to rehearse the new communication skill.

> **Therapist Tips 10.2**
> In situations where the preadolescent and parent appear hesitant to follow-up on rehearsing "Use Good Timing" in the upcoming week, assist the dyad in thinking about situations where they feel they could practice with each other.
> - Making an appointment to talk with each other at a later time
> - Observing that the other is busy, and asking to talk when he/she is available
> - Asking if a conversation could be postponed for a few minutes, so the preadolescent or parent can calm down

THERAPIST: In the next week, I'm going to ask you and Dad to practice making appointments to talk to each other. Jessica, I'd like you to make two appointments to talk with your father, and Dad, I'd like you to make two appointments to talk with Jessica.

DAD: What if there aren't any hot situations that come up in the next week?

THERAPIST: I'd like you both to make appointments to talk anyway. It's easier to practice a new skill when things are calm rather than when they are not.

Summary

You have completed the first session of the middle phase of FB-IPT in which you have outlined the structure for subsequent sessions and have begun addressing aspects of the problem area that may be contributing to the preadolescent's depressive symptoms. Using an example of a recent conflict, you have introduced a focus on communication skills and have demonstrated the effects of communication on the preadolescent's mood through construction of the depression circle. As part of this work, you shared the Tween Tips communication strategies and started to practice the skill of "Use Good Timing," using role-play as a way of rehearing new communication skills in sessions. Importantly, you initiated dyadic practice with the preadolescent and parent and have given them assigned practice for home. You will continue to introduce communication skills and problem-solving techniques in later sessions in the middle phase of FB-IPT, building upon the session structure and exercises you have established in this session. See Therapist Tips 10.3 for concerns about not completing all of the goals outlined for this session.

Therapist Tips 10.3

Help! I was only able to complete the depression circle with my preteen in this session and didn't even introduce a new communication skill. What do I do?

Completing all the tasks in Session 6 may not be possible, depending upon the degree of complexity of the preteen's situation, continued severity of symptoms, and her talkativeness in session. Remember, there are six sessions in the middle phase of treatment—what you do not address in Session 6 can be continued in Session 7. Doing a thorough depression circle will be helpful for presenting new communication skills. Also, remember that certain skills will be more relevant for some preteens. Although all of the Tween Tips are helpful, you may find that you end up focusing on and rehearsing one or two of them in greater depth during the middle phase of FB-IPT.

CHAPTER 11 Session 7: "Give to Get"

Goals for FB-IPT Session 7

- Review preadolescent's depressive symptoms and mood thermometer
- Discuss significant events in the past week in relation to the identified problem area
- Begin discussion of communication skills ("Give to Get")
- Dyadic meeting to focus on rehearsing communication skills/ problem solving

Materials

- 1–3 pages of blank paper
- Markers, pens

Structure for FB-IPT Session 7

- Check-in with preadolescent and parent (10 minutes)
- Meet with preadolescent (20 minutes)
- Meet with preadolescent and parent (20 minutes)

Preadolescent and Parent with Therapist

Mood Check-in with Preadolescent and Parent

Use the same format for checking in with the preadolescent and parent as described in Session 6. Follow-up on the at-home practice of new communication skills (e.g., "Use Good Timing") from the past week. Reinforce the preadolescent's and the parent's efforts to practice new skills at home. Ask about how it felt for each to approach the other—did they recognize the other's attempts to make appointments to talk? How did that make each of them feel? If the preadolescent or parent did not practice in the last week, talk about what made it difficult to approach the other and rehearse this communication skill. Ask the dyad if they would like to use some time today during the dyadic meeting to practice this communication skill. Assess whether the time spent in session today should continue with "Use Good Timing" or can be used to introduce another skill.

Preadolescent Alone with Therapist

Discuss Events in the Past Week as Related to the Problem Area

Begin the meeting with the preadolescent alone focusing on interpersonal events or interactions in relationships with his parents, family members, and peers as they relate to the identified problem area and goals. Assess interpersonal events in the past week and how they were related to the preadolescent's mood. Follow up on patterns of communication in interactions with family members or friends in the past week. Pick one interaction or conversation that influenced his mood and construct a depression circle to identify the words, intention, tone of voice, and implied meanings in the preadolescent's interactions with the other person. Again, the depression circle will help illustrate where different communication skills may improve the outcomes of these exchanges.

Introduce a New Communication Skill/Problem-Solving Technique

"Give to Get" is another communication strategy we introduce to preadolescents. (Refer to the Tween Tips in Appendix E.) This communication strategy reminds the preadolescent to demonstrate an empathetic understanding of another's perspective before presenting an opposing opinion or request. When a preadolescent acknowledges and validates another person's point-of-view, it helps that person be more open to hearing the preadolescent's perspective, even if it is different. The result is a discussion about different opinions rather than an argument. As one parent who participated in FB-IPT with her son stated, a preadolescent demonstrating some understanding of a parent's perspective has a "softening effect": when a preteen can acknowledge his parent's point-of-view, the parent is less likely to be defensive about her position or feel the need to lecture her child about the validity of the parent's perspective. This softening often results in parents being able to listen to their preadolescents' points-of-view and being more likely to engage in a discussion. In addition, parents often perceive a preadolescent who can acknowledge a different point-of-view as being more mature and respectful—which allows parents to respond in kind. See Therapist Tips 11.1 for additional clarification of the use of "Give to Get" with preadolescents.

Therapist Tips 11.1

Wait a minute—"Give to Get" sounds a little like mentalizing. Are preadolescents developmentally able to use this skill?

There are different levels of understanding another person's intentions. For preadolescents, we frame "Give to Get" as perspective taking in a defined context—what is your parent or your friend's point-of-view on this particular topic? Preteens, even those on the younger end of the age range, are able to engage in perspective taking with guidance. Also, remember that preteens often have experienced conflicts with family members or peers over the same issues discussed in FB-IPT sessions and may already know the other person's opinion/preference.

THERAPIST: Today we're going to talk about another communication skill that might be able to smooth out some of the conflict between you and Mom. It's called "Give to Get" and usually involves a situation where two people see a situation differently. Can you think of a situation where you and Mom see things differently?

OLIVER: Not really.

THERAPIST: A situation where you and Mom want different things? (pause) Video games?

OLIVER: Well, yeah. I like to play video games and my mom hates them.

THERAPIST: Has that been an issue in the past week?

OLIVER: Well, my mom isn't too happy that I want to spend my birthday money on video games.

THERAPIST: Tell me more about that.

OLIVER: Mom thinks that I'm addicted to video games and that they get in the way of my doing homework or chores around the house. She has a rule that I'm only allowed to play video games on the weekends and won't let me play games that are rated M.

THERAPIST: How does that affect your decision about how to spend your birthday money?

OLIVER: It makes me feel like I can't ask her to take me to the store to buy the game I really want.

THERAPIST: What are you worried will happen if you ask?

OLIVER: That she'll start saying that I spend too much time playing video games and don't do my homework.

THERAPIST: And how will that make you feel?

OLIVER: Mad.

THERAPIST: Got it. This is where we can use "Give to Get." Sometimes when we show someone else that we understand her point-of-view, even if it's different from our own, she is better able to listen to us.

OLIVER: Huh?

THERAPIST: Basically, you'd like Mom to drive you to the store so you can buy a video game with your birthday money, but you don't want to have a big argument with her. What do you think would happen if you showed Mom that you understand her point-of-view about video games before asking her to take you to the store?

OLIVER: Not sure . . .

Role-playing with Preadolescent

Spend some time writing out a script with the preteen using "Give to Get" in the situation identified earlier in the session. Again, assign roles before beginning the initial role-play, with you taking on the role of the preadolescent and the preadolescent taking on the role of the other person. Then switch roles.

THERAPIST: How about we role-play an example? I'll be you and you be Mom.

OLIVER: Okay.

THERAPIST (ROLE-PLAYING PREADOLESCENT): Hey, Mom—can I talk to you for a few minutes?

OLIVER (ROLE-PLAYING HIS MOTHER): Sure.

THERAPIST (ROLE-PLAYING PREADOLESCENT): I know that you really don't like me playing video games and spending money on them . . .

OLIVER (ROLE-PLAYING HIS MOTHER): Uh-huh.

THERAPIST (ROLE-PLAYING PREADOLESCENT): But I was wondering if you could take me to the store sometime this weekend. I'd really like to buy a new game with the money I got for my birthday.

OLIVER (ROLE-PLAYING HIS MOTHER): Well, that's a lot of money to spend on video games.

THERAPIST (ROLE-PLAYING PREADOLESCENT): Well, what if I just used some of my birthday money to buy one game, and then I can save the rest?

OLIVER (AS HIMSELF): It seems pretty easy. I'm not sure what my mom would say.

THERAPIST: Tell me more about what you mean.

OLIVER: I'm not sure she'd say yes.

THERAPIST: That's true – "Give to Get" doesn't always mean that we get what we want. Do you think she'd get upset with you and argue about you playing video games?

OLIVER: No –I don't think she'd get upset, but I'm not sure she'd let me spend my money on the video game.

THERAPIST: What about revising your script to let her know that you just wanted to buy one game and not spend all of your birthday money?

OLIVER: That might help.

Prepare Preadolescent for Dyadic Meeting

Refer back to Session 6. See Therapist Tips 11.2 for additional issues to consider when preparing the preteen for rehearsing "Give to Get" with his parent in the dyadic meeting.

> **Therapist Tips 11.2**
> "Give to Get" is a communication skill that maximizes the likelihood that the other person can hear the preteen's point of view, but it is not a guarantee that the situation will end in the preteen's favor. Hence, any discussion of "Give to Get" has to focus on the goal of *having a calm discussion instead of getting what you want.*
>
> Introduce the possibility that the preteen needs to be prepared to "Take the No" in response to his request. Role-playing a calm reaction to a "no" is helpful along with rehearsing some follow-up responses:
> - *Can we talk about it again at another time?*
> - *Is the "no" for right now?*
> - *Is the issue negotiable?*
> - *Is there anything that I can do to change your mind?*

Preadolescent and Parent with Therapist

Introduce the Communication Skill to the Parent

As in Session 6, begin by giving the parent an overview of the communication skill rehearsed in the meeting with the preadolescent and how it can improve interactions and decrease conflict. Help the preadolescent define and describe "Give to Get."

THERAPIST: Thanks for joining us, Mom. Oliver and I were talking about ways the two of you could work together and reduce misunderstandings, hurt feelings, and arguments at home. One of the new communication skills that we were talking about today is "Give to Get." Oliver, why don't you tell your mom a little bit more about it.

OLIVER: Um, it's like before you ask for something you want, you show that you understand what the other person wants. I guess it's a way to show that how what the other person thinks or feels is important.

MOM: Okay . . .

THERAPIST: Exactly. "Give to Get" involves acknowledging the other person's feelings or the other person's opinion before giving your own opinion or making a request of the other person. The goal is to help that other person be better able to listen to what you have to say since you've already shown that you know where she or he is coming from.

MOM: The one thing I don't like is the idea that if Oliver communicates with a "Give to Get" that I have to give him what he wants.

THERAPIST: Actually, it doesn't work that way. You're still the parent and have final say over what Oliver gets. The goal is to have a calm talk and to avoid an argument. Maybe we can do an example and you can see what it's like.

Introduce Role-play to the Parent

As in the previous session, share the scenario and script you and the preadolescent developed that demonstrates "Give to Get." If the parent agrees that the script is acceptable for the preadolescent to use, have the parent role-play it with you first. If the parent does not feel the script is acceptable, ask her to help you shape it into something that feels more comfortable for her, trying to ensure that it uses the same "Give to Get" concept.

If this role-play with you is successful and the parent feels comfortable with the script, scaffold a role-play between the preadolescent and parent. Ask the parent to come up with some examples where she could apply this skill in her interactions with her preteen (e.g., asking him to do a chore, following up about homework or a responsibility). Ask the parent to role-play how she could use "Give to Get" with her preadolescent.

THERAPIST: Let's just practice how you can make "Give to Get" statements—that way you'll have a basic script to use that you both will recognize.

MOM: I'm not sure . . .

THERAPIST: What about if you wanted him to help you with something around the house?

MOM: Maybe I'd say, "Oliver, I know you like to relax a bit after you get home from school, but could you help me move some of these boxes to the basement?"

THERAPIST: That's it. What do you think, Oliver?

Assign Practice at Home for the Upcoming Week

As in Session 6, assign the preadolescent and parent a goal to practice making "Give to Get" statements in the upcoming week. Again, identify some possible situations where each could rehearse their "Give to Get" scripts.

THERAPIST: In the next week, I'm going to ask you and your mom to practice using "Give to Get." What do you think might be some situations where "Give to Get" might be helpful?

MOM: Umm, maybe when Oliver asks me for help with his homework when I'm in the middle of making dinner?

THERAPIST: So what would that look like?

MOM: Well, I would love it if Oliver would say something like, "Mom, I know you're in the middle of making dinner, but I really need some help with my math homework. Would you be able to help me now or later?"

THERAPIST: That works! Oliver, do you think this is something you could try?

OLIVER: I could try.

Summary

You have completed Session 7 of FB-IPT. Building upon the foundations established in Session 6, you are actively teaching new communication skills to the preadolescent and parent. After describing the skill of "Give to Get," you have begun to explore how it may fit into scenarios where the preadolescent needs to express a different point-of-view, opinion, or request and wants to avoid conflict. Dyadic role-plays between preadolescents and parents will continue to help with their adoption of these skills, and assigning practice at home will increase their uptake. You will continue to introduce communication skills and problem-solving techniques in subsequent sessions in the middle phase of FB-IPT.

CHAPTER 12 Session 8: "Make 'I Feel' Statements"

Goals for FB-IPT Session 8

- Review preadolescent's depressive symptoms and mood thermometer
- Discuss significant events in the past week in relation to the identified problem area
- Begin discussion of communication skills ("Make 'I Feel' Statements")
- Dyadic meeting to focus on rehearsing communication skills/ problem solving

Materials

- 1–3 pages of blank paper
- Markers, pens

Structure for FB-IPT Session 8

- Check-in with preadolescent and parent (10 minutes)
- Meet with preadolescent (20 minutes)
- Meet with preadolescent and parent (20 minutes)

Preadolescent and Parent with Therapist

Mood Check-in with Preadolescent and Parent

Use the same format for checking-in with the preadolescent and parent as described in Sessions 6 and 7.

Discuss Events in the Past Week as Related to the Problem Area

Refer back to Session 7.

Introduce a New Communication Skill/Problem-Solving Technique

The next communication strategy to present is "Make 'I Feel' Statements." This communication strategy reminds preadolescents to express their feelings in response to situations that affect their mood, by using the phrase, "I feel . . ." (e.g., "*Mom, I feel sad and mad when you yell!*"). Emphasize to the preadolescent that others cannot read her mind and letting another person know how she is feeling has the potential to influence the way that person responds to the situation.

"Making 'I Feel' Statements" can help minimize interpersonal conflict, as such statements give the preadolescent a way to communicate her feelings that is less accusatory and less blaming and subsequently less likely to result in an argument (e.g., "*You make me so mad! You never let me watch TV!! I hate you!*"). Therapist Tips 12.1 provides suggestions for helping preadolescents communicate "softer" feelings that may underlie their irritability. "Making 'I Feel' Statements" can also help segue into problem-solving. Preteens may be pleasantly surprised to find that their parents are eager to find a solution to the problem. One family who participated in FB-IPT reported "Making 'I Feel' Statements" was code for "let's work this out peacefully" (i.e., if the preadolescent made the effort to communicate, the parent made an extra effort to listen and respond positively).

THERAPIST: Maya, today during check-in you brought up the big fight you got into with your mom when you and your sister were arguing. Tell me what made you so upset about the situation.

MAYA: I don't know. I feel like she is never on my side. She always takes Bri's side when there's a problem and tells me to go to my room.

THERAPIST: Did you share these feelings with your mom?

MAYA: No. I started yelling at her and saying, "It's not fair. You always take Bri's side." Then she told me to go to my room.

THERAPIST: That sounds really hard. How were you feeling when you said that?

MAYA: Mad.

THERAPIST: Anything else?

MAYA: I'm not sure.

THERAPIST: Were you feeling sad, too?

MAYA: Yeah, maybe a little.

THERAPIST: Do you think Mom knew how you felt?

MAYA: I think she knew I was mad.

THERAPIST: Do you think she knew you felt a little sad?

MAYA: (pause) No.

THERAPIST: Today we're going to talk about another communication skill called "Making 'I Feel' Statements." It reminds us to make sure we tell someone how we're feeling in a situation. An example of "Making an 'I Feel' Statement" would be if you told Mom that you feel sad when she tells you to go to your room before hearing your side of the story.

MAYA: That sounds weird. We don't talk like that in my family. I might get in trouble.

THERAPIST: It might be really different from what you're used to, and I know it might feel a little weird at first, but as much as she might try, your mom can't read your mind. "Making an 'I Feel' Statement" can be really helpful for bringing your mom into the loop about how you're feeling. Also, because you start talking about how something makes you feel, most parents don't see it as back-talk or being sassy.

MAYA: I don't know.

THERAPIST: How about we role-play an example. I'll be you and you be your mom.

Therapist Tips 12.1

Many depressed preadolescents are able to express anger when communicating with others but often do not see how only communicating this feeling can negatively affect parents and peers and put a premature end to a productive discussion. Likewise, there are parents who readily communicate anger to their preteens and then wonder why their children do not share with them how they are feeling. Often, the degree of anger the preteen or parent expresses toward each other reflects the emotional climate of the family.

When working with a preadolescent or parent who typically reports feeling and communicating anger ("I feel mad"), try to draw out other softer feelings that may be present (e.g., sadness, disappointment). Sometimes communicating a softer feeling has a better result for preteens who wish to express displeasure with a situation, allowing the other person to remain engaged in a less defensive way and able to hear the preteen's perspective. Identifying softer feelings to communicate is also a good exercise to use with younger preadolescents (7- to 9-year-olds) who may have a restricted vocabulary about emotions (e.g., "I feel bad").

Role-playing with Preadolescent

Again, spend some time writing out a script for "Making 'I Feel' Statements" in the situation identified earlier in the session.

THERAPIST: I'd like us to practice this skill using the argument you brought up during check-in today. Maya, how do you think you could start "Making an 'I Feel' Statement"? What words would you use?

MAYA: I'll say something like, "I felt really sad and angry when you told me to go to my room."

THERAPIST: That's a great start. Let's write it down (ask preadolescent to write it down). Now, is there anything else we want to explain to your mom about why you were feeling sad and angry? Is it because she asked you to go to your room?

MAYA: Yes. She always makes me go to my room because she thinks I'm the one who started the fight.

THERAPIST: I think that's the part we might want to make sure she knows –that you feel sad and angry because it seems like she thinks you are the problem?

MAYA: I guess . . . she doesn't even let me tell her my side.

THERAPIST: That's a good point. How about we put that into your script. How might you do that?

MAYA: I don't know.

THERAPIST: How about, "I felt sad and mad because you told me to go to my room before you even asked what was going on between Bri and me." Does that sound like something you could say?

MAYA: I could try, but I might forget.

THERAPIST: That's why we're going to practice first.

Assign roles before the initial role-play (you taking on the role of the preadolescent and the preadolescent taking on the role of the other person) and then switch roles. During these role-plays, be sure to encourage the preadolescent's efforts and make suggestions for improving her delivery (see Therapist Tips 12.2).

THERAPIST (ROLE-PLAYING PREADOLESCENT): Hey, Mom—can we talk about that fight we had the other night? Is now a good time? ("Use Good Timing")

MAYA (ROLE-PLAYING HER MOTHER): Okay, Maya.

THERAPIST (ROLE-PLAYING PREADOLESCENT): I felt really sad and angry when you told me to go to my room before you even asked what was going on between Bri and me.

MAYA (ROLE-PLAYING HER MOTHER): Well you guys always fight and I can't handle the yelling. I just wanted to separate you.

THERAPIST (ENDING ROLE-PLAY): Let's stop here. How do you think our script sounded?

MAYA: Pretty good.

THERAPIST: Did you get a bad feeling from what I said when you were role-playing your mom? Remember, we want the script to be something that your mom is open to hearing.

MAYA: No. I think it was good.

THERAPIST: I think keeping my voice calm helps. Are you ready to give it a try? Let's switch roles: you try out the script and I'll role-play your mom.

MAYA: Okay.

THERAPIST: You start. And, action!

MAYA (ROLE-PLAYING HERSELF): I feel sad and mad when you send me to my room whenever Bri and I fight.

THERAPIST (ROLE-PLAYING MOTHER): I don't mean to hurt your feelings, Maya. I just want to separate you and Bri.

MAYA (ROLE-PLAYING HERSELF): But she's so annoying! She also messes up my stuff on purpose. Sometimes I feel like you don't care about what Bri does to me.

THERAPIST (ENDING ROLE-PLAY): Great job, Maya. How did that feel?

MAYA: Good, I guess.

THERAPIST: I think you did a fantastic job—you even made a second "'I Feel' Statement" that was completely unrehearsed. Okay, back to something you said: do you think your mom doesn't care about Bri annoying you?

MAYA: Sometimes I do, but a lot of the time, I think she just wants us to stop fighting.

THERAPIST: So she may send you to your room to stop the fighting, not because she cares more about your sister?

MAYA: Yes.

THERAPIST: You know, I think this is an interesting point. We could invite Mom in and ask her, if you'd like. What do you think about sharing some of these ideas with Mom?

Therapist Tips 12.2

Remember that preteens (and their parents) often need to practice multiple times to feel confident using a new communication skill, such as "Making 'I Feel' Statements."

Monitor their frustration and praise their efforts! The first few attempts are always the most awkward.

Prepare Preadolescent for Dyadic Meeting

Refer back to Session 6.

Introduce the Communication Skill to the Parent

As in Session 6, begin by giving the parent an overview of the communication skill rehearsed in the meeting with the preadolescent and how it can improve interactions and decrease conflict. Help the preadolescent to define and describe "Making 'I Feel' Statements."

THERAPIST: Thanks for joining us, Mom. Maya and I were talking about ways the two of you could work together to reduce misunderstandings, hurt feelings, and arguments at home. One of the new communication techniques that we were talking about today is "Making 'I Feel' Statements." I'm going to have Maya tell you a little bit more about it.

MAYA: Um, so when I get upset or something, I'll tell you how I'm feeling instead of just keeping it inside. I guess you can't read my mind, so it's a way to tell you what's going on.

MOM: (nodding) Okay . . .

THERAPIST: That's great, Maya. "Making 'I Feel' Statements" is just what it sounds like. Instead of trying to guess what the other person is feeling, you'll just tell her or him how you feel. Does that make sense?

MOM: I think so. As a family, we're not that good at sharing our feelings so it would be a big adjustment. It would be nice not to have to try to read Maya's mind, though.

Introduce Role-play to the Parent

Encourage the preadolescent to share the depression circle that maps out the situation with her parent, as it can help set the stage for sharing the script with the parent and conducting the role-play. If the preadolescent does not want to share the depression circle, reference the conflict or situation when staging the role-play.

THERAPIST: Maya, I'd like you to take a break while your mom and I practice. Is it ok if I take your part and Mom will role-play herself?

MAYA: Okay.

Depending upon the degree of scaffolding the parent-child dyad requires (as evidenced by their ability to role-play/practice skills at home from previous sessions), you may wish to first role-play with the parent. When role-playing with the parent, assume the role of the preadolescent and have the parent role-play herself. With the feedback provided by the parent, revise the script with the preadolescent and then have the preadolescent role-play with her parent.

THERAPIST: I'd like us to practice this skill using the argument you and Maya brought up during check-in today. Maya and I worked on a script of how she could "Make an 'I Feel' Statement." I was wondering if you and I could role-play the conversation first, to make sure the script Maya and I came up with sounds appropriate. I'll role-play Maya and you can be yourself.

MOM: Okay.

THERAPIST: I'll set the scene first. Mom, you tried to talk with Maya after sending her to her room for arguing with her sister. Do you remember what you said?

MOM: Yes. I think I said something like, "I'm getting tired of not being able to leave you two alone in the same room for a minute without a fight breaking out."

THERAPIST: Let's start the role-play with you saying that. Action!

MOM (ROLE-PLAYING HERSELF): Maya, I'm getting tired of you and your sister fighting with each other every time I leave the room.

THERAPIST (ROLE-PLAYING MAYA): Mom, I feel sad and angry when you tell me to go to my room before you even ask what was going on with Bri and me. It makes me feel like it's my fault.

MOM: That's because you're the one who—

THERAPIST (INTERRUPTING): Let's stop there. Mom, do you have any changes to make to the script before you and Maya role-play it as yourselves?

After making any revisions suggested by the parent, ask the preadolescent and parent to role-play "Making 'I Feel' Statements." This will be the first time that the preadolescent practices using the new communication skill with her parent. As the therapist, you will be scaffolding the role-play between the preteen and parent, providing support and asking for clarification, as well as interrupting the role-play if the preadolescent and parent begin to have an argument (see Therapist Tips 12.3).

THERAPIST: Great. Now I'd like you and Maya to role-play this conversation "Making an 'I Feel' Statement." Once again, I'll set the scene: Mom, you come into Maya's room to talk with her about the argument with her sister. You say, "I'm tired of you and your sister arguing every time I leave you two alone." Maya, take it away. Action!

MAYA (ROLE-PLAYING HERSELF): I'll say something like, "I felt really sad and angry when you told me to go to my room before you even asked what was going on between Bri and me."

THERAPIST: That's great, Maya. How might you respond to that, Mom?

MOM (ROLE-PLAYING HERSELF): Um, wow. I knew you were mad that I told you to go to your room, but I didn't know that you were so upset that I didn't ask what was going on between you and Bri.

MAYA: Yeah, it's like you always think it's my fault. No matter what. And then I'm the one who has to go to my room and Bri gets to keep playing.

MOM: I guess I do blame the fighting on you. You're six years older than Bri, so I expect a lot more from you than I do from her.

MAYA: But that's not fair! She still shouldn't be able to wreck my stuff.

Therapist Tips 12.3

What happens if the preadolescent and the parent start to go "off script" during the dyadic role-play and actually start arguing with each other? This can happen, and although it may be uncomfortable at the time, it's better for the dyad's communication to unravel with you present.

Why? You can interrupt the argument and change the course of communication in ways that can help both the preteen and parent get some perspective.

- *Is this what happens at home when you try to talk about this issue?*
- *How is each of you feeling right now? Can you "Make an 'I Feel' Statement"?*
- *Can we map out the communication you both just had to see where emotions got strong and feelings got hurt?*
- *Can we come up with a different way of having this conversation? Can we write it out?*

Often, moving the focus from the content of the argument to the process helps both the preteen and parent calm down. Above all, validate the difficulty in having these conversations and that you are proud that the preteen and parent are willing to try to make their communication better. It takes time to figure out the best way to say how you are feeling or what you want in ways that do not trigger the other person.

THERAPIST: Let me interrupt you two right here. I want to call a time-out so we don't lose our focus on how to talk about this tricky situation calmly. How does it feel to be talking about this issue?

MOM: It's okay. I feel bad that I haven't been trying to help you get along better with Bri. I know I've just been stressed out and overwhelmed and I haven't had the energy to do it. I think I could try though.

MAYA: So you could ask me what happened?

MOM: Yeah, I could try. Even better, maybe you could tell me when Bri first starts bothering you so that it doesn't become a big fight.

THERAPIST: That's a really good idea, Mom. Do you think you might feel less overwhelmed at that point?

MOM: Yes, definitely. I could try to help then before it turns into a yelling match.

Assign Practice at Home for the Upcoming Week

THERAPIST: Maya, in the next week, I'm going to ask you and your mom to practice "Making 'I Feel' Statements." It's fine to "Make 'I Feel' Statements" with all kinds of emotions. Sometimes it's easiest to start with a low-stress situation, or even a positive feeling. Maya, I'd like you to "Make 'I Feel' Statements" to your mother two times, and Mom, I'd like you to "Make 'I Feel' Statements" two times to Maya. Something like, "Mom, I feel good when we get to hang out just the two of us," or "Maya, I feel really proud of how hard you worked on your art project."

Summary

You have completed Session 8 of FB-IPT and have introduced how to "Make 'I Feel' Statements" to the preadolescent and parent. In this session, you have encouraged the preadolescent and parent to directly communicate feelings in response to situations related to the identified problem area. (See Therapist Tips 12.4 for role-playing how to "Make 'I Feel' Statements" if the problem area involves relationships with peers). By expressing their feelings, including softer feelings of sadness, worry, or disappointment, preadolescents can experience what it is like to let a parent or peer understand where she is coming from and possibly increase his or her support of the preadolescent. Dyadic role-plays between preadolescents and parents will continue to help with their adoption of "Making 'I Feel' Statements," and assigning practice at home will increase the automaticity of using this skill. In the next sessions, you will use these communication skills to help introduce problem-solving techniques: "Meet in the Middle" and "Let's Make a Deal."

Therapist Tips 12.4

What about if the preteen has good communication with her parent but needs to work on how to "Make 'I Feel' Statements" with friends or classmates?

In these situations, you would script out "Making 'I Feel' Statements" as related to specific situations the preteen has encountered with peers. Adjust the role-plays so that you and the parent take on the roles of the peers in question and provide the preteen with the same amount of time and attention in session to script out communication and rehearse using different communication skills. Practice at home would still involve the preteen rehearing these skills with the parent as a way to build confidence and mastery. Therapy would build toward having the preteen implement this communication skill with peers.

CHAPTER 13 Session 9: "Have a Few Solutions in Mind"

Goals for FB-IPT Session 9

- Review preadolescent's depressive symptoms and mood thermometer
- Discuss significant events in the past week in relation to the identified problem area
- Begin discussion of problem-solving techniques ("Have a Few Solutions in Mind")
- Dyadic meeting to focus on rehearsing problem-solving techniques

Materials

- 1–3 pages of blank paper
- Markers, pens

Structure for FB-IPT Session 9

- Check-in with preadolescent and parent (10 minutes)
- Meet with preadolescent (20 minutes)
- Meet with preadolescent and parent (20 minutes)

Preadolescent and Parent with Therapist

Mood Check-in with Preadolescent and Parent

Use the same format for checking-in with the preadolescent and parent as described in Sessions 6 and 7. Follow-up on "Making 'I Feel' Statements" in the past week.

Preadolescent Alone with Therapist

Discuss Events in the Past Week as Related to the Problem Area

Refer back to Session 7.

Introduce New Problem-Solving Techniques

After the communication skills have been introduced and rehearsed, present different strategies that the preadolescent can use when trying to solve a problem or reach a resolution with his parent, family member, or peer ("Have a Few Solutions in Mind"). In FB-IPT, we present problem-solving with a two-pronged approach: "Meet in the Middle" and "Let's Make a Deal."

"Meet in the Middle" is a reminder for preadolescents to think about ways that they can compromise with a parent or peer in order to reach a solution. Because the idea of compromise is still abstract for many preadolescents, we define compromise as when each person gives a little to come up with an acceptable solution. In that way, preadolescents are encouraged to think about solving problems as "win-win," with each person getting a little of what he would like, instead of as "win-lose," where one person's needs are met and the other person's needs are disregarded.

Present "Let's Make a Deal" to preadolescents as a way of working together with a parent, family member, or peer to come up with a solution to a problem, wherein the preadolescent first offers to do something to help the other person in the situation. Oftentimes, doing something helpful for the other person makes it easier for the other person to reciprocate. "Let's Make a Deal" is often effective in situations where the parent wishes to see changes in the preadolescent's behavior that involves taking increased responsibility for developmentally appropriate tasks—such as completing homework or household chores—before allowing a privilege, such as going to a movie with a friend or having a cell phone. See Therapist Tips 13.1 for suggestions for helping preadolescents talk with parents about problems for which parents cannot compromise or negotiate.

> **Therapist Tips 13.1**
>
> There are times when preteens and parents disagree on an issue that parents deem nonnegotiable, thus limiting the preteen's ability to compromise or negotiate an outcome that is preferred. In these situations, it is helpful to talk with parents separately about their perspective on any such issues or to clarify their concerns.
>
> - Does the preteen wish to have privileges/autonomy that the parent does not think he can handle at this age?
> - Are there safety or financial concerns?
>
> In the case of a nonnegotiable issue, ask parents about whether they are open to listening to the preteen express his perspective on the topic. Oftentimes, listening to the preteen's perspective can demonstrate parents' warmth and understanding even if the outcome is not what the preteen wants. Preteens can work on "Making 'I Feel' Statements" and parents can demonstrate active listening.
>
> Ask if parents would work with you and their preteen to outline goals for behavior and responsibility that the preteen needs to demonstrate before a privilege would be negotiable (see "Let's Make a Deal"). This may help the preteen figure out ways that he could earn the goal he wants, even if it is not attainable at this time.

These techniques frame the discussion of contentious issues in solution-focused ways. However, it is important to stress that the goal of these problem-solving techniques is to try to resolve an issue without arguing, rather than to obtain the outcome the preadolescent wants (although that may happen). This is often disappointing to the preadolescent but it can push him to think about how to work toward earning his goal(s).

Therapist Tips 13.2 clarifies the goals for introducing problem-solving skills in younger preadolescents (ages 7-9).

Therapist Tips 13.2

Can preadolescents, especially younger ones, figure out how to compromise or negotiate?

Younger preadolescents definitely need a lot of scaffolding in their abilities to use problem-solving strategies since these involve a shift in how children approach their parents about problems (e.g., leading with possible solutions instead of simply identifying a problem). Rehearsing these skills allows younger preteens to begin interacting in a more mature way with parents, in that they must understand a perspective outside of their own and be more active in resolving problems. Keep in mind that we are not expecting preteens to master problem-solving as adolescents would.

Prior to introducing a specific technique, work with the preadolescent to identify a recent conflict or a desired outcome that requires another person's agreement or buy-in. Constructing a depression circle helps recognize patterns of communication that contribute to the preadolescent's interpersonal conflicts and can also be used to identify the larger, unresolved issues relating to independence or responsibility that may spark conflict. Therapist Tips 13.3 provides additional suggestions and strategies for helping preadolescents identify what each person wants in a problem situation.

The following vignette demonstrates how to introduce "Meet in the Middle" with a depressed preadolescent interested in earning an age-appropriate privilege—a later bedtime. For Jessica, who has just transitioned to living with her father and with whom there has been conflict over rules regarding homework and bedtime, skills that help her to approach her father to ask for what she would like are consistent with strategies for improving depression and functioning within the interpersonal problem areas of role transitions and role disputes.

THERAPIST: Jessica, you've said that one of the things that makes you feel down is that your dad has very strict rules about bedtime on school nights and that you still have an 8:00 bedtime.

JESSICA: It's not fair. My seven-year-old step-sister Tali goes to bed at the same time as I do. Plus, I can't watch a lot of the shows that the kids at school talk about at lunch. It makes me feel like it's another punishment.

THERAPIST: What time do you think is a reasonable bedtime for a 10-year old?

JESSICA: Most of my friends go to bed around 9:00 or 9:30.

THERAPIST: A possible solution is "Meet in the Middle" – picking a new bedtime that may be somewhere between where Dad would like it to be, 8:00, and where you'd like it to be, around 9:30.

JESSICA: So maybe around 9:00.

THERAPIST: Exactly. Now what words could you use to approach Dad with this possible solution?

JESSICA: You mean for a role-play asking my Dad?

THERAPIST: Yes. Do you want to take a try at role-playing?

JESSICA: Okay. "Dad, could I go to bed at 9:00 from now on?"

THERAPIST: Nice try. You may want to start with a "Give to Get" in order to show your dad that you understand his perspective on this issue.

JESSICA: Could you remind me again?

THERAPIST: Sure. A "Give to Get" is when you tell the other person that you understand his or her position or point-of-view on the issue. Do you know why your dad wants your bedtime to be 8:00?

JESSICA: Yeah. He wants me to get up on time for school.

THERAPIST: Okay. What words could you use to show him you know that?

JESSICA: You mean, like saying, "Dad, I know you want me to go to bed early because you want me to get enough sleep for school"?

THERAPIST: Yes. Show your dad you know where he's coming from and then ask about meeting in the middle.

JESSICA: How about: "Dad, I'm 10 years old now and would like to have a later bedtime. Most of my friends have 9:30 bedtimes. Could we "Meet in the Middle" and try a 9:00 bedtime?"

THERAPIST: That's a great start. The only part I'm not sure about is talking about your friends' bedtimes. Your dad might think you just want to be like them.

JESSICA: Yeah, my dad would hate that.

THERAPIST: How about, "Dad, I know you want me to go to bed early so I get enough sleep for school. I don't have any trouble getting up for school in the mornings and I'm 10 now. I'd like to have a later bedtime than my little sister. Could we 'Meet in the Middle' and find a new bedtime?"

JESSICA: That sounds like a lot.

THERAPIST: Let's write it down and work on it more.

Therapist Tips 13.3

What if the preteen knows what he wants but has no idea of how to "Meet in the Middle" with someone else?

The first part of "Meet in the Middle" can be defining what each person wants in a given situation. Often, it is necessary to help the preteen figure out what he would like to be different in a situation that makes him unhappy. You are off to a good start if the preteen can identify the outcome he wants in a specific interaction, even if the likelihood of obtaining the outcome is low. Typically, preteens need assistance in identifying the outcome that the other person—parent or peer—would like to see happen. This can certainly be a focus during the preadolescent's one-on-one meetings with you. Once these two perspectives are clarified, you can guide the preteen in identifying ways to "Meet in the Middle" and together you can write a script for role-playing.

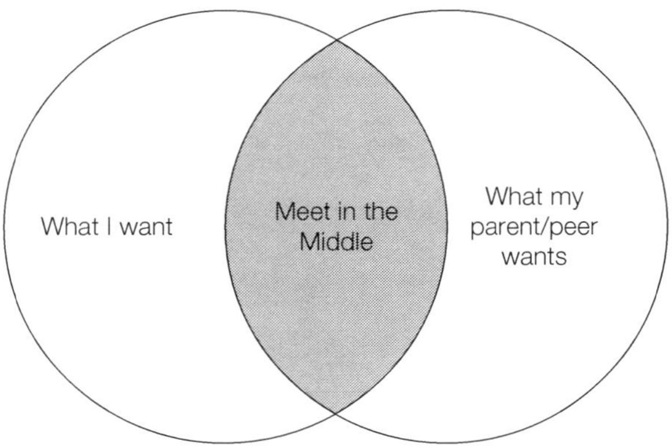

The next vignette demonstrates how to introduce "Let's Make a Deal" to a preadolescent interested in asking her mother for a cell phone. In this scenario, Maya is a preadolescent who has been experiencing depressive symptoms related to transitions stemming from her mother's return to the workforce and Maya's transition to middle school that require her to demonstrate increased independence. As a part of this developmental transition, Maya has been increasingly interested in having a cell phone for socializing with her friends. Her mother, Michelle, has expressed strong opposition to Maya's requests and often refuses to even talk about this issue. This stance causes conflict between Maya and her mother, which contributes to Maya's low mood and feelings that her mother "doesn't care about me."

THERAPIST: Maya, it sounds like you and Mom are not on the same page about you having a cell phone. Let's take a step back and look at this as a part of the changes that are taking place as you get older. You are now in middle school and want a cell phone in order to socialize with friends. That wasn't so important in elementary school, so this is something related to being a preadolescent. What's Mom's perspective?

MAYA: Well, she thinks I'm too young for a phone. She's also worried that I'd lose it, or run up huge cell phone bills, or do something stupid like send naked pictures of myself to boys . . . you know, things that you hear about.

THERAPIST: Sounds like she is afraid you are not old enough for the responsibility of a phone.

MAYA: Yeah, but that's not fair! Lots of kids my age have phones!

THERAPIST: How are you feeling right now?

MAYA: Frustrated . . .

THERAPIST: How does your mom respond when you tell her that it's not fair and that other kids your age have phones?

MAYA: She gets mad—she'll say, "Well, Maya, life isn't fair," and "I don't care what other kids have."

THERAPIST: How does that make you feel?

MAYA: Bad – it's like she doesn't care.

THERAPIST: It sounds like you both might be feeling bad. You know, I'm wondering if you could approach your mom differently about the cell phone issue. This would mean trying to talk to her like a preteen and less like a younger kid.

MAYA: What do you mean?

THERAPIST: Well, younger kids often approach a disagreement with someone by just saying what they want when a parent says "No." Preteens handle the situation a little differently—sometimes they try to figure out why the other person is saying no and then see if there's anything they can do differently. We call this "Let's Make a Deal." Sometimes when the other person sees a change in your behavior or attitude, he or she might be willing to agree to what you want. Are you following me?

MAYA: Not really.

THERAPIST: Okay, let's use a concrete example with the cell phone issue. How could you show Mom that you could handle the responsibility of a cell phone?

MAYA: I'm not sure.

THERAPIST: What about showing Mom that you can handle some of your responsibilities at home without being reminded?

MAYA: Like cleaning my room and feeding the dog?

THERAPIST: Yes. We could talk about how these are ways of showing Mom that you are "stepping up" now that you are a preteen.

MAYA: Maybe I could do things around the house to help pay for the cost of it . . . and I would hand it over to her every night at 9:00 so she could check who I've been talking to.

THERAPIST: Nice job, Maya!

MAYA: Yeah, I'm not sure she'll go for it though . . .

THERAPIST: You're right. She may not go for it. Sometimes that's the chance you have to take when you try "Let's Make a Deal" with your mom or another adult. Sometimes "Let's Make a Deal" helps you get what you want; sometimes it doesn't. The thing to remember is this: even if you don't get what you want, you and your mom could talk about the cell phone without arguing and maybe you might feel like she understands why having a cell phone is important to you.

Role-playing with Preadolescent

After introducing "Let's Make a Deal," work with the preadolescent to write a script for presenting a possible solution to the other person.

THERAPIST: Okay, Maya. Let's figure out how to start talking to your mom about the cell phone. Maybe you can start by telling her the reasons why you want a cell phone?

MAYA: Well, I'm getting older and I'd like to be able to call or text my friends. All of my friends have cell phones, and I sometimes feel left out.

THERAPIST: Are there any other reasons why a cell phone could be helpful? Do you ever need to contact Mom or does she ever need to contact you during the day?

MAYA: Well, sometimes I stay after school for softball or do the afterschool program at our church. It would be good to be able to call Mom if I get sick or have a problem.

THERAPIST: Okay. Let's write that down—you are getting older, you'd like a cell phone to call and text friends, and you also think that it would be a good way to keep in contact with Mom when you're doing afterschool activities. Try to write it down using your own words.

MAYA: (writing)

THERAPIST: Now we need to figure out what you're willing to do to earn the cell phone. What do you want to tell Mom?

MAYA: Well, I'd be willing to do extra chores to help pay for it.

THERAPIST: That sounds like a reasonable start. How could you say that to your mother?

MAYA: "Mom, I could do some chores around the house to help pay for a cell phone?"

THERAPIST: What about telling her that you know that a cell phone is expensive and that you'd like to help pay for it? Then add the bit about extra chores.

MAYA: Okay (writing).

THERAPIST: What about showing Mom that you're responsible? What could you suggest doing to show Mom that you'd be responsible with a cell phone?

Role-play using the "Let's Make a Deal" script, first with you taking on the role of the preadolescent to model presentation and tone of voice and the preadolescent taking on the role of his parent/peer. Switch roles with the preadolescent and continue to practice. Remember that this is an iterative process, and the script often requires some editing and reshaping after role-playing.

Prepare Preadolescent for Dyadic Meeting

Refer back to Session 6.

Preadolescent and Parent with Therapist

Structure the dyadic meeting between the preadolescent and parent the same way as in previous sessions: introduce the problem-solving technique to the parent, introduce the role-play that will be rehearsed to illustrate the technique, and assign practice at home for the upcoming week. In the following we present each of the problem-solving techniques separately.

Meet in the Middle: Introduce the Problem-Solving Technique to the Parent

Refer back to Sessions 6 to 8.

THERAPIST: Thanks for joining us, Dad. Jessica and I were working on a problem-solving technique today that focuses on how to negotiate or "Meet in the Middle." Jessica is going to tell you a little bit more.

JESSICA: Um, "Meet in the Middle" is like I give a little and you give a little so both of us can solve a problem.

THERAPIST: Exactly. "Meet in the Middle" is a reminder that if each person compromises, maybe a problem can be solved and each person can feel like he or she is getting a little of what he or she wants.

DAD: I'm listening . . .

Introduce Role-play to the Parent

Present the identified problem to the parent and set the stage for the dyadic role-play.

THERAPIST: Jessica and I talked about one issue that we could use for practice—the issue of her bedtime. Would that be something that we could talk about?

DAD: Yes, that would be okay.

THERAPIST: Jessica, why don't you start the conversation?

JESSICA: Well, I'm getting older and I'd like to have a later bedtime. I'd like to have some relaxing time after I finish my homework and before I have to go to my room. I also don't think that it's fair that I have to go to bed at the same time as my seven-year-old sister.

THERAPIST: Dad, do you have any concerns about Jessica having a later bedtime?

DAD: I think that she needs a good night's sleep in order to do well in school.

THERAPIST: Okay. Jessica, why don't you try talking to your dad about bedtime using "Meet in the Middle"?

JESSICA: All right. Dad, I know you're worried that I won't get enough sleep, but I think 9:30 is a reasonable bedtime for a kid in fifth grade. Could I go to bed sometime between 8:00 and 9:30? Maybe at 8:30 or 9:00 just to see how it works?

DAD: Jessie, 9:30 is out of the question. I'm willing to give 8:30 a try for a week to see how it goes—meaning how easy you can get up in the morning and how focused you are doing your schoolwork.

JESSICA: Thanks, Dad!

THERAPIST: We might have a possible solution at hand. First give me some feedback—how did this conversation feel to each of you?

Follow-up Questions 13.1

Examples of follow-up questions for dyadic problem-solving

It is important to highlight the emotional process of both the preteen and the parent when they are role-playing different problem-solving techniques. Doing so underscores the goal of communicating differently—that there is less conflict and less negative emotion, even when a problem cannot be easily resolved.

- *Was this conversation different from ones you had in the past? How so?*
- *Jessica, do you feel like your dad is listening to you?*
- *Dad, how does it feel to hear Jessica presenting some solutions to this problem?*
- *Jessica, how are you communicating differently with your dad?*
- *Dad, did you feel pressured into agreeing to something that you were not comfortable with?*

Help the parent and preteen make connections about what happens when the conversation feels better—the relationship feels stronger and both feel more on the same team even if a situation is not resolved. This process of strengthening relationships is a key mechanism in reducing the preteen's depressive symptoms.

Assign Practice at Home for the Upcoming Week

If the dyad outlined a compromise for a particular problem using "Meet in the Middle" during the session, encourage them to implement this plan at home in the upcoming week. This provides an opportunity to assess whether or not this plan was helpful or if it needs additional clarification or modification in future sessions. If a consensus was not reached on a plan to try at home in the upcoming week, ask the preadolescent and parent to table this issue until the next week's session. In the meantime, it may be helpful to ask the dyad to identify different issues that arise during a typical week that might be resolved by "Meeting in the Middle." These issues can be addressed in subsequent sessions and negotiations outlined before the preadolescent and parent make changes at home.

THERAPIST: Dad, do you feel comfortable trying out this "Meet in the Middle" solution with Jessica having an 8:30 bedtime in the upcoming week?

DAD: I'd be willing to give it a try.

JESSICA: Yes!

THERAPIST: Okay—let's do a trial run to see how it works out. How will we know if the later bedtime is a good idea?

JESSICA: It is a good idea—what do you mean?

THERAPIST: Well, think about what you both want in this situation—Jessica, the later bedtime is what you want, do you remember what your dad wants?

JESSICA: Oh, yeah—that I can get up for school and I'm not tired.

THERAPIST: Is that right, Dad?

DAD: Yes—that's my bottom line about whether we'll keep this bedtime going.

THERAPIST: What do you think, Jessica? Are you up for the challenge? Later bedtime, but no problems getting up in the morning.

JESSICA: I think so.

Let's Make a Deal: Introduce the Problem-Solving Technique to the Parent

Refer back to Sessions 6 to 8.

THERAPIST: Thanks for joining us, Mom. Maya and I were working on a new communication technique today that focuses on how to start a conversation for problem-solving using negotiation. I'm going to hand it over to Maya to tell you a little bit more.

MAYA: Um, it's called, "Let's Make a Deal."

MOM: Okay . . .

MAYA: "Let's Make a Deal" is like suggesting that I could do something to help you so that I could get something I want.

THERAPIST: Exactly. "Let's Make a Deal" is a way to remember that sometimes each person needs to do something so that a resolution to a disagreement or problem can be reached.

MOM: I'm kind of concerned about "Let's Make a Deal." I don't want Maya thinking that I owe her something in return when I ask her to do something like clean her room or set the table.

THERAPIST: Tell me more about that.

MOM: I'm just saying that she's not the parent and I make the ultimate decision—I'm all for negotiating, but sometimes the answer to a question is just "No."

THERAPIST: Has there been an issue that you and Maya have been struggling with where the answer is always a firm "No"?

MOM: Not really—I mean she keeps asking me for a cell phone, and I keep telling her no, because she's too young.

THERAPIST: I think the important thing to stress about preadolescents using "Let's Make a Deal" is that the goal is to have a calm discussion about ways a problem could be resolved. Ultimately, it's the parent who decides whether to give a potential solution a try or not. It doesn't mean that the parent is automatically locked into doing anything or that the kid is calling the shots.

Introduce Role-play to the Parent

Present the identified problem to the parent and set the stage for the dyadic role-play. See Therapist Tips 13.4 for suggestions for beginning dyadic role-plays with issues that have a greater likelihood for resolution before moving on to more challenging and emotional issues.

Therapist Tips 13.4

Sometimes it is helpful to identify a less volatile topic for the preteen to role-play with a parent. This may mean that you do not practice the role-play previously scripted with the preteen at this time and work with the dyad to identify a less complicated topic to practice clarifying what each person wants.

- Suggest making a list of problems where the preteen and parent frequently disagree.
- After coming up with four or five issues, ask the preteen and parent to pick a problem to discuss.
- Take a directive role in deciding upon a topic if the dyad struggles to come up with one on their own ("*I seem to remember some disagreements over video game/computer time? Do you think we should put that on the list?*").
- Sometimes you may want to meet individually with the parent before presenting an identified topic to assess his or her concerns and see how open he or she is to discussing this issue. During this time, you can help prepare the parent for what will happen in the session and rehearse potential responses.

THERAPIST: Before we can rehearse "Let's Make a Deal," we need to identify a problem. Maya and I talked about one issue that we could use for practice—the issue of a cell phone.

MOM: Oh, boy—here we go.

THERAPIST: You've said that this conversation hasn't been too productive in the past.

MOM: (nodding) Yes, but I'm willing to give it a try.

THERAPIST: Okay, let's focus on the problem of the cell phone. Maya, you really want a cell phone and Mom, you're not sure that it would be a good idea. Maya, maybe you can start by telling Mom the reasons why you want a cell phone?

MAYA: Well, sometimes I stay after school for softball or do the program at church. It would be good to be able to call you if I get sick or have a problem.

MOM: That is one time I think it would be helpful for you to have a phone.

THERAPIST: Okay. Mom—can you talk about why you don't think Maya should have a cell phone? What are your concerns?

MOM: Well, I'm worried that she's too young to handle the responsibility.

THERAPIST: Tell me what you mean.

MOM: I'm afraid that she'll lose the phone . . . that's like losing $150. I'm also worried that she won't be able to stop herself from calling and texting—I don't want her to run up a big phone bill because, as a single mother, I don't have the money. I'm also worried that Maya might do something stupid with a phone, like talking to people she doesn't know or sending naked pictures of herself.

THERAPIST: So two primary concerns—will Maya be able to handle the responsibility and is she mature enough to make good choices with using the cell phone?

Remind the preadolescent of the role-play rehearsed previously and encourage her to read the script if doing so would be more comfortable.

THERAPIST: Now I'd like Maya to initiate a conversation with you, Mom, about the cell phone issue using "Let's Make a Deal."

MAYA: Mom, I know that you're really worried about whether I'm old enough to handle having a cell phone. I'd like to show you that I am. What about if I started doing more chores around the house?

THERAPIST: Let's stop right there for now. First, how does it feel to hear Maya approach you about a cell phone in this way?

MOM: Well, this is much better than how she usually starts off—no whining.

THERAPIST: Great. Now what do you think about what she said?

MOM: Well . . . I guess we could try seeing how you do with taking on more chores at home. That would certainly help me out. Still, that doesn't mean I'm ready to get you a cell phone tomorrow. It doesn't make me feel less worried about you being on the phone too much or getting into situations that you're too young to be handling.

THERAPIST: What I hear you saying is that Maya's taking on extra chores at home might help you in making a decision about letting her get a cell phone?

MOM: Yes, but I'm still worried about whether she will make good choices with a cell phone.

THERAPIST: Maya, can you think of another possible solution for this problem?

MAYA: Um, maybe we could make a deal that if you let me try having a cell phone, I could give it to you every night?

MOM: Yes, that makes sense. That way I could figure out how you were doing staying within the plan each week—and maybe we could sit down together and see who you're talking to on the phone.

THERAPIST: Let me interrupt for a minute. How does this conversation feel for each of you? Does it feel different than previous conversations you've had about this issue?

Assign Practice at Home for the Upcoming Week

See example for "Meet in the Middle."

Summary

You have completed Session 9 of FB-IPT and have begun engaging the preadolescent and parent in problem-solving. You have revisited the depression circle to define a problem to solve and have talked about how to compromise ("Meet in the Middle") and negotiate ("Let's Make a Deal"). In working with the preadolescent to propose a solution, you incorporated many of the communications skills presented in earlier sessions, such as "Give to Get" and "Make 'I Feel' Statements." Dyadic role-plays between preadolescents and parents have focused on helping each identify and communicate their wants and/or concerns about problematic issues, as well as to come up with a possible solution to the problem that can be implemented and revised. Subsequent sessions will allow you to continue with these problem-solving techniques and further refine solutions. See Therapist Tips 13.5 for reminders about prioritizing techniques that are most relevant to the preadolescent's problem area and session planning.

Therapist Tips 13.5

Wow. There is a lot of information to get through in Session 9. What if I can't do it all in a single meeting?

Remember that the middle phase of FB-IPT is longer than in IPT-A. You do not have to introduce both problem-solving strategies in a single session. One option would be to introduce these strategies in Session 9 and rehearse them in Sessions 10 and 11.

Also remember that you may need to prioritize the skills most relevant to helping the preteen with his identified problem area in the middle phase of FB-IPT. You have the flexibility to concentrate on a few communication skills or individual problem-solving techniques when working with a specific preteen and parent. Therefore, if problem-solving is most relevant to the preteen's identified problem area, devote more middle phase sessions to practicing these techniques and introduce individual communication skills in the context of rehearsing "Meet in the Middle" and "Let's Make a Deal."

CHAPTER 14 Sessions 10 and 11: Designing Interpersonal Experiments for Comorbid Anxiety

Goals for FB-IPT Session 10

- Review preadolescent's depressive symptoms and mood thermometer
- Discuss significant events in the past week in relation to the identified problem area
- Discuss interpersonal approach strategies and introduce interpersonal experiments
- Enlist parent's assistance in preadolescent's use of interpersonal approach strategies in the upcoming week

Materials

- 1–3 pages of blank paper
- Markers, pens

Structure for FB-IPT Session 10

- Check-in with preadolescent and parent (10 minutes)
- Meet with preadolescent (20 minutes)
- Meet with preadolescent and parent (20 minutes)

Preadolescent and Parent with Therapist

Mood Check-in with Preadolescent and Parent

Use the same format for checking-in with the preadolescent and parent as described in Sessions 6 and 7. Follow-up on the use of previously rehearsed problem-solving strategies in the past week.

Preadolescent Alone with Therapist

Discuss Events in the Past Week as Related to the Problem Area

Refer back to Session 7.

Introduce Interpersonal Approach Strategies

Talk with the preadolescent about how increasing the frequency of interactions with peers or establishing new friendships is often necessary when resolving her identified problem area and/or reducing depressive symptoms. Grief role transitions, and role disputes often result in preteens having less social support. Preadolescents with interpersonal deficits may have long-standing difficulties establishing friendships with peers or may avoid social situations due to social anxiety. Even with preteens who have a history of good peer relationships, depression often increases preadolescents' social withdrawal which may result in heightened social anxiety when faced with the goal of re-engaging with friends.

Explore the possibilities of the preadolescent increasing her peer interactions or expanding her friend group by engaging in interpersonal approach strategies. Such strategies involve the preadolescent initiating social interactions, such as a conversation or an activity, with a peer or potential friend. Depressed preadolescents often express ambivalence or anxiety about taking the lead in initiating with peers. Discuss any concerns the preadolescent may have about increasing her interpersonal approach strategies. For preadolescents who are socially anxious, discuss the ways in which interpersonal avoidance is related to her depressive symptoms. Many anxious preteens avoid social situations that cause them to be anxious. While this coping strategy decreases their level of anxiety in the short term, it often prevents them from engaging with peers and establishing meaningful friendships over time. Feeling lonely or disconnected from peers is often a significant contributor to preadolescent depression.

THERAPIST: We've been talking a lot about your adjustment to a new school.

OLIVER: Yeah, it's been really hard.

THERAPIST: Do you think it would be easier to go to school if you had a group of friends or kids who you could talk to?

OLIVER: Yeah. I'd like to have someone to sit with at lunch.

THERAPIST: I thought maybe we could talk about how you could put yourself out there a little bit more with kids at school.

OLIVER: What do you mean?

THERAPIST: I was thinking about ways that you could start talking more with kids and work up toward asking if you could sit with a group in the cafeteria.

OLIVER: I don't know about that. I'm really nervous about who I should sit with and what I should say.

THERAPIST: You've always been a little nervous about reaching out to kids; you've said that before. Do you think those worries stop you from approaching and getting to know friends?

OLIVER: Maybe.

THERAPIST: I think you told me that you feel like you end up spending a lot of time alone. Do you think being nervous and not approaching kids sometimes ends up with you being by yourself?

OLIVER: Yeah, but I just don't feel comfortable doing that.

THERAPIST: I know. Maybe one of things we could do is talk about how you could put yourself out there a little bit more.

Role-playing with Preadolescent

First, spend some time with the preadolescent identifying potential peers he could approach. For preadolescents who have friends, identify those with whom he would like to reconnect. For preadolescents who need to make new friends, ask him to list peers who seem accepting, share interests, or overlap in terms of classes, neighborhood, or extracurricular activities. Most preadolescents can identify one or two peers who they see on a regular basis (on the bus, in class) and with whom they could start a conversation. With the preadolescent, identify different ways that he could approach peers at varying levels of interaction: making eye contact, saying hello, asking a question about school, paying a compliment (e.g., "*Cool shirt*"), or inviting them to participate in a shared activity. Script out ways that the preadolescent could approach the identified peer.

THERAPIST: Oliver, who at school might be a good person to practice talking to?

OLIVER: Maybe this kid named Jake. He was on my soccer team last year and now he's at the same school as me.

THERAPIST: Good. Do you run into Jake at all during the school day?

OLIVER: Yeah, I see him in my math class.

THERAPIST: Do you usually say hello to him or talk to him?

OLIVER: Not really.

THERAPIST: Maybe saying hello would be a good place to start? How do you think you could do that?

OLIVER: I don't know . . . he might think I'm weird if I just start saying, "Hi, Jake" when I see him in class.

THERAPIST: Is there another way that you could start a conversation?

OLIVER: I don't think so.

THERAPIST: How about asking about the math homework or about whether he's still playing soccer?

OLIVER: I guess I could. I know he's a big sports fan—

THERAPIST: Let's go with that then. What could you say?

OLIVER: Maybe something like, "Did you catch the game last night?"

THERAPIST: Write it down. Now let's practice (role-play).

Introducing Interpersonal Experiments

Develop a plan with the preadolescent to implement an interpersonal approach strategy that has been scripted and rehearsed during in-session role-plays. Provide the rationale that road-testing interpersonal approach strategies can help revise and improve scripts and can allow you and the preteen to see if initiating more with peers has a positive effect on the preadolescent's mood. Many preadolescents, even those without comorbid anxiety disorders, express anxiety about actually implementing interpersonal approach strategies. It helps to explain that one of the most effective ways to decrease anxiety that often accompanies social initiation is to practice. Describe this to preadolescents as "going out of your comfort zone" or "stretching a muscle" to emphasize that increasing approach strategies can feel uncomfortable at first but gets easier with practice. See Therapist Tips 14.1 for suggestions on how to encourage preadolescents to increase their use of interpersonal approach strategies.

THERAPIST: We know that in your last school your mood was better when you had a group of other kids to hang out with and do things with. This is a really important goal to work up to. Are you up for the challenge?

OLIVER: What do you mean?

THERAPIST: What do you think about practicing some of the things we talked about during the upcoming week? That way, we could figure out if we're on the right track or not.

OLIVER: I don't know. I'm already feeling anxious just talking about it.

THERAPIST: That's totally understandable. Anxiety makes us want to avoid doing things like talking to someone new even when that could really help us feel better.

OLIVER: (shrugs)

THERAPIST: It may sound weird, but one way to deal with anxiety is to try to do some of the things that make us anxious, and with practice we become less anxious about doing them.

OLIVER: I'm not sure I understand.

THERAPIST: Let me give you an example. Talking to someone new, like Jake, is like going out of your comfort zone or stretching a muscle because it doesn't necessarily feel good at first. But the more you practice, the anxiety will go down and you'll be more confident about talking to new kids.

OLIVER: Okay, I think I get it, but I'm not sure I want to do that.

THERAPIST: I know it might make you uncomfortable at first, but I think it will be important to begin to step out of your comfort zone so that you can have the type of friendships you want. It's hard to push yourself to do something like this at first. You're still not on your A-game and a little out of practice.

OLIVER: Yeah and maybe nothing good will happen.

THERAPIST: What do you mean?

OLIVER: Well, maybe Jake will blow me off.

THERAPIST: How would that make you feel?

OLIVER: Lousy.

THERAPIST: Do you think Jake's that kind of kid? If he is, maybe we should think about you talking to someone else.

OLIVER: No. I think he's a good guy.

THERAPIST: I think that's your anxiety talking then . . .

OLIVER: Probably.

THERAPIST: It's okay to be nervous. It gets easier the more you practice putting yourself out there.

Therapist Tips 14.1

Sometimes a preteen needs some additional encouragement to consider stepping out of her comfort zone. Remind her that avoidance works to keep anxiety at bay in the short term but learning how to cope when she's feeling anxious helps to decrease her anxiety in the long term. Strategize about taking very small steps toward reaching out to peers. Small successes build confidence and help preteens engage in more challenging interpersonal experiments as time goes on.

Prepare Preadolescent for Dyadic Meeting

Refer back to Session 6.

Preadolescent and Parent with Therapist

Introduce Interpersonal Approach Strategies to the Parent

Outline for the parent the rationale for increasing the preadolescent's initiaton of social interactions with peers as a strategy for decreasing depressive symptoms and improving the preteen's social support. Discuss the challenges that social anxiety presents in the preadolescent's ability to initiate with peers and its contribution to the preadolescent's interpersonal avoidance.

THERAPIST: Thanks for joining us, Mom. Oliver and I were just talking about ways he can become more comfortable initiating social interactions with kids at his new school.

MOM: Oh, that's great. I think that would definitely help him feel better about being at his new school.

THERAPIST: Oliver and I have been talking about taking some first steps even if it means him going outside his comfort zone. Oliver, do you want to tell you your mom the plan we came up with?

OLIVER: Well, we talked about how I could start off by trying to talk to that kid Jake who was on my soccer team last year. He's in my math class and seems cool—he likes sports like I do.

MOM: That sounds like a good idea. I think I remember him from your team.

THERAPIST: Oliver and I talked about how he could approach Jake—either by saying hello or asking him a question about last night's game.

MOM: Do you think you could do that, Oliver?

OLIVER: I'm not sure . . .

THERAPIST: Well, we role-played what it would be like but were just discussing an interpersonal experiment for the upcoming week.

MOM: A what?

THERAPIST: Oliver, do you want to explain what an interpersonal experiment is to your mom?

OLIVER: It's like trying out what we role-played in real life.

THERAPIST: That's right—it would involve Oliver implementing the interpersonal approach strategy we practiced, so we can see how it works out.

Enlist the Parent's Assistance in Conducting Interpersonal Experiments

Parents play an important role in helping their preadolescent rehearse and implement interpersonal approach strategies outside of therapy. Encourage parents to act as coaches and help their preteen engage in the interpersonal experiments. Address any parental concerns about encouraging interpersonal approach strategies in their preadolescents, particularly if the parent is unsure of how to support the child in the event of distress or refusal (see Therapist Tips 14.2).

Explain to parents that permitting their preadolescent to avoid social situations actually makes the anxiety stronger, and the more that their preadolescent practices interpersonal approach strategies, the less intense the anxiety will become. Discuss with the parent how to handle elevated emotional distress or resistance the preadolescent may evidence when attempting interpersonal experiments.

Therapist Tips 14.2

Since parents do not like to see their children struggle, sometimes they inadvertently reinforce avoiding as a way to spare the preteen the stress of going out of her comfort zone. Parents often become frustrated by the extent of their preteen's interpersonal avoidance, which can become a big source of conflict between parents and kids, and between the parents, if they themselves are not on the same page.

Assign Practice at Home for the Upcoming Week

You should reach an agreement on an interpersonal experiment that the preadolescent will attempt in the upcoming week. Reiterate that success on these interpersonal experiments is in the trying, not in the outcome. That means the goal is for the preadolescent to try to initiate an interaction with a family member or peer in a positive way, and success is not measured by how the other person responds to her. Highlight the possibility that the identified experiment may prove too challenging for the preadolescent and that it may not be successful in its first attempt (see Therapist Tips 14.3). In this event, the interpersonal experiment may need to be revised in a subsequent session before it can be attempted again and the goals met. Share this plan with the parent and identify how the parent will support the preadolescent in attempting the interpersonal experiment.

THERAPIST: Okay, so the interpersonal experiment for the upcoming week will be asking Jake if he caught the game last night.

MOM: Wow, Oliver – that would be awesome.

OLIVER: Mom—I don't know if I can.

THERAPIST: Oliver, you sound unsure. What's going on?

OLIVER: I guess I'm afraid of trying it.

THERAPIST: It makes sense. What are you most worried about?

OLIVER: Um. I'm not sure. It's not like anything bad can happen—not worse than what I've already been through anyway. I guess it's just new.

THERAPIST: You're right. It is new and your anxiety is kicking in. I'm wondering if we can ask your mom to be part of the team. Could you to act as a coach for Oliver to encourage him to talk to Jake even if he feels nervous?

MOM: Sure.

THERAPIST: Oliver's probably going to feel nervous and may try to put it off. It would be great if you can remind him about some of the things we've been talking about. What things would be helpful for Mom to remind you, Oliver?

OLIVER: Well, she could remind me that if I want to make new friends I have to go out of my comfort zone.

THERAPIST: Anything else?

OLIVER: That Jake's a nice guy and probably won't be mean. And that I can practice with my mom too.

THERAPIST: Okay, so you want your mom to remind you that you want to talk to Jake, but you need to go out of your comfort zone; that Jake's a nice guy and probably won't blow you off; and that it might help to practice what you want to say with your mom, right?

OLIVER: Yeah.

MOM: I can do that.

Therapist Tips 14.3

What should I do if the preteen and parent come into our next session and the preteen was unable to complete the interpersonal experiment?

This is a common concern, especially for preadolescents with comorbid anxiety. Explore the degree to which anxiety and avoidance contributed to the preteen's inability to initiate with a peer. Validate that the experience of putting oneself out there is anxiety provoking, but not trying to reach out to potential friends may be what ultimately keeps her feeling lonely and disconnected from peers. Reevaluate if the interpersonal experiment was too much of a challenge for the preteen. Do you need to work on a less anxiety-provoking type of initiation strategy? Do you need to elicit assistance from the parent in setting up social activities for the preteen? If so, what sort of activities would the preteen be open to trying? It is important for you to model problem-solving and persistence for the reluctant preteen.

Summary

In Session 10, you have introduced interpersonal approach strategies as ways to help socially isolated or avoidant preadolescents increase the frequency of initiating with peers. Working collaboratively with the preadolescent, you have identified peers and situations where the preadolescent could initiate even a brief interaction, and you have scripted examples of saying hello, asking a question, or giving a compliment. After role-playing the interpersonal approach strategy, you encouraged the preteen to implement this approach in the upcoming week as an interpersonal experiment, with the hope that more frequent initiation with peers will result in more positive moods. You have enlisted the preadolescent's parent as a support and coach for the preadolescent in completing the interpersonal experiment in the upcoming week, and suggested the possibility of the parenting a more active role in increasing the child's opportunities for social interactions. For preadolescents who experience comorbid anxiety and social isolation, interpersonal approach strategies would likely be the focus of the middle phase of FB-IPT, and sessions such as the one outlined in Session 10 would be prioritized and repeated in subsequent sessions as noted in the next section.

FB-IPT Session 11

This extra session can be used to complete the introduction and rehearsal of effective communication skills in cases where (a) the initial phase of treatment extends beyond five sessions (e.g., interpersonal inventory requires extended time or crisis situations emerge and must be addressed in session) or (b) preadolescent or family crises arising in the middle phase of FB-IPT require extended sessions in order to complete presentation of communication skills.

The structure of the session will be identical to the other FB-IPT sessions in the middle phase and will include a 10-minute check-in with the preadolescent and parent, a 20-minute individual meeting with the preadolescent to introduce/review skills, and a 20-minute dyadic meeting to enlist the parent's assistance rehearsing the communication skills.

PART FOUR

Termination Phase of FB-IPT

CHAPTER 15 Session 12: Planning for the End of FB-IPT

During the termination phase of treatment, you will prepare the preadolescent and parent for the completion of FB-IPT. The four primary goals of the termination phase include

1. linking the preadolescent's symptom improvement to the use of new communication and problem-solving skills,
2. developing a plan for the conclusion of treatment or the next step in treatment based on the preadolescent's current symptoms and functioning,
3. providing psychoeducation about the risk of relapse in depression, and
4. helping the preadolescent and parent identify specific behavioral or mood changes that signify the re-emergence of depressive symptoms and develop a plan to intervene quickly.

As in the middle phase of FB-IPT, sessions during the termination phase of FB-IPT are divided between the individual meetings with the preadolescent and dyadic meetings with the preadolescent and parent. Individual meetings with the preadolescent consist of reflecting on his degree of improvement experienced over the course of treatment. During this phase you will help the preadolescent see the relationship between symptom improvement and his use of new communication and problem-solving skills. You will also discuss the preadolescent's feelings about ending treatment or transferring to a different clinical service, depending on whether the preadolescent is still experiencing significant symptoms of depression. It is important to help the preteen to differentiate normal feelings of sadness about ending his relationship with you from returning symptoms of depression. You will also provide psychoeducation about depression recurrence, problem-solve potentially stressful upcoming situations, and develop a plan for the preadolescent to follow should symptoms return. Throughout these sessions, you will encourage the preadolescent to use the FB-IPT skills to problem-solve and plan for the conclusion of treatment.

Similarly, in the dyadic meetings you will ask for the parent's assessment about the progress the preteen has made in treatment. You will incorporate preadolescent and parent feedback to identify and discuss the most appropriate next step after completing weekly FB-IPT. The options include ending treatment, continuing FB-IPT for a longer but time-limited period, or a referral to another clinical service. You will talk to parents about their feelings about ending treatment, reinforce their ability to maintain treatment gains at home by using new skills, and develop a plan to intervene should the preadolescent's symptoms recur.

Goals for FB-IPT Session 12

- Review preadolescent's depressive symptoms and mood thermometer
- Discuss significant events in the past week and how preadolescent used skills to communicate better or solve a problem
- Introduce termination and make a plan for next steps
- Psychoeducation about depression recurrence with preadolescent and parent

Materials

- 1–3 pages of blank paper
- Markers, pens

Structure for FB-IPT Session 12

- Check-in with preadolescent and parent (10 minutes)
- Meet with preadolescent (20 minutes)
- Meet with preadolescent and parent (20 minutes)

Preadolescent and Parent with Therapist

Mood Check-in with Preadolescent and Parent

Just as in the middle phase, begin the session by meeting with both the preadolescent and parent together. Ask the preadolescent to rate his mood on the mood thermometer in the last week; follow up with the parent's report of the preteen's mood and symptoms. Introduce the transition to the termination phase of treatment, for example:

> *Believe it or not, we're moving into the last three sessions of our work together. So today we're going to start talking about the progress you've made in therapy and what we need to put in place for moving ahead.*

Preadolescent Alone with Therapist

Discuss Interpersonal Events in the Past Week and Implementation of Communication Skills or Problem-Solving Techniques

Ask the preadolescent to update you on any significant events involving family members or peers in the past week that affected his mood. By the time you reach the termination phase of FB-IPT, many preadolescents have experienced improvement in their mood and shifts in their behavior that have resulted in better relationships with parents and peers. Listen carefully to any positive reports of interactions with parents or friends so that you can link symptom improvement to new ways of communicating (see Therapist Tips 15.1). Help the preadolescent identify ways in which changes in his communication and/or behavior have contributed to positive outcomes in his relationships.

> **Therapist Tips 15.1**
> If the preadolescent continues to report distress related to interpersonal events, continue to work with him to use communication skills and problem-solving techniques.
>
> - Construct the depression circle to map out interactions where the preadolescent tries to use new communication skills. Does he need more practice?

- Determine whether the preteen needs more practice using his skills in his relationships with parents, family members, or peers.
- Talk with the preadolescent about what may be getting in the way of using some of the new skills. Preadolescents who continue to experience high levels of distress in their relationships may not be implementing new skills at home or at school.
- Assess whether the depressive symptoms continue to interfere with the ability to try new communication skills or take an active approach to solving problems. This information is important in determining whether you will refer the preadolescent to continuing clinical services at the end of treatment.

Construct Wellness Circle

A wellness circle (see Appendix G) helps illustrate how the preadolescent's communication and behavior can result in better outcomes during conflicts and in resolving disagreements with parents and peers, thereby improving these relationships. A wellness circle utilizes communication analysis by creating a series of text boxes that represent each point in an interpersonal interaction that the preadolescent experienced with a parent or peer. Help the preadolescent to recreate the interaction, remembering what he said and how the other person responded. Throughout the process, assist the preadolescent in making connections between how he was feeling during different points in the interaction and how his mood affected his responses to the person with whom he was interacting.

Whereas a depression circle emphasizes the types of events and responses that relate to a low mood, a wellness circle emphasizes the types of communication and problem-solving strategies that can help the preadolescent have an improved mood (see Therapist Tips 15.2). The exercise of the wellness circle can remind preadolescents of how they feel when they use positive communication techniques (e.g., "*It seems like you tried to 'Use Good Timing' here. I'm glad you asked to talk with your dad after he was finished helping your little sister with her math homework. It seems like he could focus his full attention on what you were saying and you felt like he really cared*").

THERAPIST: It sounds like going ice-skating with your friends really boosted your mood. How did that happen?

JESSICA: Well, I really wanted to go to ice-skating with some friends, and I knew I needed to ask my dad for permission. I knew that if I asked him when he was in the middle of doing something else, he probably wouldn't say yes, so I asked him if we could find a time to talk after dinner.

THERAPIST: Good for you! What skill did you use?

JESSICA: The making-an-appointment one.

THERAPIST: Yes—"Use Good Timing." Okay, so what did you say to him?

JESSICA: I said, "Dad, I know you're busy helping Tali with her homework now, but could we talk later on?"

THERAPIST: Let's write that down in this first text box. What was your mood like when you said that to Dad?

JESSICA: It was okay– about a 4 on my mood thermometer. I was kind of nervous because I was afraid he would say no.

THERAPIST: So how did your dad respond?

JESSICA: He said, "Is everything all right, Jess?" I told him it was, but I wanted to talk to him about something when he wasn't in the middle of helping Tali with her homework.

THERAPIST: (writes that down in square). How did your dad react?

JESSICA: He said, "Sure, how about right after dinner?"

THERAPIST: So you decided to make an appointment with your dad (writes that down in square). How were you feeling?

JESSICA: I was still nervous, but I felt good.

THERAPIST: How did it go during your appointment?

JESSICA: I asked if I could go ice-skating with my friends on Friday night. My dad asked what time ice-skating was and who I wanted to go with.

THERAPIST: (writes that down in square). When your dad asked you those questions, how were you feeling?

JESSICA: Still a little nervous, but happy that he didn't say no. He just seemed like he wanted to know more details.

THERAPIST: (writes that down above arrow). How did your dad respond to what you said?

JESSICA: He said that he'd try to make it work even though he'd be getting home late on Friday night.

THERAPIST: Okay, I'll write that down here. How were you feeling then?

JESSICA: So happy—I couldn't believe that he didn't just say no.

Therapist Tips 15.2

Use the wellness circle to help identify the skills that were helpful during the preadolescent's interaction with his parent or peer.

- Did the preadolescent engage in perspective taking?
- Did he use a new communication skill?
- Did he attempt to compromise or negotiate to solve a problem?

Make the link between communicating differently and any positive outcome he experienced. Relate the positive outcome with his parent or peer to improvements in his mood.

Even if the preteen does not experience a positive outcome, reinforce his hard work and willingness to improve interactions with important people in his life. Tell him, "Don't give up!" Learning new skills takes time and patience.

Initiate Conversation about Termination

Talk with the preadolescent about how weekly FB-IPT sessions will be ending soon and the need to make a plan about next steps. Spend time talking with the preadolescent about his depressive symptoms and assess the degree of improvement experienced over the course of treatment. Have there been significant improvements in the preadolescent's depression? Is he experiencing significant improvement in his relationships with his parents and peers? These questions will determine whether the preadolescent will take a break from treatment at the end of FB-IPT or will continue psychotherapy.

Ask the preadolescent about his feelings as his time working with you is ending. Regardless of symptom improvement, many preadolescents are eager to end treatment and return to routines that do not involve weekly therapy appointments. Termination is a time to celebrate the gains made by the preteen and his hard work in implementing new communication and problem-solving skills. Inquire about aspects of treatment that he found helpful and areas that he still may need to work on.

THERAPIST: It may be hard to believe, but we're coming to the end of our time working together.

JESSICA: I know. When we were driving in, my dad told me that we only have about three sessions left.

THERAPIST: How are you feeling about that?

JESSICA: Good, I guess.

THERAPIST: Do you feel ready to take a break from therapy?

JESSICA: Well . . . I'm not sure.

THERAPIST: Let's compare how things are now to how things were when we met for the first time.

JESSICA: Things are going a lot better at school.

THERAPIST: What about your mood?

JESSICA: I haven't been crying at night.

THERAPIST: Anything else that's different now?

JESSICA: I'm not really sure.

THERAPIST: What about your relationship with your dad?

JESSICA: (shrugs) I don't know. I guess we aren't fighting as much.

THERAPIST: Yes, your dad has also said you two aren't fighting as much. Do you think that has helped your depression improve?

JESSICA: I think so.

THERAPIST: Do you think the relationship just got better on its own, or did you do anything differently to make things better with your dad?

JESSICA: I tried to not fight with him.

THERAPIST: I agree—I think you tried really hard. What sort of things did you do?

JESSICA: All the stuff we talked about in here.

THERAPIST: Let's pinpoint some of the skills we used here. What about "Making 'I Feel' Statements"? Do you think they helped you and Dad fight less?

JESSICA: Um, maybe.

THERAPIST: When we met with your Dad at the beginning of our session today, he said that you've been letting him know how you're feeling.

JESSICA: Yeah, I do think that's true.

THERAPIST: How does that help you and your dad get along better?

JESSICA: Well, I don't know. Dad says we're not trying to read each other's minds as much.

Prepare Preadolescent for Dyadic Meeting

Before asking the parent to join you and the preadolescent, let the preadolescent know about issues you will bring up in the dyadic session. Explain how you will ask the parent to give his or her feedback on the preadolescent's current depressive symptoms and functioning as weekly FB-IPT sessions will be ending in the upcoming weeks. Tell the preadolescent that the three of you will need to decide upon a plan for how to proceed and that today's meeting will be one of the first steps in making that plan.

Preadolescent and Parent with Therapist

Initiate Conversation about Termination

As with the preadolescent, begin the dyadic session with the parent by observing that FB-IPT sessions are ending. Ask the parent to share his or her feelings about ending sessions. Some parents may be anxious that therapy, and extra support, is ending and express the desire to continue treatment. Acknowledge that parents and preadolescents are likely to experience a range of feelings upon termination, and they may even have conflicting feelings about ending therapy.

Discuss the need to make a plan about next steps. Review the preadolescent's current depressive symptoms with the parent and assess the degree of symptom improvement. Introduce a discussion about (a) planning for the preadolescent to terminate all treatment at the end of

FB-IPT, (b) continuing FB-IPT, (c) possibly augmenting with medication for partial responders, or (d) transferring to another clinical service. Present the consensus on the preadolescent's current symptoms and functioning based on your meeting with the preadolescent and feedback from the parent. Explain how the preadolescent's symptom status at this time maps onto one of the following treatment recommendations:

- Ending or taking a break from treatment is indicated in the case of a preadolescent who has demonstrated an improved mood and return to functioning prior to depression onset, or
- Continued treatment (at the same level of care or higher) or possibly a different treatment approach is indicated for preadolescents who continue to evidence depressed mood and poor psychosocial functioning.

Get feedback from the preadolescent and parent about the recommendation for ending or continuing treatment (see Therapist Tips 15.3 for some additional suggestions).

THERAPIST: Maya and I were just talking about how much work she's done over the past few months and how much improvement we've seen in her depressive symptoms.

MOM: Yeah, we were just talking about it in the car as well. Hard to believe we have just three sessions left.

THERAPIST: I know. How do you think she's doing now?

MOM: I think Maya's doing better. She is definitely less irritable and we're not fighting as much. She is still more tired than usual though. There are still some issues with homework and fighting with her sister, but she's talking to me more about things when she's upset.

THERAPIST: Maya's definitely made a lot of progress, and you both have been working really hard to help her recover from the depression and work on your relationship. Still, it sounds like there are some symptoms of depression that are being stubborn. We need to figure out if ending all treatment makes sense or if Maya would benefit from continued treatment.

MAYA: Wait, more therapy? I thought you said I was only going to have three more sessions.

THERAPIST: Both you and your mom told me that you are still struggling with some symptoms of depression—still feeling more tired than usual, sometimes having a hard time finishing homework. You've had a good response to treatment, so a couple of extra sessions may help get some of these symptoms under better control.

MOM: I'm not sure about that either. It's been hard to come in for these sessions every week.

THERAPIST: Well, let's keep an eye on how Maya's doing with her energy and attention over the next week or so. Maybe we can talk about other types of treatment that might be helpful to resolve these stubborn symptoms.

MOM: Like what?

THERAPIST: We could start by adding a few more sessions and see if that helps. We can always explore a medication evaluation in addition to therapy and consider tutoring support for Maya's homework.

MOM: Let me think about that.

Therapist Tips 15.3

The preteen I'm working with has made some progress in therapy but still is struggling with low mood, low motivation, poor concentration, and poor school performance. I want to refer him for continued treatment to another clinical service, but he wants to be finished with therapy. What should I do?

Some preadolescents require longer, more intensive psychological interventions to alleviate their depressive symptoms. FB-IPT may not be effective in treating depression in all clients, despite the best efforts of the therapist, preteen, and parent. Making a recommendation for continued treatment is often met with disappointment and frustration on the part of the preadolescent, who may feel pessimistic about getting better and tired of weekly therapy appointments. Encourage him to express his feelings about continued treatment. Validate the disappointment that his expectations for ending treatment have not been realized at this time. Blame the depression for being stubborn, and highlight the preadolescent's hard work. Provide psychoeducation about adjunctive treatments for stubborn depression in preadolescents, such as psychiatric medication. Model good problem-solving and reassure the preadolescent (and parent) that you will work with them over the remaining weeks to come up with a plan for continued treatment.

Provide Psychoeducation about Depression Recurrence

Preadolescents who have experienced depression appear to be at an increased risk for recurrence in adolescence, particularly if they have a family history of mood disorders. Because of the episodic nature of depression, introduce the need for the preadolescent to monitor his mood and symptoms after ending treatment. Outline ways that the parent can continue to check in with the preadolescent to assess for returning symptoms of depression. Review the link between the use of new communication and problem-solving skills and improvements in mood that can help the preadolescent maintain treatment gains and hopefully protect against future episodes of depression (see Therapist Tips 15.4).

Therapist Tips 15.4

Psychoeducation regarding the recurrence of depression in preadolescents can include

- Discussion of how to distinguish between normal episodes of sadness and a recurrence of depression
- Reviewing the skills learned in treatment and their role in maintaining the preadolescent's improved mood
- Steps to take if preadolescent and/or parent feel there is a recurrence

Summary

In Session 12 of FB-IPT, you have continued to support the preadolescent's practice of interpersonal skills and have begun to reflect with the preadolescent and parent upon the progress that the preadolescent has made in treatment. During the session, there is continued emphasis on the link between improvement in the preadolescent's depressive symptoms and the role that FB-IPT communication and problem-solving skills have played in his symptom improvement.

In addition, you have begun to talk with both preadolescent and parent about the next step after FB-IPT ends: the termination of outpatient therapy, referral to a maintenance group or individual therapy, or to a more intensive treatment, depending on the preadolescent's individual symptoms.

CHAPTER 16 Session 13: Identifying Early Warning Signs for Depression Recurrence

Goals for FB-IPT Session 13

- Review preadolescent's depressive symptoms and mood thermometer
- Discuss significant events in the past week and how preadolescent used skills to communicate better or solve problems
- Identify preadolescent's early warning signs for depression
- Review plan for anticipating and planning for stressful situations
- Review the preadolescent's early warning signs with parent

Materials

- 1–3 pages of blank paper, index cards
- Markers, pens

Structure for FB-IPT Session 13

- Check-in with preadolescent and parent (10 minutes)
- Meet with preadolescent (20 minutes)
- Meet with preadolescent and parent (20 minutes)

Preadolescent and Parent with Therapist

Mood Check-in with Preadolescent and Parent

Use the same format for checking in with the preadolescent and parent as described in Session 12.

Discuss Interpersonal Events in the Past Week and Implementation of Communication Skills or Problem-Solving Techniques

Refer to Session 12.

Help the Preadolescent Anticipate Stressful Situations

As the preadolescent prepares to end treatment or transition to another clinical service, focus on how she can continue to apply the communication skills and problem-solving techniques in different situations. Begin by asking the preadolescent to develop a list of stressors/events coming up in the next couple of months that may negatively affect her mood (e.g., new school year, poor report card, argument with friend, excluded from birthday party, disagreement with Dad, holiday without Mom, going to summer camp). Explain that anticipating stressors allows the preadolescent to plan for how to respond to these situations. Use an example of an upcoming stressor provided by the preadolescent. If she struggles with identifying upcoming stressors, suggest scenarios similar to situations she has found stressful in the past. Talk about which types of communication skills she could use or which techniques she could use to resolve a problem.

THERAPIST: We're going to spend some time today talking about how to help you remember to use your skills even after we stop therapy. One way you can do that is to not let stressful situations sneak up on you. What do you think I mean when I say that?

OLIVER: That you don't want to get surprised?

THERAPIST: Right – you want to be prepared for situations that might be difficult so you have a plan for what you can do. I'd like us to put our heads together to think about what sorts of things might be coming up for you that could make you stressed out.

OLIVER: I don't know . . .

THERAPIST: Anything at school or at home?

OLIVER: Well, I do have an overnight trip with my class coming up . . . and I have to go on that weekend trip with my mom and dad.

THERAPIST: Those are some good examples. Let's start with the overnight trip—what sorts of things could be stressful for you?

OLIVER: Well, I have to share a room with three other guys. I'm just afraid I'm going to get stuck with kids I don't like.

THERAPIST: What would happen then?

OLIVER: I'd be stuck . . . and have a lousy time.

THERAPIST: Any other concerns?

OLIVER: Yeah – I'm afraid I won't have anyone to hang out with during the day when we visit the museum.

THERAPIST: How would that feel?

OLIVER: Lonely.

THERAPIST: Any ideas of ways to avoid those outcomes?

OLIVER: I'd like to share a room with Jake. He's someone at my new school that I've been getting to know better.

THERAPIST: Sounds reasonable. How could you go about making that happen?

OLIVER: I'm not sure.

THERAPIST: Take a look at the Tween Tips. Could any of these be helpful?

OLIVER: I could come up with a way to handle the problem, like "Have a Few Solutions in Mind."

THERAPIST: Great idea—"Have a Few Solutions in Mind" is a good way to start. How would you do that?

OLIVER: I guess I could talk with my teacher about sharing a room with Jake.

Identify Early Warning Signs of Depression

The preadolescent's ability to monitor changes in her mood, motivation, attention, sleep, appetite, energy, self-esteem, and thoughts about death or suicide can help her know if her depression is coming back. Provide the rationale that early detection of these changes can serve as alerts that she is feeling overwhelmed. If these symptoms are persistent and/or intensify, the preadolescent can be proactive in talking to a parent about her symptoms, utilizing some of the therapy skills, or getting back into treatment. Explain the importance of catching a relapse or recurrent episode of depression early, as it is easier to treat an illness in its beginning stages than when it is farther along.

Present the idea that the preadolescent can learn what depressive symptoms to watch out for based on her previous experience with depression (see Therapist Tips 16.1). What sort of depressive symptoms did she endorse when she first began treatment? Help the preteen write a list of symptoms she can monitor (see Therapist Tips 16.2).

Therapist Tips 16.1

Be prepared to help the preadolescent identify her depressive symptoms prior to treatment, if she struggles remembering specific details. It may be helpful to review self-report measures from the beginning of treatment (e.g., "*It looks like when you were depressed you were having a lot of trouble falling asleep. Let's add that to our list*") or to help anchor this time in terms of seasons or events (e.g., summer, back to school, around your birthday).

THERAPIST: Another thing I wanted to talk about today is how depression sometimes comes back, especially when we're stressed out.

OLIVER: That stinks.

THERAPIST: I know. It's not fair at all. But being able to identify the first signs of depression can help us catch it earlier. That way we can do something about it and stop it from getting as bad as it was before. What do you think?

OLIVER: (nods)

THERAPIST: I think it's helpful to write out a list of early warning signs for you to have when you leave therapy. It's a list of changes in your mood and behavior that happened when you were depressed. It can help remind you what sorts of things to pay attention to and when to ask for help.

OLIVER: Okay.

THERAPIST: Do you remember some of the first things that started changing when you were depressed?

OLIVER: Not really.

THERAPIST: Think for a few minutes—how were you feeling when you first came in for your assessment back in February?

OLIVER: I was really angry—I just wanted to be alone all the time.

THERAPIST: Let's write down, "Wanting to be alone all the time." What about feeling angry? Was that all the time too?

OLIVER: I guess. I was angry a lot because nothing was going right for me. I was getting in trouble all the time and felt like nobody liked me. I felt left out a lot, too.

THERAPIST: That's what happens when depression sinks its teeth into you. Let's write that down. Anything else?

OLIVER: I'm not sure.

THERAPIST: I remember your mom saying that you were really tired and not hungry at all.

OLIVER: Yeah, that's right I guess.

THERAPIST: Do you want to talk to your mom about some of these warning signs so she can help you pay attention to these symptoms?

OLIVER: Yeah.

Therapist Tips 16.2

Assist the preteen in making a list of her early warning signs. It may help to put these on an index card that she can refer to later.

What are the early warning signs that I might be getting depressed?

Changes in mood ______________________________

Changes in sleep ______________________________

Changes in appetite ______________________________

Changes with how I'm getting along with friends ______________________________

Changes with how I'm getting along with my family ______________________________

Prepare Preadolescent for Dyadic Meeting

Talk with the preadolescent about sharing some of the work you have done together when the parent joins the session. Frame this collaboration as a way to make sure that the parent and preadolescent continue to be on the same page with monitoring early warning signs for depression. Also, introduce the goal of the preadolescent and parent making a plan for what to do if the depressive symptoms return in the future.

Preadolescent and Parent with Therapist

Collaborating with the Parent for Monitoring the Preadolescent's Stress and Early Warning Signs

Initiate a discussion with the parent about the importance of anticipating upcoming situations or events that may trigger an increase in the preadolescent's stress and depressive symptoms. Help the preadolescent share with the parent possible situations that may be stressful and some ideas of how she could problem-solve or ask for help in preparing for these situations.

THERAPIST: Thanks for joining us, Mom. Oliver and I were planning ahead, trying to anticipate events that could be stressful for him and brainstorm ways to handle them.

MOM: That's great. Even though he's doing really well now, I'm just nervous that he's going to get depressed again.

THERAPIST: That's a valid concern, and one that Oliver and I have talked about. However, we've learned a lot about how Oliver acts differently when he's depressed, and we can use that information to help identify any future problems early. First thing we need to do is help Oliver anticipate stressful situations and have a plan for how to handle them. Oliver, do you want to tell your mom what we talked about?

OLIVER: We talked about going on the overnight trip with my class. I'm nervous about getting stuck in a room with kids who aren't nice. I think that would make me feel really bad. I know that I started getting depressed when the kids at school weren't nice to me and I felt left out a lot. I don't want the same thing to happen again.

MOM: Yes, I was thinking about that too. I do think things are a little different this year though.

OLIVER: How?

MOM: Well, you've been working really hard on some new friendships this year so you're going into this trip in a really different situation than last year.

OLIVER: That's true.

MOM: And as a family we've gotten a lot better at talking about our feelings, so if you're feeling frustrated or sad, maybe you would let me know instead of keeping it inside. We could try to do some problem-solving.

THERAPIST: Great point, Mom. I agree that Oliver has a whole bunch of tools in his tool box that he didn't have last year when he was going through difficult times. Oliver and I also talked about how to approach the overnight trip, and he came up with some great suggestions.

OLIVER: Like talking to Mrs. C about sharing a room with Jake.

Ask the parent to help identify the preadolescent's early warning signs for a future depressive episode. Talk with the parent about his or her role in helping the preteen monitor stress and changes in functioning.

MOM: Those are really good ideas. What happens if several months from now you seem like you are getting depressed again?

OLIVER: Um, we talked about catching it early so it doesn't get so bad. Like some early signs of getting depressed for me are starting to get really mad and wanting to be alone all the time.

THERAPIST: That's right. Mom, we'd like to pick your brain about Oliver's early warning signs for depression. What changes in Oliver's mood or behavior do you think might mean that he may be getting depressed?

MOM: Well, I remember that Oliver had a hard time falling asleep at night. That isn't typical for him. And he didn't eat very much. That's a big clue.

THERAPIST: Does that seem right, Oliver? Should we write those things down?

OLIVER: (nods)

THERAPIST: Two sets of eyes are better than one. Mom, it would helpful if you could continue to check in with Oliver about how he's doing even after therapy ends. Would you be willing to do that?

MOM: Of course.

THERAPIST: That way, Oliver wouldn't be the only one paying attention to see if these symptoms of depression are returning. If we catch them earlier, hopefully things won't get as bad as they did for Oliver this fall.

MOM: And if we notice that, we could give you a call and make a plan for returning to therapy?

THERAPIST: Exactly.

Summary

In Session 13 of FB-IPT, you have helped the preadolescent identify potential stressors that may trigger another depressive episode, emphasizing the need for her to be aware of early warning signs (e.g., not sleeping well, loss of appetite) that may signal a relapse or recurrence. The preadolescent also has been supported in talking about these stressors and early warning signs with her parent. With your help, the preadolescent has enlisted the parent's assistance to monitor her stress and changes in functioning to catch any future episodes at an earlier point in the illness.

CHAPTER 17 Session 14: Reviewing Progress and Saying Goodbye

Goals for FB-IPT Session 14

- Review preadolescent's depressive symptoms and mood thermometer
- Encourage preadolescent to talk about his feelings ending treatment or transferring to another clinical service
- Highlight the successful work of both preadolescent and parent
- Identify the need for treatment should depression recur in the future
- Say goodbye

Materials

- 1–3 pages of blank paper
- Markers, pens

Structure for FB-IPT Session 14

- Check-in with preadolescent and parent (10 minutes)
- Meet with preadolescent (20 minutes)
- Meet with preadolescent and parent (20 minutes)

Preadolescent and Parent with Therapist

Mood Check-in with Preadolescent and Parent

Use the same format for checking in with the preadolescent and parent as described in Session 12. Since this is the final FB-IPT session, confirm both the goals and structure for the preadolescent and parent; for example:

> *Today is our final session. First I'll meet with Maya individually to talk about the progress she's made in treatment, about how she feels about ending treatment, and then we will finalize the plan for monitoring depressive symptoms and catching early warning signs. Then we'll all meet together and talk about this with Mom.*

Preadolescent Alone with Therapist

Review Preadolescent's Progress during Therapy

Begin by asking the preadolescent to identify any changes that have occurred in his mood, behavior, and interpersonal relationships since he first started treatment. Review the ways that he has modified his behavior by using new communication skills and problem-solving strategies to elicit increased support from parents (e.g., asking for help), decreasing conflict when disagreeing with parents or peers, and increasing his interpersonal approach strategies (e.g., initiating social interactions with family members or peers). Therapist Tips 17.1 provides additional suggestions for helping the preteen assess his progress with communication skills and problem-solving strategies.

Therapist Tips 17.1

- For younger preadolescents, it may be helpful for you to list the symptoms and difficulties they presented with at assessment in a column on a piece of paper or white board. Then ask the child to assess the changes that have been made in these areas in a second column. A third column may be included to identify the specific types of communication or problem-solving skills they used to help bring these changes about.
- Refer to the Tween Tips in Appendix E when reviewing the skills that the preadolescent has been using.
- Ask for examples of successes and failures the preadolescent has experienced when using each of these skills.

- Ask about other situations where the preadolescent could apply these skills, and draw upon examples discussed in Session 13 (anticipating stressful situations).
- Explain that even when there is significant improvement in depressive symptoms, there may still be other areas where the preadolescent wants to see improvement (e.g., initiating interpersonal approach strategies).

Encourage Preadolescent to Share Feelings about Ending Treatment

Initiate a conversation on the preadolescent's feelings about ending treatment (i.e., happy, worried, mixed feelings). It helps to preface this conversation with the observation that preteens often have mixed feelings about ending therapy—happy and proud of the hard work they did but also maybe sad about saying goodbye. This allows the preadolescent to discuss his positive feelings about ending treatment without the potential worry that doing so will hurt you. Encourage the preadolescent to "Make an 'I Feel' Statement" about ending therapy. If he struggles doing this, model an example of this by sharing your own feelings about the preadolescent ending therapy, such as:

THERAPIST: Maya, I'm really happy that you're graduating from therapy and feeling better. I also feel a little sad that I won't get to see you every week and hear about how you're doing. I really enjoyed getting to know you and your mom. The three of us made a good team.

MAYA: (nodding) Me too.

THERAPIST: How are you feeling about ending therapy?

MAYA: Okay, I guess. At first I didn't really want to do therapy, but it ended up not being that bad. I guess it might even be weird not to come here anymore.

THERAPIST: It is pretty normal to have mixed feelings when you are ending therapy. Lots of kids feel sad that they won't be seeing the therapist anymore, but they might feel proud of all that they accomplished. There is also a difference between feeling sad that therapy is over and feeling depressed again.

MAYA: What do you mean?

THERAPIST: Our moods are constantly changing as you can see on your mood thermometer. Even after therapy ends, there are still going to be times when you feel sad, angry, or bored. You may still have bad days here and there. The thing to watch out for is when your mood is down and it's getting stuck low on the mood thermometer. A sad, angry, or bored mood that doesn't seem to get better for a few weeks would be something to share with your mom.

> **Follow-up Questions 17.1**
>
> Examples of follow-up questions to elicit the preteen's feelings about ending therapy:
>
> - What did you like about therapy?
> - What didn't you like about therapy?
> - What was helpful about therapy?
> - How did therapy change ways you deal with negative feelings?
> - How did therapy change the way you deal with problems with your family and friends?

Prepare Preadolescent for Dyadic Meeting

Refer to Session 13.

Preadolescent and Parent with Therapist

Review Preadolescent's and Parent's Progress in Therapy

When the parent joins the session, ask the preadolescent to share his list of changes that he has made since starting therapy. This conversation should build upon the previous session's identification of early warning signs for depression, wherein the preadolescent and parent have listed the changes each has noticed in the preadolescent's mood and behavior since starting treatment. Help the preteen present the specific communication skill or problem-solving strategy he has used that has contributed to improved relationships with family members or peers. Elicit the parent's feedback on the preadolescent's progress in therapy. Regardless of the disposition (termination of treatment or referral for continued treatment), help the parent to express pride and support for the preadolescent's hard work and accomplishments in therapy (see Therapist Tips 17.2).

Therapist Tips 17.2

I'm transferring my preteen to another clinical service for a more intensive program of treatment. Ending FB-IPT has been disappointing for the preadolescent and his mother. How do I summarize treatment gains? First, identify the depression as the problem. Sometimes a short-term treatment is not enough to combat a stubborn depression, despite the best efforts by you, the child, and the parent. In such cases, you need to support the continued efforts of the preadolescent to get well and of the parent to continue supporting the child. It is often helpful to verbalize the disappointment felt by the preadolescent and the parent (e.g., *"I know you and your mom are disappointed and just want to go back to feeling like your old self"*), while highlighting that continued treatment does not render the hard work by the preadolescent as worthless or as a failed experience. Highlight the improvement in the preadolescent's symptoms, closeness in relationships, and willingness to communicate his needs to others. Encourage the preadolescent and parent to continue their hard work, and reassure them that their persistence will result in progress.

Ask parents to reflect on their own changes during treatment. Have they implemented any of the new communication skills or problem-solving strategies to improve their relationship with their preteen? It may be helpful to have a copy of the Parent Tips on hand (refer to Appendix D) for the parent to review. Elicit the preadolescent's feedback on the parent's support and successful modeling of new communication and problem-solving skills. Help the preadolescent express appreciation for the parent. Praise the preadolescent and parent's collective efforts to improve their relationship.

Review the Early Warning Signs of Depression

Revisit the preadolescent's early warning signs for depression that were discussed in Session 13. Outline a plan for the preadolescent and parent to check-in with each other regularly after therapy ends. Encourage the parent to take the lead in proactively checking-in with the preadolescent and to reinforce the preadolescent's use of communication skills after treatment ends.

THERAPIST: What things can we do to make sure that you two continue to check-in about Maya's mood like we do in therapy?

MAYA: Well, I can tell my mom if I'm upset about something.

THERAPIST: Absolutely. That's really important. I'm thinking it might also be good to check-in regularly about your mood even if you're not upset about something. That way, you and Mom will be able to notice if there are changes in your mood or changes in your sleep.

MOM: So you mean, do a check-in like we do in here?

THERAPIST: That is exactly what I was thinking. You can check-in with Maya about her mood and things going on at home or school and also ask her about the early warning signs we identified to see if there have been changes.

MOM: How often do you think we should try to do this?

THERAPIST: I would say maybe once a week. I think it might help to decide on a good time of the week for both of you and then put a reminder in your phone so that you don't forget.

MOM: We can do that. Maya, maybe a good time to check-in would be after I drop your sister off at Grandma's on Saturday afternoons. It's usually just you and me at home then.

MAYA: Yeah, that works.

Parent's Feelings about Ending Therapy

As the last FB-IPT session draws to a close, give parents an opportunity to discuss their feelings about treatment ending. You may get more detailed responses from the parent than from the child. Many parents will express some anxiety about their preadolescent's depression returning and concerns about ending treatment. Normalize these concerns (e.g., *"It's pretty common for parents to worry about their preadolescent backsliding"*) and offer reassurance that with good communication, continued problem-solving, and regular symptom monitoring, both the parent and the preadolescent will be ready should the depression return. Acknowledge parents' hard work and willingness to work with you to help their preadolescent. Praise parents' efforts to support their preadolescent and their continued commitment to check-in with the preteen after therapy ends.

Saying Goodbye

Transition to end the session and initiate saying goodbye to the preadolescent and the parent. Summarize what they have accomplished in therapy, and express your feelings about having worked with the dyad (e.g., "*It has been a pleasure working with you both, and I'm honored to have been a part of Maya's team,*" or "*The three of us made a good team! I will miss seeing you guys every week but know that it's time for Maya to get back to doing things that a preteen needs to do*"). Refer to the early warning signs that the preadolescent and parent have compiled, and express confidence in their ability to catch any future depressive episodes early. Reassure the preadolescent and the parent that they can contact you at any time in the future (e.g., "*Saying goodbye now doesn't mean that it's goodbye forever. My door is open if you want to contact me in the future*").

THERAPIST: It seems like you have a good plan to stay on top of depression. Maya, you and your mom are going to continue using the new ways of communicating and problem-solving. Maya, I'd really like you to remember how being open with Mom about your feelings seems to decrease arguments and help with problem-solving. We've also identified some early warning signs that could mean you're getting depressed again—like having trouble sleeping, loss of appetite, and being more irritable. In addition, we've also set up times for your mom to check-in with you about your mood and other important things going on in your life. Together, these strategies can help you feel good about your relationship with your mom and give you a way to let her know if your depression seems to be coming back.

Summary

In Session 14 of FB-IPT, the preadolescent has reviewed with you the ways in which he has implemented new communication and problem-solving skills and how these skills could help him in future situations. You also have provided the preadolescent with the opportunity to explore his feelings about ending therapy. Together with the preadolescent, you have reviewed his early warning signs and contracted with the parent to regularly check-in with the preteen after treatment ends. You also have acknowledged the parent's role in treatment and given the parent an opportunity to share his or her feelings about ending therapy. Lastly, you have expressed appreciation to the parent-child dyad for their hard work. Although you say goodbye, you have also invited the family to contact you at any time in the future with questions or concerns.

PART FIVE

Implementation of FB-IPT

CHAPTER 18 Special Topics in FB-IPT

FB-IPT is an effective treatment for preadolescent depression, but the success of its formulation and implementation depends on careful consideration of the home environment, school factors, and individual strengths and weaknesses of both the preadolescent and the parent as they relate to their ability to engage in the treatment process. In our experiences, there are several clinical challenges that are unique to working with this age group and inherent in working dyadically with preadolescents and their parents. In this chapter we outline seven specific clinical challenges common to working with depressed preadolescents: school avoidance, therapy noncompliance, identification of comorbid diagnoses during treatment, suicidality, divorce and custody issues, multiple caregiver involvement in treatment, and parental psychopathology. We describe these challenges and strategies to manage each issue when conducting FB-IPT.

Managing School Avoidance

One of the most common issues brought up by parents of depressed preadolescents is difficulty attending school. We define school avoidance in depressed preadolescents as a problem attending school that is directly related to symptoms of depression. It is not classic school refusal stemming from a primary anxiety disorder related to separation anxiety, generalized worries about performing academically in the school setting, or fears of being negatively evaluated by teachers and peers.

As listed in Therapist Tips 18.1, school avoidance secondary to depression can be related to sleep disturbance, amotivation, poor concentration, and/or problems with peers. Preadolescents who have difficulty falling asleep at night may have trouble getting up for school. They may be fatigued and have difficulty concentrating in school, which can impair their ability to understand the information being presented in class. Additionally, decreased motivation can impair the quality or completion of homework. Depressed preadolescents often experience somatic complaints such as headaches and stomachaches that also can contribute to missing school. Many depressed preadolescents have difficulty initiating and sustaining positive peer relationships, which can make school a very lonely place and lead to school avoidance. Sometimes preadolescents fall into a pattern in where they start missing significant amounts of school and/or fall behind on academic work. Falling behind or doing poorly in schoolwork may be additional stressors that further increase depressed preadolescents' reluctance to attend school.

Therapist Tips 18.1

Why do depressed preadolescents avoid going to school?

- Sleep disturbance
- Low energy and motivation
- Poor concentration
- Falling behind in school
- Problems with peers

When there are consistent problems attending school or falling behind academically, you may have already addressed its link to depression in the context of the limited sick role during the initial phase of treatment. If problems with school avoidance persist, you will need to revisit the problem in the middle phase with the preadolescent and parent. Remind them that the problem attending school is related to depression, which can impair the preteen's ability to carry out the responsibilities normally expected of her. See Therapist Tips 18.2 for questions to ask the parent to help understand the link between depression, any school problems, and school attendance. The goal is to help identify ways the parent can help the child get to school. This often requires a good understanding of the circumstances surrounding the preadolescent's school avoidance.

Therapist Tips 18.2

Helpful questions to ask parents about school avoidance:

- *How is your preteen doing academically?*
- *Has there been a change in her school work? Her relationships with peers?*
- *Has she been having problems with friends at school?*
- *Is she being bullied? How do you handle these complaints?*
- *Is she sleeping at night? Has she been having a hard time getting up in the morning?*
- *Is she complaining of frequent headaches or stomachaches? How do you handle these complaints? Has she been missing a lot of school related to frequent headaches and stomachaches?*

Once you have a good understanding of the factors contributing to the school avoidance, you will engage in active problem-solving to address the issues at hand. You may say to the preadolescent,

> *Sometimes when preteens get depressed, they fall into a pattern of having trouble completing homework and attending school regularly. This can happen because the symptoms of depression make it hard to fall asleep at night and can get in the way of concentrating, which is necessary to understand the schoolwork. Let's make a plan for helping you sleep better, which may help with getting your schoolwork done and let you feel better about going to school.*

Oftentimes school avoidance in depressed preadolescents necessitates communicating with the preteen's school. If the parent feels comfortable contacting the school directly, you can ask the parent to call the teacher to discuss the preadolescent's situation. Coach the parent to provide the teacher with some psychoeducation about depression and to ask for help in securing appropriate accommodations for the preadolescent. If the parent is not comfortable speaking with the school or if you are concerned that the parent is not able to contact the school directly, request permission to contact the school. It also can be very helpful to have an initial school meeting involving you, the parent, and teachers. One of the benefits to a school meeting is that you can ensure that the parent(s) and teachers understand their roles in helping the preadolescent regularly attend school, as well as discuss more formal academic accommodations that may be appropriate for preadolescents with medical conditions.

When you speak to the school on the phone or during a school meeting, provide psychoeducation about the impact of depression on the preteen's ability to complete school work and/or attend school. Talk to the teacher about potential accommodations he or she can offer that may help the preadolescent get back on track academically and improve her ability to be successful at school. This may include a modified class schedule or extra time for completing homework assignments. For preadolescents with many somatic symptoms, educate involved school personnel that depressed preadolescents do have more headaches and stomachaches but that we do not want them to leave school when they feel this way. You can negotiate a plan that the preadolescent can go to the school nurse for 5 to 10 minutes, but she then needs to return to class unless she has a fever or vomits. The teacher can also take a more active role in helping the preadolescent have more positive social interactions by strategically placing her with other students with similar interests. Identifying a support person at school—such as a school counselor, school nurse, or teacher—with whom the preadolescent can talk during the school day can also be helpful in keeping her in school when she feels sad or frustrated. Encourage the parent to become more involved in the preadolescent's schoolwork and to start having more frequent communication with the school so he or she can track the child's progress. See Therapist Tips 18.3 to identify helpful strategies to promote more regular school attendance in depressed preadolescents.

Therapist Tips 18.3

Strategies for addressing school avoidance:

Talk to the school:

- Provide psychoeducation about depression to the teacher and/or school personnel.
- Ask for accommodations such as a modified class schedule or extra time to complete assignments.
- Request a school meeting to get everyone on the same page if necessary.

Plan at home:

- Ensure extra support from the parent to help the preteen complete homework assignments.
- Increase parental monitoring to help the preteen improve sleep habits.
- Make a contract with the preadolescent to attend school consistently with the understanding that certain accommodations are in place at school.

Once the school is involved in helping the preadolescent manage her difficulties attending school, work closely with the parent and the preadolescent to adhere to the plan. If homework is a part of the problem, have the preteen work on homework at night with a parent's support. If there have been problems with peers, begin setting up interpersonal experiments to help the preadolescent develop new friendships. If involving the school and parent more closely does not improve the preadolescent's school attendance, you may consider alternative options. At certain times it may be helpful to talk to the parents about contacting the school district to request a 504 plan, which will ensure that teachers follow certain accommodations and modifications for students with a medical condition.

Therapy Noncompliance or Strategies for Engaging Ambivalent Preadolescents

Therapy for depressed preadolescents is usually adult-initiated, either because parents or teachers notice changes in a preadolescent's mood or functioning or because of an event like a suicidal gesture or disclosing thoughts of death to another child or adult. Preadolescents often have ambivalent feelings about attending therapy appointments, and they usually need some coaching to become engaged in therapy. They may not know what to expect and may even view therapy as a punishment for misbehavior. While you will provide psychoeducation about depression and the purpose of therapy at the initial assessment, some preadolescents may remain uneasy and reticent. Here we describe several strategies to engage ambivalent preadolescents in FB-IPT.

Preadolescents vary greatly in their desire and cognitive/emotional ability to engage in meaningful therapy work. The inclusion of parents through the dyadic structure of FB-IPT is designed to improve preadolescents' engagement in treatment. Preadolescents are expected to meet with you individually for just 20 minutes of the session, and parents share participation dyadic sessions. This decreases pressure on the preadolescent to be focused and engaged and increases the parent's responsibility for generalizing the therapy skills to situations outside of the sessions. Within the FB-IPT framework, there is flexibility, so that you can adjust sessions to the cognitive and emotional level of each preadolescent.

You want to coach parents to be mindful about how they talk to their child about attending therapy. Preadolescents will notice parents' negative comments about therapy. Remind parents to give their preadolescent permission to talk about what is going on at home, even if it does not paint the parent in the most positive light. We also suggest that the parent can make therapy a more positive experience by scheduling an enjoyable activity before or after therapy (i.e., stopping for a hot chocolate or a meal) or trying to make the most of the time they spend traveling to therapy appointments (i.e., listening to music together, talking about mutual interests).

For preadolescents who do not want their parents to leave sessions, you can allow the parent to stay for the individual component of the session, but try to coach the preadolescent to take a more active role even though the parent is present. As the preadolescent gets to know you better and begins to talk more in therapy, suggest that she try meeting with you individually. Remember to praise the preadolescent for her efforts in making changes or trying something new, no matter how small.

For a preadolescent who does not want to talk or frequently says, "*I don't know*," you may reassure her that you will only meet with her individually for half the session to allow time to talk to her parent individually or to have her parent join a dyadic session. The shortened session may remind the preteen that the session is a manageable period of time and the time frame may encourage her to actively participate (i.e., "*I know meeting one-on-one is hard for you. It's hard for a lot of kids to talk to a grown-up by themselves about their feelings. The good news is that we only have about 20 minutes of one-on-one time before we meet together with your mom. Do you think you could tell me more about the fight with your brother now and then I'll do more of the talking when we meet with Mom?"*). Alternatively, you may want to increase parental involvement in sessions after have tried these strategies and the preadolescent remains hesitant/resistant to engage in individual meetings. Spend more time meeting with the parent and preadolescent together during the initial part of the session, gather more information about the events in the past week, and then elicit feedback from the preadolescent based on the parent report (i.e., "*Your dad said you seemed really angry when you guys didn't go to Pizza Hut for dinner. Tell me more about what happened*"). With preadolescents who completely refuse to come into the room or who are developmentally less mature, meet with the parent individually, teach him the FB-IPT skills, and have the parent model using them with the preadolescent, either in session or at home.

Using rewards for working hard in therapy is another strategy to engage preadolescents in treatment. Since the length of time that you will be meeting individually with the preadolescent is only 20 minutes, we recommend that you start with the therapy tasks and then use playing a game as a reward for participating in therapy. "*I know it's hard to talk about what's been going on at school. How about we agree to talk about it for 15 minutes and then we can play Uno for the last 5 minutes before we meet with your mom?*"We do not recommend bringing out a game in the beginning of the meeting because you will run out of time to teach and rehearse the FB-IPT skills. By offering a compromise, you are also modeling the FB-IPT skills you are trying to teach. Therapist Tips 18.4 reviews strategies for preadolescents who are difficult to engage in sessions.

Therapist Tips 18.4

Strategies for engaging ambivalent preadolescents:

- Use the 20-minute individual meeting time as motivation.
- Help the preadolescent understand the positive impact therapy could have on her life if she views sessions as a punishment.
- Increase parental involvement or rely more heavily on working with the parent individually or dyadically.
- Consider the use of a reward for participation in meetings.

MAGGIE: I'm not coming into the room!

MOM: This is ridiculous Maggie. I took off of work to take you to this appointment. Just come into the office.

MAGGIE: No, I told you I don't need to go to therapy.

THERAPIST: Okay, Maggie. I'm gathering that you and your mom aren't on the same page about coming to see me.

MAGGIE: Good guess.

THERAPIST: Does this happen a lot at home? That you and Mom aren't on the same page?

MAGGIE: All the time, yeah.

THERAPIST: So that's what this type of therapy is actually all about. Therapy is not a punishment for something you did. It's about helping you and your mom be on the same page more of the time so there is less fighting at home, which could help you feel happier. I could just meet with your mom, but I think it would be a lot more helpful if I were also able to hear your perspective on things, Maggie. Do you think you might be willing to come into my office and hear a little more of what this type of therapy is all about?

MAGGIE: Fine.

Identifying Additional Diagnoses in the Course of Treatment

Despite best efforts to complete a thorough pretreatment assessment of comorbid psychiatric issues, it is inevitable that more information will be revealed as you get to know the preadolescent better. Sometimes the resolution of depressive symptoms highlights other symptoms that can no longer be accounted for by depression. For example, problems concentrating are common among depressed preadolescents, but you would expect concentration to improve as other symptoms of depression improve. If concentration does not improve, it is important to consider whether the preadolescent is also suffering from symptoms of another disorder. Parents and preadolescents may be more forthcoming as they get to know you better and may provide information that makes you suspect that there are other issues at play. As was discussed in Chapter 4, there are some comorbid diagnoses that would require you to refer for more specialized treatment. For example, if you find out there is significant impairment due to an anxiety disorder—such as obsessive-compulsive disorder or posttraumatic stress disorder—you may need to refer the preadolescent for more specialized treatment. The two most common comorbid diagnoses that we see in our work with depressed preadolescents are attention deficit hyperactivity disorder (ADHD) and autism spectrum disorder (ASD), which we discuss in greater detail next (also see Therapist Tips 18.5).

Attention Deficit Hyperactivity Disorder

ADHD is one of the most common psychiatric problems in children, and studies have estimated rates of ADHD from 5.9% to as high as 11% in children (Polanczyk, Willcutt, Salum, Kieling, & Rohde, 2014; Thomas, Sanders, Doust, Beller, & Glasziou, 2015; Visser et al., 2014; Willcutt, 2012). Undiagnosed ADHD has been associated with academic problems, internalizing and externalizing disorders, problems with peers, and parent–child conflict (Cussen, Sciberras, Ukoumunne, & Efron, 2012; Ek, Westerlund, Holmberg, & Fernell, 2011; Lifford, Harold, & Thapar, 2008; Ostrander, Crystal, & August, 2006; Ostrander & Herman, 2006). ADHD may even be considered a risk factor for depression because depressive symptoms tend to emerge several years after the onset of ADHD symptoms (Daviss, 2008). Peer problems and parent–child difficulties have been shown to mediate the relationship between ADHD symptoms and depression (Humphreys et al., 2013).

A depressed preadolescent with underlying ADHD may have trouble completing schoolwork, managing time, and following directions from adults, all of which could be exacerbated by depressive symptoms. As the depressive symptoms improve in treatment, if there are continued problems sustaining attention, you may begin to suspect that there are underlying attentional issues. In this case, consider referring the preteen for an evaluation and possible treatment for ADHD. It is appropriate to continue to treat the preteen's depressive symptoms with FB-IPT and augment treatment with relevant recommendations from an ADHD evaluation (i.e., stimulant medication).

Autism Spectrum Disorders

Individuals with an ASD experience higher rates of comorbid internalizing and externalizing disorders (Woodman, Mailick, & Greenberg, 2016). It is not uncommon to encounter preadolescents who present with depression and who also have an underlying ASD that has been undiagnosed. This is not uncommon: ASD is more difficult to diagnose in higher functioning children (Magnuson & Constantino, 2011; Mazzone, Ruta, & Reale, 2012). During the pretreatment assessment and initial phase of treatment, you will gather a lot of information about the preadolescent's interpersonal style and history of social interactions at home, in school, and with peers prior to the onset of this depressive episode. Some preadolescents demonstrate interpersonal deficits that predate their current depression, and some preteens have difficulty engaging in perspective taking or social problem-solving skills needed for FB-IPT. In such situations, it may become clear that these interpersonal deficits are better accounted for by an ASD (i.e., rigidity, not noticing social cues, few friendships, preference for solitary activities over social interactions, difficulty with routine transitions). Take the time with the parents in the initial phase of treatment to gather information about the nature of the preadolescent's interpersonal problems, how long they have been going on, and even request permission to talk with teachers about the preadolescent's social functioning with peers.

Although it may be uncomfortable to broach this topic with parents, you should introduce the possibility that the preadolescent's long-standing difficulties with social interactions may indicate the presence of another condition an ASD. Parents may have information to share regarding previous recommendations for an evaluation, an elementary school teacher who may have asked about ASD, or a previous evaluation that produced inconclusive findings. At times, you may need to make a recommendation for neuropsychological testing or a referral for an Autism Diagnostic Observation Schedule (ADOS) assessment in order to rule-out an ASD. FB-IPT is not a recommended treatment for depressed preadolescents with comorbid ASD, primarily because difficulties engaging in perspective taking will make it hard for preadolescents with ASD to conceptualize and use FB-IPT skills. Therefore, if a preadolescent is diagnosed with an ASD, we recommend transferring her to services specific to ASD and to continue providing the preadolescent and her family with support and clinical monitoring until they establish care with a new treatment team.

> **Therapist Tips 18.5**
> Identifying additional diagnoses in the course of treatment:
> - ADHD—refer for evaluation and continue FB-IPT with adjunctive treatment (e.g., medication) for ADHD.
> - ASD—refer for testing and specialized treatment, continuing with FB-IPT or clinical monitoring until preadolescents establishes care with new treatment team.

THERAPIST: Elena, I'd like to talk to you one-on-one for a few minutes.

MOM: Okay, sure.

THERAPIST: As we've talked about before, Louis struggled in a number of areas even before he was depressed.

MOM: Yes, he's never been an easy kid.

THERAPIST: I'm beginning to wonder if some of the things he struggles with—rigidity, not picking up on social cues, trouble with friendships, preference for solitary activities over social interactions, difficulty with routine transitions—are actually related to another underlying condition. Sometimes kids who struggle from a young age with these problems are diagnosed with an autism spectrum disorder.

MOM: Wait, are you saying that Louis is autistic?

THERAPIST: I'm not saying anything for sure, but I do think that some of the issues he struggles with could fall into the category of an autism spectrum disorder. There is a tremendous range of functioning among kids with this diagnosis.

MOM: This is a lot for me to take in. First depression and now autism.

THERAPIST: You're right; but remember, we need more information to make that diagnosis. I would like you to think about it scheduling an appointment for Louis to get a formal assessment, called an ADOS, to see what's going on.

MOM: I'm going to need to talk to Louis's father about this. I don't know. I do remember one of Louis kindergarten teachers making a comment about him missing a lot of social cues. And he does have a hard time with transitions.

THERAPIST: I can certainly appreciate that this is a lot to process. You don't have to make a decision right now. We can talk more about it after you have a chance to talk to Louis dad.

Managing an Escalation in Non-Suicidal Self-Injury and Suicidality

FB-IPT is an effective treatment for preadolescents who demonstrate a passive death wish or passive suicidal ideation (SI) with a vague plan and who can contract for safety (see Therapist Tips 18.6). You will routinely monitoring depressive symptoms and suicidality during each session with the parent and preadolescent. You also need to carefully distinguish non-suicidal self-injury from suicidal intent, which is hard to do in this age group. Clarify whether there is any intent to die by asking, *"When you were ____________________, what were you thinking or feeling? Did you want to die when you were ______________________?"* If the preadolescent endorses non-suicidal self-injury (NSSI), you need to assess the triggers for the self-harm behaviors. Within the FB-IPT framework, examine whether the NSSI is an attempt to communicate feelings or whether it has another purpose. If it is being used as a form of communication, you can help the preadolescent develop other methods of communicating feelings to her family and peers that do not involve self-harm. If it is a means of managing feelings or a lack of feeling, help the preadolescent begin to link emotions to the situational triggers with the goal of improving recognition of emotions and expression of these in her significant relationships. If the frequency and level of risk associated with the self-harm increases, we recommend an evaluation for a higher level of therapeutic intervention.

When treating depressed adolescents with thoughts of self-harm, you will be relying on the preadolescent to communicate with her parent and for the parent to take the appropriate steps to ensure the child's safety. Therefore, you want to be certain that you have educated the parent to check-in regularly with the child about safety and the steps to take in the event of an emergency. You also want to spend more time talking about distraction and self-soothing techniques—such as listening to music, watching TV, or going for a walk with a parent—that the preadolescent can use to manage suicidal thoughts at home.

If there is a worsening of symptoms or if the preadolescent continues to demonstrate significant suicidality after four weeks, we recommend that you refer to a psychiatrist to evaluate the need for medication as an adjunctive treatment. There are times when, due to immediate stressors, a preadolescent's symptoms may worsen. In some cases, it may be appropriate to schedule an extra session in a week to help with the preteen cope with that particular crisis and to monitor her suicidality. It is often possible to continue with FB-IPT as prescribed once the preadolescent's suicidality has been stabilized.

Therapist Tips 18.6

Managing suicidality:

- FB-IPT is appropriate for preadolescents who demonstrate a passive death wish or passive SI with a vague plan and who can contract for safety.
- Continue to routinely monitor depressive symptoms and suicidality with the help of the parent (ask the parent to set predetermined check-ins about suicidality/NSSI to improve the chance that the preadolescent will communicate honestly with her parent).
- Differentiate between NSSI and SI.
- Teach the parent and the preadolescent the skills to manage passive SI at home and what to do in the event of immediate safety concerns.
- Refer to a psychiatrist for a medication evaluation if suicidality persists after four weeks of FB-IPT.
- Refer to a higher level of care if safety becomes a concern.

At other times, it may be necessary to refer the preadolescent to a higher level of care such as an intensive outpatient program, partial hospitalization, or inpatient hospitalization. If a preadolescent has a specific plan to kill herself or has engaged in any type of suicidal behavior, she likely needs a higher level of care and should be evaluated immediately in a psychiatric emergency room. Similarly, a higher level of care may also be needed if there is an increase in the frequency and severity of NSSI.

Divorce and Custody Issues

During the initial meeting with parents who are separated or divorced, it is important to ask about custody arrangements and ongoing legal proceedings. You will use this information to plan how to (a) manage issues of confidentiality regarding information about the preadolescent and (b) involve the parents in the treatment sessions, as well as understand the impact of the separation/divorce on the child's depression (see Therapist Tips 18.7). Custody arrangements can impact which parent brings the child for treatment and the continuity of the parental work across sessions. It is challenging to conduct FB-IPT if a different parent brings the preteen for appointments each week due to the logistics of shared custody arrangements (i.e., one week spent with mother, alternative week with father). Parents who are undergoing custody determinations through the court as part of divorce proceedings may have differing expectations for the therapist's role in sharing information about the preadolescent, as this may affect custody decisions. It is common for the parent initiating treatment for the depressed preteen to hope the therapist will be able to provide an expert opinion to support that parent's custody choice. Similarly, it is common for the parent who did not initiate treatment to want equal time in bringing the preadolescent for sessions, to share his side of the story, and/or to demonstrate his commitment to the child's therapy. Consider involving the other parent in treatment as clinically appropriate and with the custodial parent's permission. Present it as an opportunity for both parents to come together to help their child, and educate them that more cooperation among them as co-parents will only benefit their child and that their focus needs to be on the child and not on their own conflicts. It is important to ensure that the parent(s) with legal custody give consent to treatment and to clarify expectations in regard to any legal proceedings during or after the course of treatment.

Therapist Tips 18.7

During the initial evaluation:

- Ask about custody arrangements and ongoing legal proceedings.
- Ensure that parent(s) with legal custody give consent to treatment.
- Clarify your role as a support for the preadolescent, not as someone to provide expert opinion on custody decisions.
- Talk about ways to conduct FB-IPT if there is shared custody.

Throughout treatment:

- Involve the both parents as appropriate.
- Talk about the impact of the divorce on the preadolescent.

Strategies to Address Multiple Caregiver Involvement in Treatment

Ideally, FB-IPT should be conducted with the preadolescent and one identified caregiver so there can be continuity in teaching the FB-IPT skills and helping the preadolescent use the skills at home. If both parents can attend the sessions regularly, this can be even more helpful in supporting skills use outside of the sessions, but this is often not possible. Even having the same parent attend weekly can prove difficult for families who are balancing busy schedules and for families with multiple caregivers (divorced parents, grandparent involvement). When you introduce the preteen and family to the structure of FB-IPT, explain that the parent's role in the treatment is to help build communication and problem-solving skills in the child and family with a goal of strengthening the parent–child relationship. At this time, discuss the importance of having parent/guardian consistency from session to session and ask the parent if it is realistic for one parent/guardian to bring the preadolescent to weekly sessions. Emphasize that consistent parental attendance will help FB-IPT be most effective. The time-limited nature of FB-IPT may help parents manage the potential stress of regularly attending weekly therapy appointments (i.e., long commute, missing work).

If it is not realistic for one parent to attend weekly sessions with the preadolescent, problem-solve with the parents to identify ways that they can work together to promote continuity in their co-parenting, or by adding additional sessions to meet with one or both parents (see Therapist Tips 18.8). With your help, divorced or separated parents can share the work of the treatment and identify their respective roles in supporting their depressed preadolescent.

Using the phone or telepsychiatry software to communicate with the parent who cannot attend can help maintain the integrity of FB-IPT. For example,

> *So, your mom will be bringing you to most of your sessions, but we know that she's going to be traveling for work for a few weeks in March, so then your dad will be bringing you. We are going to keep Dad in the loop from the beginning by talking to him on the phone to help him understand what you're working on, so when it is his turn to bring you in for sessions he will know what we are working on.*

Other times, you may plan to work with one parent primarily but something may prevent that from actually happening (e.g., illness, work conflicts, other family obligations). Using the telephone or telepsychiatry to keep the parent abreast of what is being discussed in the sessions can be helpful, but is not a good situation for maximizing the effectiveness of FB-IPT.

In these situations, talk to the preadolescent to understand how she feels about her parent not being able to attend therapy sessions. Does her family tend to be chaotic and is an uninvolved parent part of the problem contributing to the preadolescent's depressive symptoms? If at least one parent cannot attend sessions with the preadolescent, you need to speak directly with the parent about the impact inconsistent parental involvement has on the preadolescent and the effectiveness of the FB-IPT. You may wish to refer the family to another type of treatment that requires less parental involvement.

Therapist Tips 18.8

Addressing multiple caregiver involvement in treatment:

- During the initial evaluation, explain the format of FB-IPT and identify a parent who can consistently participate in therapy.
- Be creative in problem-solving potential solutions with the family to help promote consistent parental involvement.
- Use phone or telepsychiatry software to include the parent who will not be attending weekly sessions with the preteen.

- Talk to the preadolescent about her feelings about Mom or Dad not being able to attend consistently, and consider whether parental involvement is part of a broader familial issue that is impacting the preadolescent's mood and needs to be addressed directly in treatment.

Parental Psychopathology

As noted in Chapter 1, preadolescent depression is associated with high rates of depressive disorders in parents that may contribute to negative family processes. Since FB-IPT requires significant parental involvement, it is important to understand parental psychopathology and its role in the preadolescent's depression as well as its potential impact on treatment. Parental illness can be revealed during the initial assessment phase of treatment and may be gleaned from reports of interactions or behavior by the preadolescent. Depressed parents in particular can make the work of FB-IPT more difficult as the parent may be socially withdrawn or too irritable to effectively support the practice of new communication and problem-solving skills. You may need to meet separately with the parent and discuss your impressions about the interplay between the parent's own mental health struggles and those of the preteen to lay the foundation for recommending that the parent seek his or her own treatment. As stated in the Parent Tips in Appendix D, it is important for parents to help themselves first in order to best help their child. You can present the analogy of "Putting on Your Own Oxygen Mask First,"

> *When traveling by plane, the flight attendant announces that in case of a sudden drop in cabin pressure, put the oxygen mask on yourself first, and then place the mask on your child. You can't help your depressed preadolescent if you do not take care of yourself first.*

While FB-IPT involves dyadic work with the parent and child, it may still be helpful for parents to have their own place to discuss their struggles separately in order to allow you to focus on the needs of the child. When explaining the recommendation for parents getting their own therapy, be sensitive to their possible feelings of guilt that they may have caused the child's depression. Approach parents with a nonjudgmental attitude and join with them around the common goal of helping their child to feel better. Send the message that, despite their difficulties, they still play an important role in their child's recovery. This stance will be crucial during the dyadic work in FB-IPT. In these circumstances, you also may need to provide increased coaching for the parent in using positive communication strategies with the child. Psychoeducation about the parent maintaining appropriate boundaries to avoid oversharing with the preadolescent or inadvertently using the preadolescent as support may also be helpful.

Understanding the influence of parent's psychopathology is important for setting realistic treatment goals about the parent–child relationship. If a parent is very impaired by his or her illness, you may need to either revise the goals or identify other people in the child's life with whom she can practice FB-IPT skills and obtain additional support. If only one parent is ill, you may want to meet separately with the other parent to discuss increasing his or her involvement in FB-IPT and additional sources of support for the preteen. If both parents are ill or if it is a single-parent family, identify other people in the child's life who can take on a mentor role or be a greater source of support for the child's treatment. (See Therapist Tips 18.9 for a list of strategies to address parental psychopathology.)

Therapist Tips 18.9

Parental psychopathology:

- Be prepared for high rates of depression in parents of depressed preadolescents.
- Take time to understand the parent's struggle with psychopathology and its impact on the preteen.
- Emphasize the importance of parents seeking their own therapy if their illness is untreated, being sensitive to parents' potential feelings of guilt about possibly causing the child's depression.
- Use the "Putting on Your Own Oxygen Mask First" analogy to help a parent understand that helping him or herself *is* helping the child.
- Set realistic treatment goals for improvement in the parent–child relationship in the context of parental psychopathology.
- Consider identifying another parent or another adult in the preadolescent's life who can help provide support and help her practice FB-IPT skills.

Summary

FB-IPT is an effective, flexible treatment that can be adapted for a wide range of individual preadolescents and family situations. This chapter illustrates how to manage certain clinical challenges that are common when working with preadolescents and their families, including school avoidance, therapy noncompliance, identification of comorbid diagnoses during treatment, suicidality, divorce and custody issues, multiple caregiver involvement in treatment, and parental psychopathology. We define each challenge, provide recommendations for managing each issue using FB-IPT, and advise when it is necessary to refer a child to a different treatment. While you may encounter other obstacles when working with preteens, we hope that you can apply some of the recommendations outlined in this chapter to the depressed preadolescents and their families with whom you work.

CHAPTER 19 Empirical Evidence for FB-IPT

Support for FB-IPT as an efficacious treatment for depressed preadolescents includes an open treatment trial (Dietz et al., 2008) and a preliminary randomized controlled trial (Dietz et al., 2015). We review the findings from each study in this chapter and present future directions for research on this promising treatment for depressed preadolescents.

Open Treatment Trial

The first clinical study of FB-IPT was an open treatment trial conducted to demonstrate its feasibility and acceptability, as well as to examine the preliminary clinical outcomes of depressed preadolescents treated with FB-IPT. We recruited participants through the Services for Teens at Risk (STAR) Center of Western Psychiatric Institute & Clinic in Pittsburgh, Pennsylvania. The STAR Center is a specialty outpatient clinic that assesses and treats depressed and suicidal adolescents and receives external funding from the state of Pennsylvania to provide education to community mental health professionals and outreach to schools and other community agencies. Beginning in 2004, the STAR Center triaged an increasing number of preadolescents between the ages of 9 and 12 with depression and/or suicidal ideation. FB-IPT arose from this identified need to learn more about this younger patient population and develop an intervention to successfully treat depressed preadolescents. At the same time, an increasing number of preadolescent siblings of adolescents receiving treatment for depression through the STAR Center began presenting for assessment and treatment. This trend highlighted the risk for early-onset depression in families and further supported the development of a family-based intervention for depressed preadolescents.

Participants

From December 2004 to December 2005, 20 preadolescents were evaluated for depression. Preadolescents (n = 18) were included if they met diagnostic criteria for a depressive disorder based on the Schedule for Affective Disorders and Schizophrenia for Children, Present and Lifetime Version (Kaufman et al., 1997) and evidenced impairment of functioning based on the Children's Global Adjustment Scale (CGAS; Shaffer et al., 1983). Of these, 16 parents and their preadolescents provided informed consent/assent to participate in this open treatment trial through the STAR Center, which was approved by the Institutional Review Board of the University of Pittsburgh School of Medicine.

At the time of assessment, all preadolescents were offered antidepressant medication in addition to psychotherapy. Seventy-five percent of parents chose psychotherapy only for their preadolescents who met diagnostic criteria for a depressive disorder (n = 12). Four families (25%) opted to begin a selective serotonin reuptake inhibitor (SSRI) in addition to psychotherapy for treating their preadolescents' depressive disorders. Within the initial phase of therapy, two other families requested the addition of antidepressant medication to continue outpatient therapy, as their children's depressive symptoms worsened in Week 3 and Week 5, respectively. These two subjects were then followed in the combination treatment group.

Parents overwhelmingly chose psychotherapy alone (FB-IPT) over combination treatment (psychotherapy and SSRI) for the treatment of preadolescent depression (62% FB-IPT only; 38% combination treatment). However, parents were more likely to choose combination treatment when their depressed preadolescents had a comorbid anxiety disorder. There were no significant group differences between preadolescents on antidepressant medication and medication-free preadolescents in pre- or posttreatment scores.

Delivery of FB-IPT

Preadolescents and parents received a no-cost course of psychotherapy guided by Interpersonal Psychotherapy for Depressed Adolescents (IPT-A), delivered by Dr. Dietz in collaboration with Dr. Mufson. In this trial, parents were systematically involved in their preadolescents' weekly sessions and IPT-A techniques were applied dyadically within the framework for the identified problem area. FB-IPT was administered in a manner consistent with the guiding principles of IPT-A, and treatment was driven by techniques relevant to each identified problem area. Forty-four percent ($n = 7$) experienced a family dispute, 44% ($n = 7$) identified a family transition, 6% ($n = 1$) experienced the death of a family member, and 6% ($n = 1$) were classified as having interpersonal deficits, marked by social isolation and few interpersonal relationships.

Acceptability

Eighty-eight percent of the preadolescents enrolled in this open treatment trial completed treatment (i.e., attended four sessions for Phase I and at least four sessions for Phase II of FB-IPT), suggesting that the treatment was acceptable to parents and their children. Preadolescents and their parents who completed a course of FB-IPT attended an average of 14 sessions (range 9–22). Anecdotally, parents were enthusiastic about the conjoint and dyadic session with preadolescents and reported a better understanding of their preadolescents' concerns and of the treatment strategies introduced in individual sessions with preadolescents. Three families (19%) dropped out of treatment within the initial phase of treatment. Two of these families traveled at least an hour to the STAR Center and could not consistently make appointments. One family was unable to be contacted after the second session and may have relocated.

Reasonable Clinical Outcomes

Differences in preadolescents' depressive and anxiety symptoms and in their global functioning were compared across pre- and posttreatment conditions in the open treatment trial. Preadolescents showed significant improvement in their depressive symptoms measured by the Children's Depression Rating Scale–Revised (CDRS-R; Poznanski et al., 1985) and a decrease in anxiety symptoms from pre- to posttreatment measured by the Self-Report for Childhood Anxiety Related Emotional Disorders (Birmaher, Khetarpal, Cully, Brent, & McKenzie, 2003). Preadolescents' global functioning as indexed by the CGAS also significantly improved over the course of treatment (Dietz et al., 2008).

Conclusions

The results from the open treatment trial of FB-IPT demonstrated the feasibility of enrolling and retaining a sample of clinically depressed preadolescents in a developmentally relevant psychotherapy intervention that actively involved their parents in weekly sessions. FB-IPT seemed an acceptable psychosocial intervention for depressed preadolescents and their parents, as evidenced by high treatment compliance, low attrition rates, and favorable clinical outcomes for preadolescents completing treatment. Furthermore, findings that preadolescents who received FB-IPT were as likely as those receiving combination treatment (SSRI and FB-IPT) to have significant reductions in depressive symptoms and anxiety symptoms and to experience significant improvement in global functioning were promising for pursuing future clinical research on FB-IPT.

Randomized Controlled Trial of FB-IPT

As a follow-up to our open treatment trial, we conducted a randomized controlled trial of FB-IPT in a sample of 42 treatment-seeking preadolescents (ages 7–12) who met *Diagnostic and Statistical Manual of Mental Disorders* (fourth edition) criteria for a depressive disorder. Again, youths assessed at the STAR Center were eligible for participation in the trial if they were diagnosed with a current depressive disorder (major depressive disorder, dysthymia, depressive disorder not otherwise specified), and had a parent provide informed consent to be contacted about ongoing research. Preadolescents with diagnoses of bipolar disorder, pervasive developmental disorder (PDD), posttraumatic stress disorder, and obsessive-compulsive disorder were excluded from participation. Preadolescents on a stable dose of SSRI medication for at least two months were included in the study, providing they met diagnostic criteria and would remain on the same stable dose of SSRI ($n = 2$). Preadolescents with comorbid attention-deficit hyperactivity disorder were included in this study if they met diagnostic criteria and had been on a stable dose of stimulant medication for at least one month ($n = 12$).

Treatment Conditions

Depressed preadolescents were randomized to FB-IPT or child-centered therapy (CCT), a supportive and nondirective treatment that closely approximates the standard of care for pediatric depression in community mental health (Posner et al., 2011). CCT is based on a Rogerian model of treatment, whereby changes in children's mood and behavior are initiated through their experience of a therapeutic relationship marked by unconditional positive regard, empathic understanding, and therapeutic genuineness. Specific techniques include listening and attending skills and demonstrating acceptance through reflection, clarification, paraphrasing, and summarizing statements. CCT therapists also use nondirective problem-solving, helping children to consider alternative responses to a problem without making specific recommendations or offering solutions. Although parents did not participate in sessions, they were invited to join the first 10 minutes of each session to check-in about their preadolescents' symptoms. CCT has been successfully employed as a manualized comparison treatment in efficacy studies of youth depression (Brent et al., 1997; Szigethy et al., 2014).

Preadolescents were randomized to treatment through a computer program taking sex, minority status, and comorbid anxiety disorders into account so they would be consistent across treatment condition. All preadolescents received up to 14 sessions of outpatient psychotherapy. Treatment was delivered by three psychologists, two of whom developed FB-IPT (Laura J. Dietz and Rebecca J. Weinberg) and all of whom had previous training in empirically supported psychotherapies for youth with depression.

Data analyses did not include four participants: two did not receive any treatment after randomization, and two had diagnoses of PDD confirmed in Sessions 1 through 4 of treatment. The remaining 38 participants were included in the analyses of FB-IPT ($n = 25$) and

CCT (n = 13), and there were no differences in the demographic and clinical characteristics of preadolescents in each treatment condition (see Table 19.1), nor in their pretreatment indices of depression severity, parent–child conflict, anxiety, or in social or peer impairment (see Table 19.2).

Table 19.1. Demographic and Clinical Characteristics of Randomized Sample

	FB-IPT (n = 29)	CCT (n = 13)	Statistic	p
Age (Mean, SD)	10.6 (1.2)	11.1 (1.1)	F(1, 41) = 1.54	.22
Female (n, %)	18 (62.1%)	10 (76.9%)	FET	.49
Ethnic/Racial Minority (n, %)	6 (20.7%)	3 (23.13%)	FET	1.00
Two-Parent Family (n, %)	13 (44.8%)	7 (53.8%)	χ^2(n = 42, df = 1) = 0.29	.59
Medical Assistance (n, %)	5 (17.2%)	3 (23.1%)	FET	.69
Diagnosis			χ^2(n = 42, df = 1) = 0.06	.81
Major Depressive Disorder (n, %)	19 (65.5%)	9 (69.2%)		
Depressive Disorder NOS (n, %)	10 (34.5%)	4 (30.8%)		
Suicidal Ideation (n, %)	21 (72.4%)	11 (84.6%)	FET	.47
Non-Suicidal Self-Injury (n, %)	6 (20.7%)	4 (30.8%)	FET	.70
SSRI Augmentation (n, %)	2 (33.3%)	4 (66.7%)	FET	.06
Comorbid ADHD (n, %)	9 (31.0%)	3 (23.1%)	FET	.72
Comorbid Anxiety Disorder (n, %)	15 (51.7%)	7 (53.8%)	χ^2(n = 42, df = 1) = 0.02	.90

Note. FB-IPT = family-based interpersonal psychotherapy; CCT = child-centered therapy; SD = standard deviation; NOS = not otherwise specified; SSRI = selective serotonin reuptake inhibitor; ADHD = attention deficit hyperactivity disorder.

At the request of their parents, six preadolescents ($n = 6$) started an SSRI trial in the first four weeks of the study. Although not significantly different, a higher percentage of preadolescents in the CCT condition received adjunctive treatment with an SSRI than did those in the FB-IPT condition (67% [$n = 4$] as compared to 33% [$n = 2$], respectively). Not surprisingly, SSRI augmentation was correlated with higher pretreatment scores (greater depression symptom severity) on the CDRS-R in both CCT and FB-IPT treatment conditions. SSRI augmentation was therefore controlled for in subsequent analyses.

Table 19.2. Descriptive Statistics for Treatment Outcomes in FB-IPT and CCT

Measures	FB-IPT (n = 25)		CCT (n = 13)	
	Pretreatment Mean (SD)	Posttreatment Mean (SD)	Pretreatment Mean (SD)	Posttreatment Mean (SD)
CDRS-R	44.3 (7.0)	28.8 (8.5)	47.2 (9.3)	34.9 (12.1)
MFQ-P	19.2 (10.4)	6.6 (7.2)	25.2 (13.3)	11.2 (7.3)
MFQ-C	24.7 (16.2)	6.6 (8.5)	23.6 (16.7)	10.9 (11.0)
SCARED-P	21.7 (13.6)	14.9 (10.6)	23.9 (15.3)	17.2 (9.5)
SCARED-C	28.0 (18.4)	13.5 (14.6)	26.3 (17.7)	20.9 (13.7)
CBQ-P	9.5 (5.1)	6.3 (4.6)	8.6 (5.1)	7.9 (5.7)
CBQ-C	5.4 (4.5)	3.5 (4.9)	6.8 (5.3)	4.8 (3.5)
SAS-SR FRI*	10.0 (6.0)	6.8 (4.4)	10.1 (4.5)	9.0 (6.4)
SAS-SR SOC*	11.8 (6.4)	7.8 (4.6)	11.5 (5.2)	10.2 (6.3)

Note. FB-IPT = family-based interpersonal psychotherapy; CCT = child-centered therapy; CDRS-R = Children's Depression Rating Scale–Revised; MFQ-P = Mood and Feelings Questionnaire–Parent ; MFQ-C = Mood and Feelings Questionnaire–Child; SCARED-P = Self-Report for Childhood Anxiety Related Emotional Disorders–Parent; SCARED-C = Self-Report for Childhood Anxiety Related Emotional Disorders–Child; CBQ-P = Conflict Behavior Questionnaire–Parent; CBQ-C = Conflict Behavior Questionnaire–Child; SAS-SR FRI = Social Adjustment Scale–Self Report, Friends Subscale; SAS-SR SOC = Social Adjustment Scale–Self Report, Social ability Subscale. * Lower scores indicate less impairment.

Results

Preadolescents in the FB-IPT condition were more likely to achieve remission at posttreatment than those in CCT (16 [66%] vs. 4 [31%]). The FB-IPT group had significantly lower posttreatment CDRS-R scores and on parent-reported and preadolescent-reported scores on the Mood Feeling Questionnaire (Adrian Angold et al., 1995) compared to the CCT group. Preadolescents receiving FB-IPT exhibited a greater decrease in CDRS-R scores from pre- to posttreatment compared to those receiving CCT, as depicted in Figure 19.1.

Compared to those in the CCT condition, preadolescents in the FB-IPT condition evidenced a greater decrease in self-reported anxiety symptoms from pre- to posttreatment. There were no differences

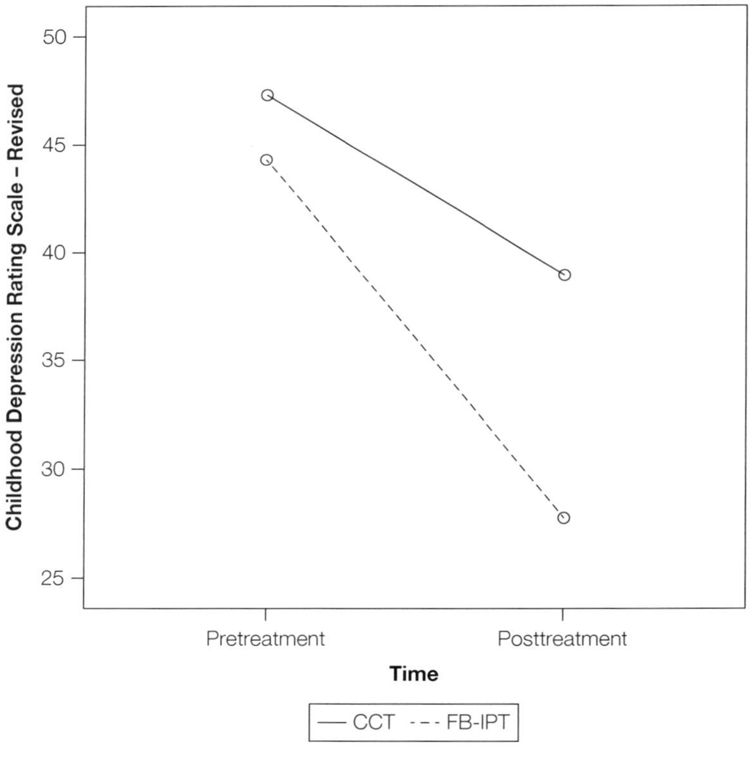

Figure 19.1.

Preadolescents receiving FB-IPT evidence significantly greater decrease in depressive symptoms across treatment as compared to those receiving CCT.

between the FB-IPT and CCT groups in the rate of change in parent–child conflict as indexed by the Conflict Behavior Questionnaire (Robin & Weiss, 1980) from pre- to posttreatment, although a nonsignificant trend suggested a greater decrease in parental report of conflict from pre- to posttreatment for preadolescents treated with FB-IPT compared to preadolescents treated with CCT. As predicted, preadolescents in the FB-IPT condition had a significantly greater decrease in social impairment, as measured by two subscales of the Social Adjustment Scale–Self Report (Weissman & Bothwell, 1976), from pre- to posttreatment than did preadolescents in the CCT condition (see Figure 19.2).

Furthermore, a significant association between posttreatment CDRS-R scores and changes in preadolescents' report of social impairment was found, indicating that lower depression scores at posttreatment were associated with greater decreases in preadolescents' social and peer

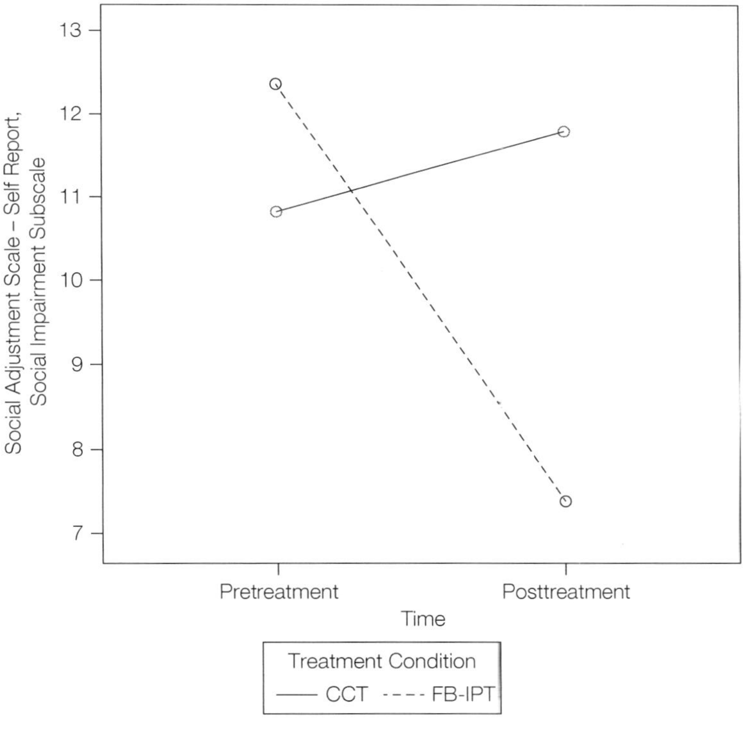

Figure 19.2.

Preadolescents receiving FB-IPT evidence significantly greater decrease in social impairment across treatment as compared to those receiving CCT.

impairment across treatment. Additionally, preadolescents' social impairment mediated the association between FB-IPT and posttreatment CDRS-R scores. Changes in social impairment accounted for the association between FB-IPT and preadolescents' depressive symptoms at posttreatment.

Conclusions

These findings provide strong support for FB-IPT as an effective treatment for preadolescent depression. Preadolescents receiving FB-IPT also evidenced a greater reduction in anxiety symptoms and interpersonal impairment across the treatment course than did those receiving CCT. Of these variables, only changes in social and peer impairment were associated with preadolescents' posttreatment depressive symptoms. There was a significant indirect effect for decreased social impairment mediating the association between the FB-IPT and preadolescents' posttreatment depressive symptoms. This may suggest that reducing social impairment is one mechanism by which FB-IPT may decrease preadolescents' depressive symptoms.

Our results support the efficacy of FB-IPT in increasing the likelihood of remission and reducing preadolescents' depressive symptoms over the course of treatment and suggest a genuine advantage of FB-IPT over supportive therapy. Preadolescents in the FB-IPT condition demonstrated significant decreases in anxiety and in interpersonal impairment as compared to preadolescents receiving CCT, suggesting that FB-IPT was effective in changing constructs targeted by treatment. Results also provide preliminary support for decreases in preadolescents' social impairment as a specific treatment mechanism of FB-IPT in reducing depressive symptoms. Given the lack of temporal precedence in our hypothesized mediator measures, it may be possible that decreases in depressive symptoms accounted for the decreases in preadolescents' social impairment in the FB-IPT group, and therefore further studies are needed to confirm mediation. It is likely that low statistical power obscured our detection of significant changes in parent–child conflict between treatment groups.

Summary

Psychotherapy for preadolescents with depression presents an opportunity to reduce family and interpersonal risk factors that may increase the likelihood of recurrent depression in adolescence. The results of these trials suggest that FB-IPT is an efficacious psychotherapy for increasing remission and decreasing preadolescents' anxiety and interpersonal impairment. These promising findings need to be replicated in additional studies to confirm its efficacy. Future research should test the effectiveness and transportability of FB-IPT, as well as longitudinal outcomes of preadolescents with depression treated with FB-IPT.

Appendices

Appendix A

Mood Thermometer

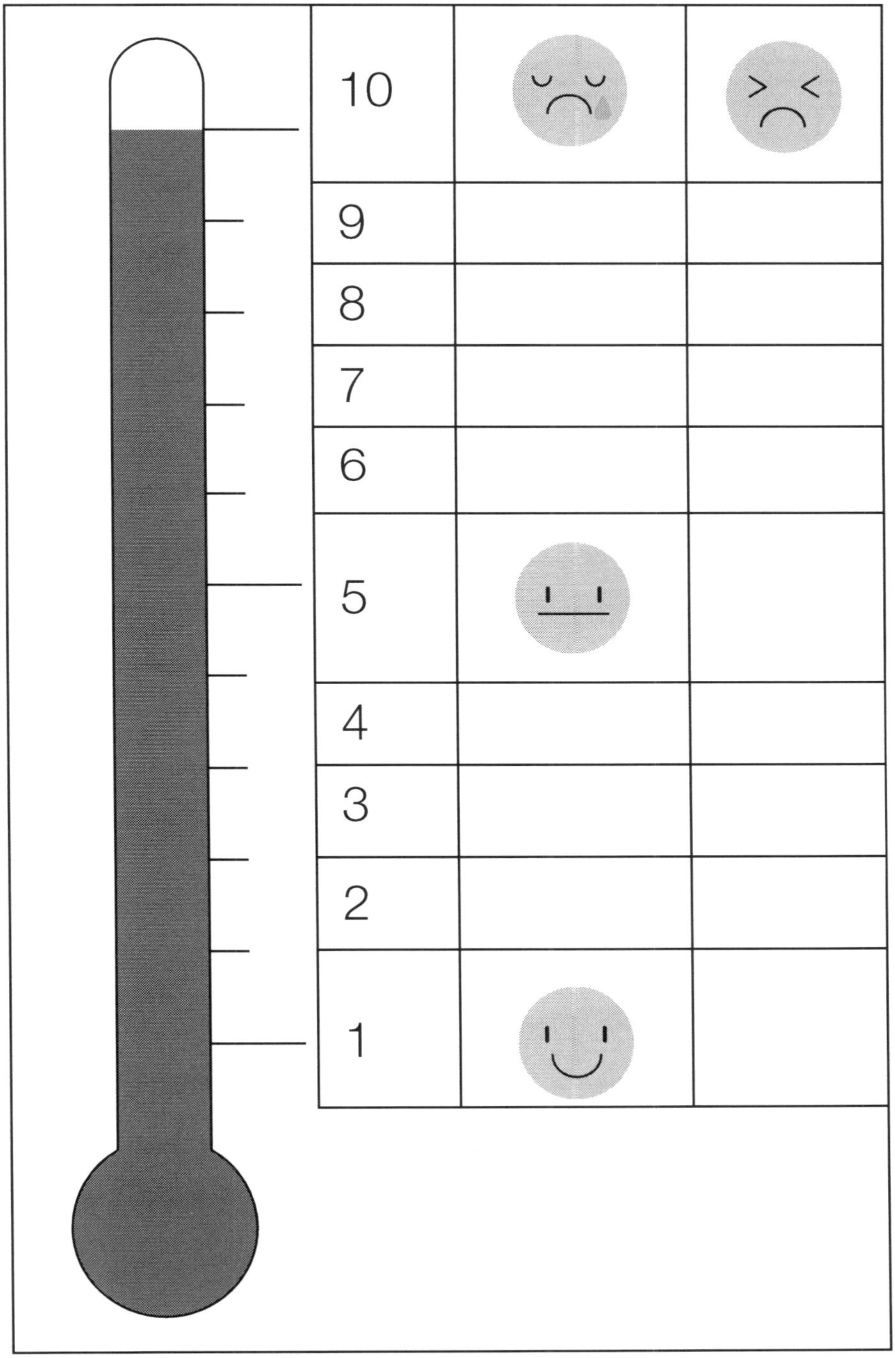

Appendix B

Closeness Circle

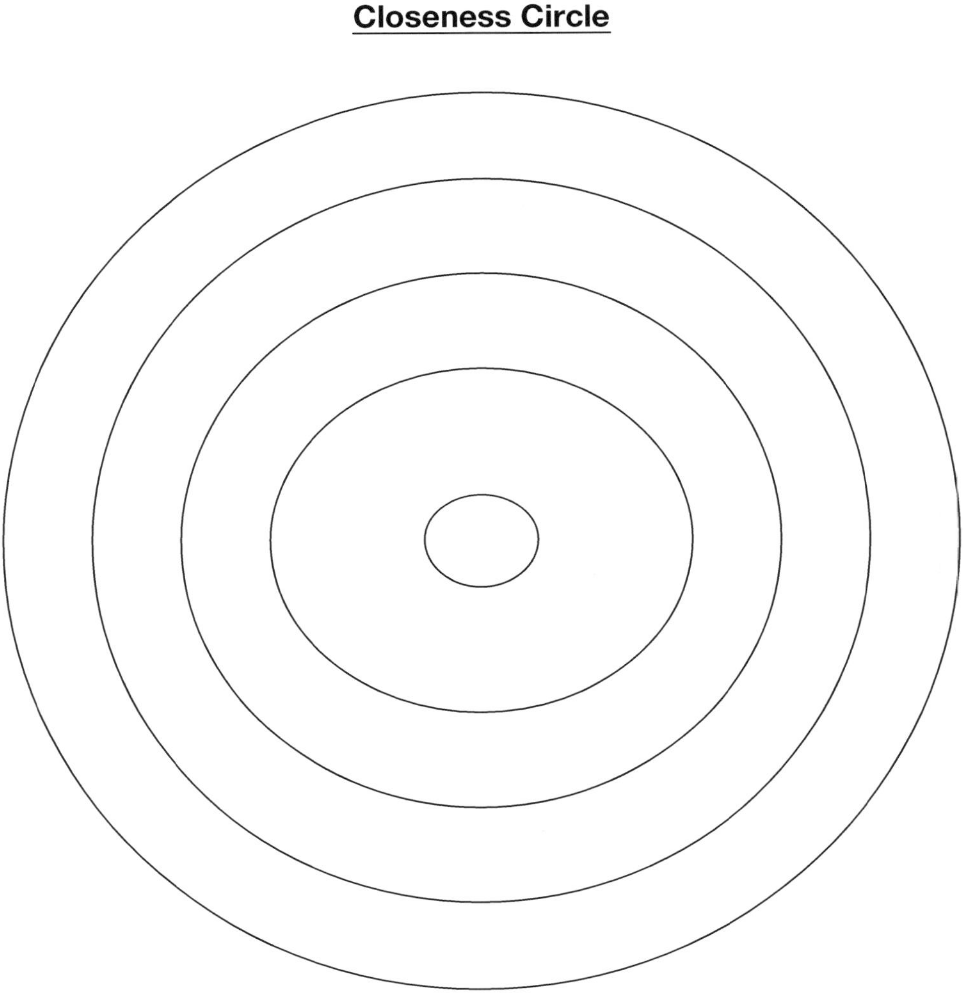

Sample Closeness Circle for Maya

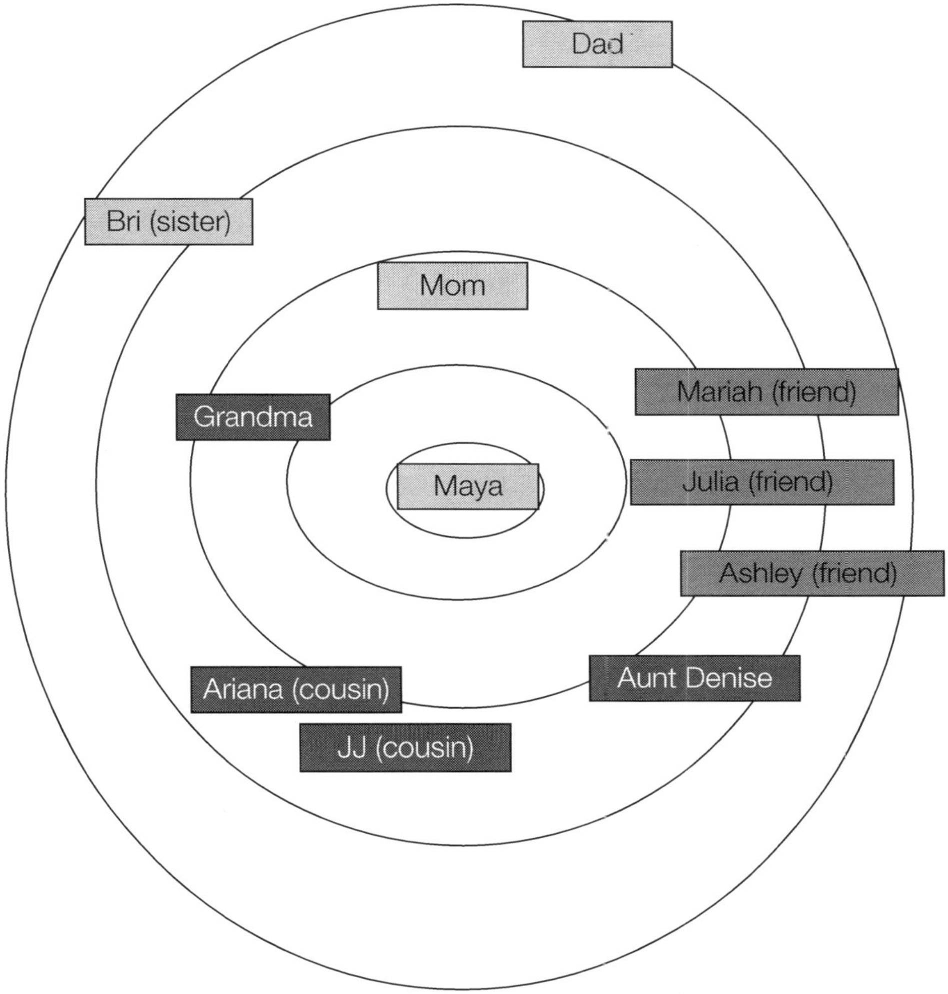

Appendix C

Interpersonal Inventory

Sample Closeness Circle for Jessica

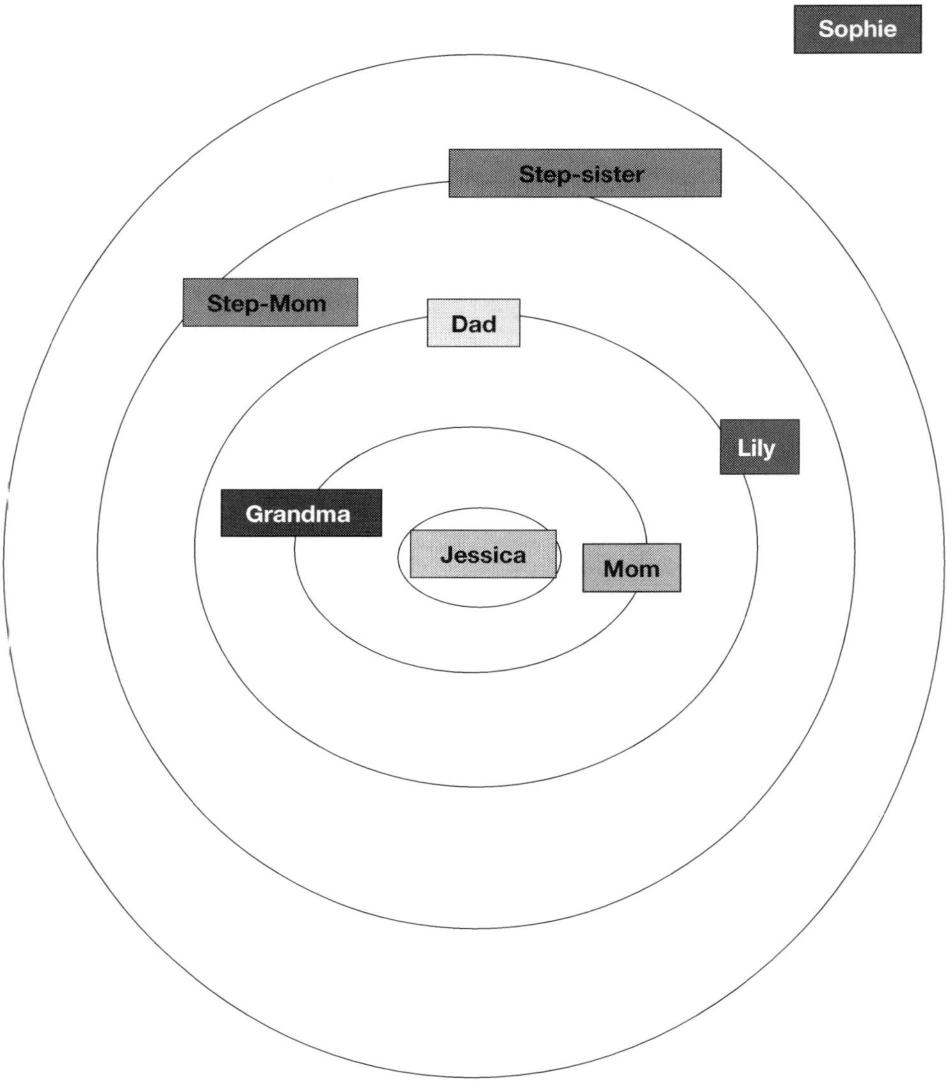

Questions to Guide the Interpersonal Inventory

The goal of the interpersonal inventory is to get a detailed picture of the preadolescent's significant relationships in order to identify patterns about communication and problem-solving that may be negatively impacting on the preadolescent's mood. The questions typically start out more general and gradually become more specific to elicit details about specific types of interactions, problems within the relationship, and desired changes for the relationship.

Questions about Events Related to the Interpersonal Problem Areas:

Has anything happened recently that you think has made you feel more sad?

Have there been any big or small changes in your life in the past year or more? New school? New home? Different friends? Changes with your parents?

Have you been having trouble getting along with people? Getting into fights or arguments? About what? With friends and/or family? At home or in school?

Have you been having trouble making friends in school? In the neighborhood?

Has anyone you have been close to died recently or died a while ago but you still think about that person a lot?

Types of Questions to Ask about Each Relationship:

Tell me a little about ____________? What do you like about ____________? What don't you like about ____________?

How much time do you spend together? What kinds of things do you do together?

Do you like to talk to _____________ about what is going on in your life?

What kinds of things can you talk about with _____________?

Are there things you feel you can't talk about with _____________? How come?

How do you feel when you and _________________ are together? Happy? Sad?

What do you do together with _________________ that makes you feel happy?

What happens when you are together with _________________ that makes you feel sad?

Do you get into arguments with _________________ a lot?

What happens when you argue or fight with _________________?

Do you get the chance to solve the conflict with _________________, or do you just drop it because you are so angry with each other?

Does _____________ know that you have been feeling sad? If yes, how does he/she talk to you about it? If no, would you like him/her to know?

Is there anything you would like to change about your relationship with _________________?

Additional Questions for Exploring Grief as a Problem Area:

Can you tell me about your relationship with _____________? How long ago did he/she die?

How did you find out about it? Have you been able to talk to anyone about your feelings? Now or when it happened?

How much time did you spend with _____________? Did you speak to him/her a lot? Was this someone who you could tell your feelings to?

How has it been to be without this person? What do you miss about him/her?

When you think about him/her, how do you feel? Has this loss caused changes in your other relationships?

Additional Questions for Exploring Interpersonal Role Disputes as a Problem Area:

What happens when you try to talk to ____________ about your feelings or when you want something?

How often do you disagree or fight with ____________? What happens?

Have you ever tried to talk to ____________ about how that makes you feel? What happened when you tried?

What stops you from talking to ____________ about your feelings?

What about this person makes you so angry?

Have you ever tried to come up with a solution to your disagreements with ____________? What happened?

When you disagree with ____________ about something, have you ever been able to come to a new agreement?

Additional Questions for Exploring Role Transitions as a Problem Area:

Have there been changes in your life lately? At home? At school?

What feels different to you?

What is okay about the changes? What feels hard to you about the changes?

Anything you like about the change?

Has the change made you worry about things? Like what?

Anything about the changes that has made you feel sad?

Have you been able to talk to anyone about what feels bad about the changes? What stops you from talking to someone?

Additional Questions for Exploring Interpersonal Deficits as a Problem Area:

Would you say it is hard for you to make friends? What is hard about it?

Do you feel lonely or uncomfortable in some social situations? Which ones? How so?

How do you feel when you are in a new situation like when you are put into a new group at school? Is that hard for you?

How do you feel when you are with groups of kids your age? Do you feel like part of the group or more like an outsider?

Do you ever feel like other kids pick on you?

Are there friends who you feel close to and who you can talk to?

How is it for you to try to make new friends? Do you wait for someone to come to you and be friendly or can you go up to someone new?

What do you think would help you to feel more comfortable with people?

Appendix D

PARENT TIPS

Strike While the Iron's Cold

- It's never a good idea to talk about a problem or conflict when tempers are raging.
- It's okay to step away from the situation and take time to calm down. It's okay to say "I'm feeling really angry right now. Let me take some time to calm down and then we can talk about what happened . . ."
- Remember that this is a great opportunity for you to model for your preteen how to approach problems when you are calm.

Consider the Intention, Not the Outcome

- Your child may not be performing on his/her "A-game" in school, in activities, or at home. Try to see past the outcome and praise the effort.
  - **Example:** *"Hey . . . I know that just doing the day-to-day stuff is hard right now. I think you are doing a great job."*
- Your child may ask for reassurance; please take any opportunity to tell him or her that you understand that he or she is struggling but things will get better.

- Don't use this as an opportunity to inform your child of where she or he is still coming up short ("Yes, you've been doing your homework again but you still can't keep your room clean")

Kind and Firm (Find the Balance)

- It's easy to get frustrated with a depressed tween.
- Depressed tweens are not always aware of how their words and their tone of voice elicit negative responses from others. It takes patience and practice for parents to take the "high road" when communicating with a depressed child.
- Make "I feel" statements and let your tween know if he or she has said something that upsets you instead of responding in an angry way.
  - **Example:** *"I feel bad when you say things like you never have clean clothes or that dinner was disgusting. Sometimes it makes me want to say mean things back to you, and that only makes the two of us feel worse. I know that you are feeling lousy, but that kind of talk is not acceptable."*
- Depressed tweens are sensitive to the tone of voice parents take when responding to them. Sarcasm ("Good work, genius" or "You're right—everything stinks around here") is completely lost on depressed kids—they only hear parents' negative tone, which they may interpret as "My parent doesn't like me."
- Maintain a neutral tone of voice when talking to a moody tween—you will present a model of good emotion regulation that you can insist they demonstrate back to you.
- Reach out to your child and talk about the things they are doing right, even if he or she is not on their A-game.
- Create situations where your depressed tween can succeed—don't set your expectations so high that she or he gives up.
- Remember, your depressed tween still wants to please you even if he or she is irritable, unmotivated, and oppositional right now. In a few short years, your tween will be a teenager and

will want to please their friends, particularly if the parent-child relationship is marked by tension and conflict.

Put on Your Own Oxygen Mask First

- One of the difficult aspects of having a depressed tween is that they need a lot more support, structure, direction, and praise from parents.
- The stress of caring for a depressed child is sometimes overwhelming for parents. It can get in the way of empathic and kind communication with your child.
- Remember what they tell you in case of sudden drops in cabin pressure when traveling by plane: "Put the oxygen mask on yourself first, and then place the mask on your child."
- You can't help your depressed tween if you do not take care of yourself first.
- Parents need support from other adults, time away from stressful situations at home, and guidance about parenting a depressed preteen.
- Vent to a spouse, friend, family member, or therapist.

Appendix E

TWEEN TIPS

Use Good Timing

- Make "appointments" with people you need to talk to.
- Avoid starting conversations at times when people are tired/upset/etc.

  Example: "Mom, I know you are pretty tired from working so hard today. There's something I want to talk to you about. Can we find a time to talk later on tonight?"
- Sometimes "Use Good Timing" means having to be patient and holding onto questions or reactions for when both people are calm, focused, and ready to listen.

Give to Get

- How can you help another person listen to you? Oftentimes, we are so focused on making sure that the other person understands us that we don't really listen to them.
- Start with a positive statement that shows you understand how they feel:
  - **Example:** Mom, I know you worked really hard today and you are probably pretty tired. You probably don't feel like going out to the store right now.
- Make your request/present your feelings about the situation:
  - **Example:** Would you be willing to take me to the store so I could buy something I need for my project/activity?
- Modify your request based on the answer:
  - **Example:** How about tomorrow after school?

- Show the other person that you can accept his or her answer and move on ("Take the No").

Make "I Feel" Statements

- Say how you feel about a situation or about what someone does.
- Start with "I feel."
  - **Example:** *"I feel sad when you yell at me" or "I feel frustrated when I'm doing my math homework."*
- People cannot read your mind no matter how it seems. Put it in words!
- Leading with how you feel is less likely to cause an argument because you are taking ownership of your feelings and not blaming someone else.
  - **Example:** *"I feel frustrated when you talk when I'm trying to explain something," compared to "You don't listen to me!"*

Have a Few Solutions in Mind

- If you want to work something out, do a little prep work! Come up with one or two plans for handling a situation. Here are some helpful strategies for coming up with some plans for handling a tricky situation:
  - "Meet in the Middle": Can this problem be solved by compromising? This is when each person accepts a little less than she or he would like in order to come up with a solution that is reasonable for both people.
  - **Example:** *A preteen asks to go to the movies with her friend. Her father does not feel comfortable with her going without adult supervision and wants to accompany them. "Dad, could my friend and I sit by ourselves inside the movie theatre?"*
  - "Let's Make a Deal": Can this problem be solved by negotiating, or making a plan that would result in each person getting something that he or she wants? This is when one person does

something that the other would like, and the other person does something that you would like in return.

- *Example: "Mom, I'd like to go play at my friend's house on Saturday, but I know that I promised to clean my room. If I clean my room after school on Friday, can I go over to my friend's house on Saturday?"*

Don't Give Up!

- Remember, it takes some time to change the way we communicate and try to solve problems with others. Keep trying!

Appendix F

Sample Depression Circle for Jessica

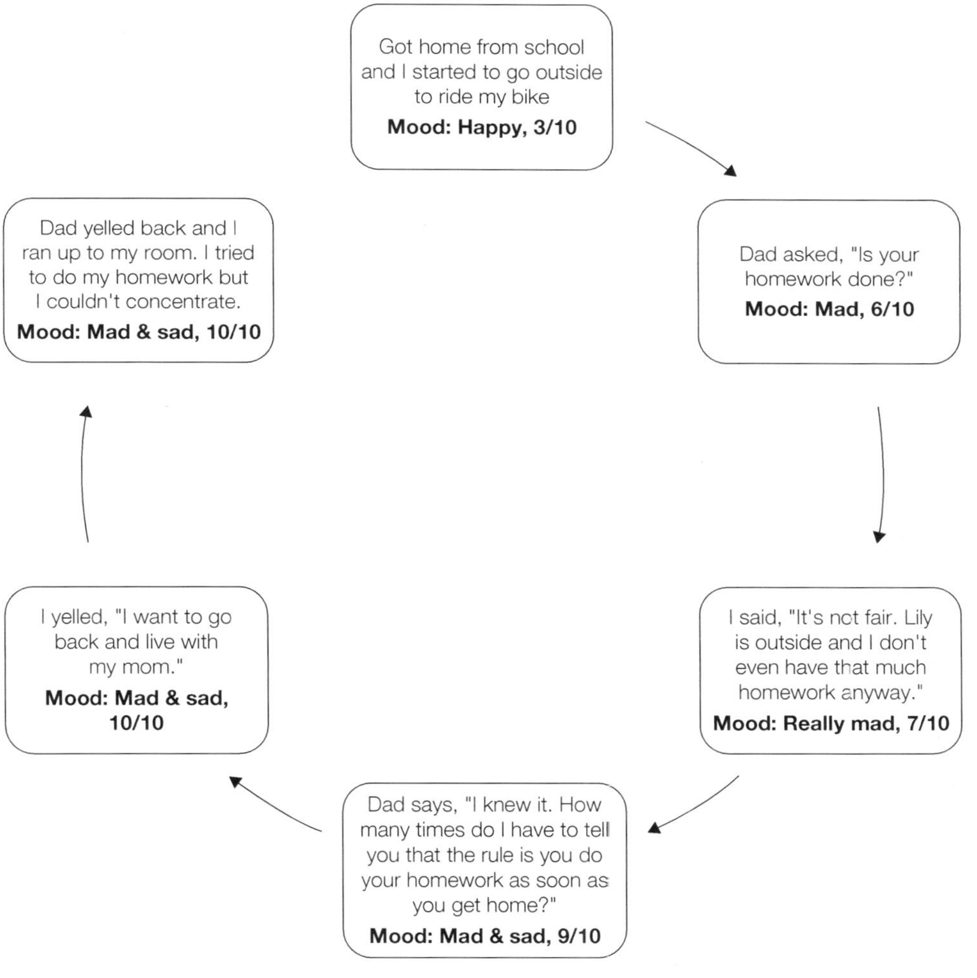

Appendix G

Sample Wellness Circle for Jessica

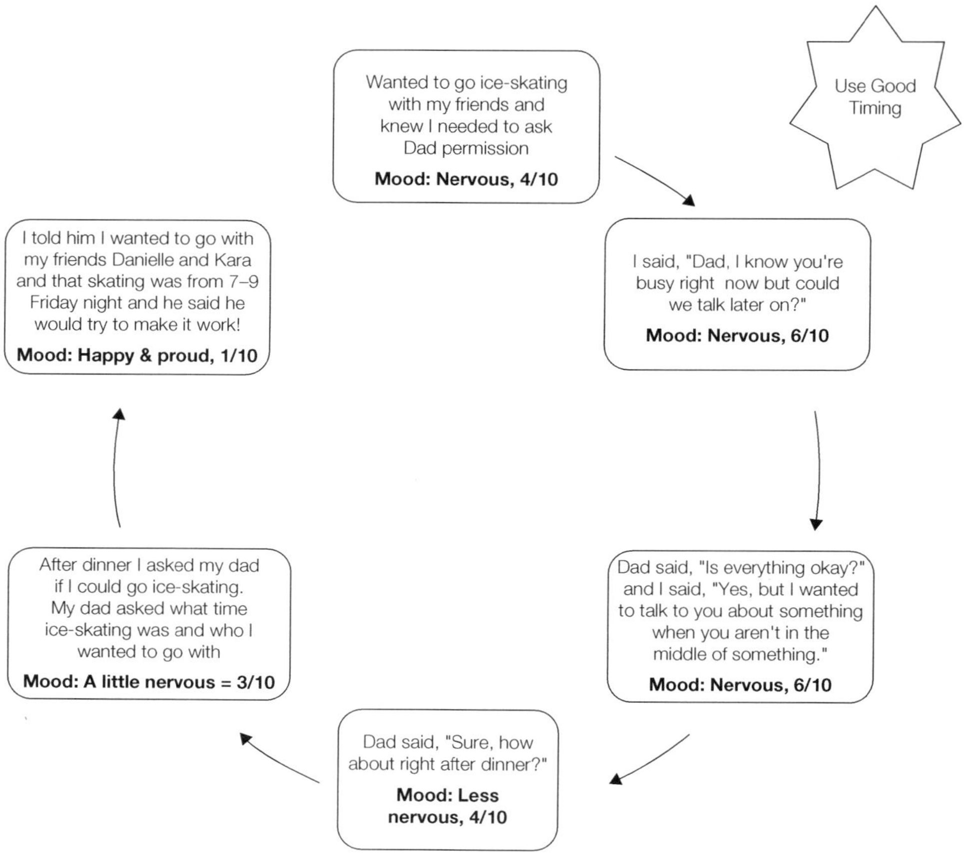

References

Allen, J. P., Insabella, G., Porter, M. R., Smith, F. D., Land, D., & Phillips, N. (2006). A social-interactional model of the development of depressive symptoms in adolescence. *J Consult Clinic Psychol*, *74*, 55–65.

Allen, N. B., & Badcock, P. B. (2003). The social risk hypothesis of depressed mood: evolutionary, psychosocial, and neurobiological perspectives. *Psychol Bull*, *129*(6), 887–913. doi: 10.1037/0033-2909.129.6.8872003-09105-009 [pii]

Alloy, L. B., Abramson, L. Y., Smith, J. M., Gibb, B. E., & Neeren, A. M. (2006). Role of parenting and maltreatment histories in unipolar and bipolar mood disorders: mediation by cognitive vulnerability to depression. *Clin Child Fam Psychol Rev*, *9*(1), 23–64. doi: 10.1007/s10567-006-0002-4

Angold, A., & Costello, E. J. (1993). Depressive comorbidity in children and adolescents: empirical, theoretical, and methodological issues. *Am J Psychiatry*, *150*(12), 1779–1791.

Angold, A., Costello, E. J., Farmer, E. M., Burns, B. J., & Erkanli, A. (1999). Impaired but undiagnosed. *J Am Acad Child Adolesc Psychiatry*, *38*(2), 129–137. doi: 10.1097/00004583-199902000-00011

Angold, A., Costello, E. J., Messer, S. C., & Pickles, A. (1995). Development of a short questionnaire for use in epidemiological studies of depression in children and adolescents. *Int J Methods Psychiatr Res*, *5*(4), 237–249.

Asarnow, J. R., Goldstein, M. J., Carlson, G. A., Perdue, S., Bates, S., & Keller, J. (1988). Childhood-onset depressive disorders. A follow-up study of rates of rehospitalization and out-of-home placement among child psychiatric inpatients. *J Affect Disord*, *15*(3), 245–253.

Avenevoli, S., Stolar, M., Li, J., Dierker, L., & Ries Merikangas, K. (2001). Comorbidity of depression in children and adolescents: models and evidence from a prospective high-risk family study. *Biol Psychiatry*, *49*(12), 1071–1081.

Axelson, D. A., & Birmaher, B. (2001). Relation between anxiety and depressive disorders in childhood and adolescence. *Depress Anxiety*, *14*(2), 67–78.

Barnett, P. A., & Gotlib, I. H. (1988). Psychosocial functioning and depression: distinguishing among antecedents, concomitants, and consequences. *Psychol Bull, 104*(1), 97–126.

Barrocas, A. L., Hankin, B. L., Young, J. F., & Abela, J. R. (2012). Rates of nonsuicidal self-injury in youth: age, sex, and behavioral methods in a community sample. *Pediatrics, 130*(1), 39–45. doi: 10.1542/peds.2011-2094

Beardslee, W. (1993). The impact of parental affective disorder on depression in offspring: A longitudinal follow-up in a nonreferred sample. *J Am Acad Child Adolesc Psychiatry, 32*(4), 723.

Beardslee, W. R., Versage, E. M., & Gladstone, T. (1998). Children of Affectively Ill Parents: A Review of the Past 10 Years. *J Am Acad Child Adolesc Psychiatry, 37*(11), 1134–1141.

Birmaher, B., Khetarpal, S., Cully, M., Brent, D. A., & McKenzie, S. (2003). Screen for Child Anxiety Related Disorders (SCARED)—Parent form and child form (8 years and older). In L. VandeCreek (Ed.), *Innovations in clinical practice: Focus on children & adolescents* (pp. 99–104). Sarasota, FL: Professional Resource Press/Professional Resource Exchange.

Birmaher, B., & Rozel, J. S. (2003). The school age child. In I. M. Goodyer (Ed.), *Unipolar depression: A lifespan perspective*. Oxford: Oxford University Press.

Birmaher, B., Ryan, N. D., Williamson, D. E., Brent, D. A., Kaufman, J., Dahl, R. E., . . . Nelson, B. (1996). Childhood and adolescent depression: a review of the past 10 years. Part I. *J Am Acad Child Adolesc Psychiatry, 35*(11), 1427–1439. doi: 10.1097/00004583-199611000-00011

Bowlby, J. (1978). Attachment theory and its therapeutic implications. *Adolesc Psychiatry, 6*, 5–33.

Brady, E. U., & Kendall, P. C. (1992). Comorbidity of anxiety and depression in children and adolescents. *Psychol Bull, 111*(2), 244–255.

Brendgen, M., Wanner, B., Morin, A. J., & Vitaro, F. (2005). Relations with parents and with peers, temperament, and trajectories of depressed mood during early adolescence. *J Abnorm Child Psychol, 33*(5), 579–594. doi: 10.1007/s10802-005-6739-2

Brent, D. A., Holder, D., Kolko, D., Birmaher, B., Baugher, M., Roth, C., . . . Johnson, B. A. (1997). A clinical psychotherapy trial for adolescent depression comparing cognitive, family, and supportive therapy. *Arch Gen Psychiatry, 54*(9), 877–885.

Brent, D. A., Kolko, D. J., Birmaher, B., Baugher, M., Bridge, J., Roth, C., & Holder, D. (1998). Predictors of treatment efficacy in a clinical trial of three psychosocial treatments for adolescent depression.

J Am Acad Child Adolesc Psychiatry, 37(9), 906–914. doi: 10.1097/00004583-199809000-00010

Bridge, J. A., Asti, L., Horowitz, L. M., Greenhouse, J. B., Fontanella, C. A., Sheftall, A. H., . . . Campo, J. V. (2015). Suicide trends among elementary school-aged children in the United States from 1993 to 2012. *JAMA Pediatr, 169*(7), 673–677. doi: 10.1001/jamapediatrics.2015.0465

Bridge, J. A., Greenhouse, J. B., Weldon, A. H., Campo, J. V., & Kelleher, K. J. (2008). Suicide trends among youths aged 10 to 19 years in the United States, 1996–2005. *JAMA, 300*(9), 1025–1026. doi: 10.1001/jama.300.9.1025

Brown, G. W., & Harris, T. O. (1978). *Social origins of depression: A study of psychiatric disorder in women.* London: Tavistock.

Campbell, S. B., Cohn, J. F., & Meyers, T. (1995). Depression in first-time mothers: mother-infant interaction and depression chronicity. *Develop Psychol, 31*(3), 349–357.

Cheung, A., Mayes, T., Levitt, A., Schaffer, A., Michalak, E., Kiss, A., & Emslie, G. (2010). Anxiety as a predictor of treatment outcome in children and adolescents with depression. *J Child Adolesc Psychopharmacol, 20*(3), 211–216. doi: 10.1089/cap.2010.0006

Connolly, M. B., Crits-Christoph, P., Barber, J. P., & Luborsky, L. (2000). Transference patterns in the therapeutic relationship in supportive-expressive psychotherapy for depression. *Psychother Res, 10*(3), 356–372.

Copeland, W. E., Shanahan, L., Costello, E. J., & Angold, A. (2009). Childhood and adolescent psychiatric disorders as predictors of young adult disorders. *Arch Gen Psychiatry, 66*(7), 764–772. doi: 10.1001/archgenpsychiatry.2009.85

Copeland, W. E., Wolke, D., Angold, A., & Costello, E. J. (2013). Adult psychiatric outcomes of bullying and being bullied by peers in childhood and adolescence. *JAMA Psychiatry, 70*(4), 419–426. doi: 10.1001/jamapsychiatry.2013.504

Costello, E. J., Angold, A., Burns, B. J., Erkanli, A., Stangl, D. K., & Tweed, D. L. (1996). The Great Smoky Mountains Study of Youth. Functional impairment and serious emotional disturbance. *Arch Gen Psychiatry, 53*(12), 1137–1143.

Costello, E. J., Mustillo, S., Erkanli, A., Keeler, G., & Angold, A. (2003). Prevalence and development of psychiatric disorders in childhood and adolescence. *Arch Gen Psychiatry, 60*(8), 837–844. doi: 10.1001/archpsyc.60.8.837

Coyne, J. C. (1976). Depression and the response of others. *J Abnorm Psychol, 85*(2), 186–193.

Cuijpers, P., Donker, T., Weissman, M. M., Ravitz, P., & Cristea, I. A. (2016). Interpersonal psychotherapy for mental health problems: a comprehensive meta-analysis. *Am J Psychiatry, 173*(7), 680–687. doi: 10.1176/appi.ajp.2015.15091141

Cuijpers, P., Geraedts, A. S., van Oppen, P., Andersson, G., Markowitz, J. C., & van Straten, A. (2011). Interpersonal psychotherapy for depression: a meta-analysis. *Am J Psychiatry, 168*(6), 581–592. doi: 10.1176/appi.ajp.2010.10101411

Cuijpers, P., van Straten, A., van Oppen, P., & Andersson, G. (2008). Are psychological and pharmacologic interventions equally effective in the treatment of adult depressive disorders? A meta-analysis of comparative studies. *J Clin Psychiatry, 69*(11), 1675–1685; quiz 1839–1641.

Cuijpers, P., van Straten, A., Warmerdam, L., & Andersson, G. (2009). Psychotherapy versus the combination of psychotherapy and pharmacotherapy in the treatment of depression: a meta-analysis. *Depress Anxiety, 26*(3), 279–288. doi: 10.1002/da.20519

Cussen, A., Sciberras, E., Ukoumunne, O. C., & Efron, D. (2012). Relationship between symptoms of attention-deficit/hyperactivity disorder and family functioning: a community-based study. *Eur J Pediatr, 171*(2), 271–280. doi: 10.1007/s00431-011-1524-4

Cyranowski, J. M., Frank, E., Young, E., & Shear, K. (2000). Adolescent onset of the gender difference in lifetime rates of major depression. *Arch Gen Psychiatry, 57*(1), 21–28.

Dahl, R. E., & Gunnar, M. R. (2009). Heightened stress responsiveness and emotional reactivity during pubertal maturation: implications for psychopathology. *Dev Psychopathol, 21*(1), 1–6. doi: 10.1017/S0954579409000017

David-Ferdon, C., & Kaslow, N. J. (2008). Evidence-based psychosocial treatments for child and adolescent depression. *J Clin Child Adolesc Psychol, 37*(1), 62–104. doi: 10.1080/15374410701817865

Daviss, W. B. (2008). A review of co-morbid depression in pediatric ADHD: etiology, phenomenology, and treatment. *J Child Adolesc Psychopharmacol, 18*(6), 565–571. doi: 10.1089/cap.2008.032

Degirmenicioglu, S. M., Urbeg, K. A., Tolson, J. M., & Richard, P. (1998). Adolescent friendship networks: continuity and change over the school year. *Merrill Palmer Q, 44*(3), 313–337.

Dervic, K., Brent, D. A., & Oquendo, M. A. (2008). Completed suicide in childhood. *Psychiatr Clin North Am, 31*(2), 271–291. doi: 10.1016/j.psc.2008.01.006

Dietz, L. J., Birmaher, B., Williamson, D. E., Silk, J. S., Dahl, R. E., Axelson, D. A., . . . Ryan, N. D. (2008). Mother-child interactions in depressed children and children at high risk and low risk for future depression. *J Am Acad Child Adolesc Psychiatry, 47*(5), 574–582. doi: 10.1097/CHI.0b013e3181676595

Dietz, L. J., Mufson, L., Irvine, H., & Brent, D. A. (2008). Family-based interpersonal psychotherapy for depressed preadolescents: an open-treatment trial. *Early Interv Psychiatry, 2*(3), 154–161. doi: 10.1111/j.1751-7893.2008.00077.x

Dietz, L. J., Weinberg, R. J., Brent, D. A., & Mufson, L. (2015). Family-based interpersonal psychotherapy for depressed preadolescents: examining efficacy and potential treatment mechanisms. *J Am Acad Child Adolesc Psychiatry, 54*(3), 191–199. doi: 10.1016/j.jaac.2014.12.011

Dorn, L. D., Dahl, R. E., Woodward, H. R., & Biro, F. (2006). Defining boundaries of early adolescence: a user's guide to assessing pubertal status and pubertal timing in research with adolescents. *Applied Developmental Science, 10,* 30–56.

Downey, G., & Feldman, S. I. (1996). Implications of rejection sensitivity for intimate relationships. *J Pers Soc Psychol, 70*(6), 1327–1343.

Ek, U., Westerlund, J., Holmberg, K., & Fernell, E. (2011). Academic performance of adolescents with ADHD and other behavioural and learning problems: a population-based longitudinal study. *Acta Paediatr, 100*(3), 402–406. doi: 10.1111/j.1651-2227.2010.02048.x

Emslie, G. J., Rush, A. J., Weinberg, W. A., Gullion, C. M., Rintelmann, J., & Hughes, C. W. (1997). Recurrence of major depressive disorder in hospitalized children and adolescents. *J Am Acad Child Adolesc Psychiatry, 36*(6), 785–792.

Fendrich, M., Warner, V., & Weissman, M. M. (1990). Family risk factors, parental depression, and psychopathology in offspring. *Dev Psychol, 26*(1), 40–50.

Fombonne, E., Wostear, G., Cooper, V., Harrington, R., & Rutter, M. (2001a). The Maudsley long-term follow-up of child and adolescent depression. 1. Psychiatric outcomes in adulthood. *Br J Psychiatry, 179,* 210–217.

Fombonne, E., Wostear, G., Cooper, V., Harrington, R., & Rutter, M. (2001b). The Maudsley long-term follow-up of child and adolescent depression. 2. Suicidality, criminality and social dysfunction in adulthood. *Br J Psychiatry, 179,* 218–223.

Forbes, E. E., Cohn, J. F., Allen, N. B., & Lewinsohn, P. M. (2004). Infant affect during parent-infant interaction at 3 and 6 months: differences between mothers and fathers and influence of parent history of depression. *Infancy, 5*(1), 61–84. doi: 10.1207/s15327078in0501_3

Forbes, E. E., & Dahl, R. E. (2010). Pubertal development and behavior: hormonal activation of social and motivational tendencies. *Brain Cogn*, *72*(1), 66–72. doi: 10.1016/j.bandc.2009.10.007

Frank, E., Kupfer, D. J., Buysse, D. J., Swartz, H. A., Pilkonis, P. A., Houck, P. R., . . . Stapf, D. M. (2007). Randomized trial of weekly, twice-monthly, and monthly interpersonal psychotherapy as maintenance treatment for women with recurrent depression. *Am J Psychiatry*, *164*(5), 761–767. doi: 10.1176/ajp.2007.164.5.761

Frank, E., Kupfer, D. J., Perel, J. M., Cornes, C., Jarrett, D. B., Mallinger, A. G., . . . Grochocinski, V. J. (1990). Three-year outcomes for maintenance therapies in recurrent depression. *Arch Gen Psychiatry*, *47*(12), 1093–1099.

Galambos, N. L., Leadbeater, B. J., & Barker, E. T. (2004). Gender differences in and risk factors for depression in adolescence: a 4-year longitudinal study. *Int J Behav Develop*, *28*, 16–25.

Geller, B., Zimerman, B., Williams, M., Bolhofner, K., & Craney, J. L. (2001). Adult psychosocial outcome of prepubertal major depressive disorder. *J Am Acad Child Adolesc Psychiatry*, *40*(6), 673–677.

Gilbert, P. (1992). *Depression: The evolution of powerlessness*. New York: Guilford Press.

Goodman, S. H., & Gotlib, I. H. (1999). Risk for psychopathology in the children of depressed mothers: A developmental model for understanding mechanisms of transmission. *Psycholog Rev*, *106*(3), 458–490.

Goodyer, I. M., Herbert, J., Secher, S. M., & Pearson, J. (1997). Short-term outcome of major depression: I. Comorbidity and severity at presentation as predictors of persistent disorder. *J Am Acad Child Adolesc Psychiatry*, *36*(2), 179–187. doi: 10.1097/00004583-199702000-00008

Graber, J. A. (2013). Pubertal timing and the development of psychopathology in adolescence and beyond. *Horm Behav*, *64*(2), 262–269. doi: http://dx.doi.org/10.1016/j.yhbeh.2013.04.003

Graham, P., & Rutter, M. (1968). The reliability and validity of the psychiatric assessment of the child: II. Interview with the parent. *Br J Psychiatry*, *114*(510), 581–592. doi: 10.1192/bjp.114.510.581

Gunlicks-Stoessel, M., Mufson, L., Jekal, A., & Turner, J. B. (2010). The impact of perceived interpersonal functioning on treatment for adolescent depression: IPT-A versus treatment as usual in school-based health clinics. *J Consult Clin Psychol*, *78*(2), 260–267. doi: 10.1037/a0018935

Hames, J. L., Hagan, C. R., & Joiner, T. E. (2013). Interpersonal processes in depression. *Annu Rev Clin Psychol*, *9*, 355–377. doi: 10.1146/annurev-clinpsy-050212-185553

Hammen, C., & Brennan, P. A. (2001). Depressed adolescents of depressed and nondepressed mothers: tests of an interpersonal impairment hypothesis. *J Consult Clin Psychol, 69*(2), 284–294.

Hammen, C., & Rudolph, K. D. (Eds.). (1996). Childhood depression. In E. J. Mash & R. A. Barkley (Eds.), *Child psychopathology*. New York: Guilford.

Hammen, C., Rudolph, K., Weisz, J., Rao, U., & Burge, D. (1999). The context of depression in clinic-referred youth: neglected areas in treatment. *J Am Acad Child Adolesc Psychiatry, 38*(1), 64–71.

Hankin, B. L., & Abela, J. R. (2011). Nonsuicidal self-injury in adolescence: prospective rates and risk factors in a 2 1/2 year longitudinal study. *Psychiatry Res, 186*(1), 65–70. doi: 10.1016/j.psychres.2010.07.056

Harrington, R. C., Fudge, H., Rutter, M. L., Bredenkamp, D., Groothues, C., & Pridham, J. (1993). Child and adult depression: a test of continuities with data from a family study. *Br J Psychiatry, 162*, 627–633.

Harrington, R., Fudge, H., Rutter, M., Pickles, A., & Hill, J. (1990). Adult outcomes of childhood and adolescent depression. I. Psychiatric status. *Arch Gen Psychiatry, 47*(5), 465–473.

Harrington, R., Fudge, H., Rutter, M., Pickles, A., & Hill, J. (1991). Adult outcomes of childhood and adolescent depression: II. Links with antisocial disorders. *J Am Acad Child Adolesc Psychiatry, 30*(3), 434–439. doi: 10.1097/00004583-199105000-00013

Harrington, R., Rutter, M., Weissman, M., Fudge, H., Groothues, C., Bredenkamp, D., . . . Wickramaratne, P. (1997). Psychiatric disorders in the relatives of depressed probands. I. Comparison of prepubertal, adolescent and early adult onset cases. *J Affect Disord, 42*(1), 9–22.

Hazel, N. A., Oppenheimer, C. W., Technow, J. R., Young, J. F., & Hankin, B. L. (2014). Parent relationship quality buffers against the effect of peer stressors on depressive symptoms from middle childhood to adolescence. *Dev Psychol, 50*(8), 2115–2123. doi: 10.1037/a0037192

Humphreys, K. L., Katz, S. J., Lee, S. S., Hammen, C., Brennan, P. A., & Najman, J. M. (2013). The association of ADHD and depression: mediation by peer problems and parent-child difficulties in two complementary samples. *J Abnorm Psychol, 122*(3), 854–867. doi: 10.1037/a0033895

Jakobsen, J. C., Hansen, J. L., Simonsen, S., Simonsen, E., & Gluud, C. (2012). Effects of cognitive therapy versus interpersonal psychotherapy in patients with major depressive disorder: a systematic review of randomized clinical trials with meta-analyses and trial sequential analyses. *Psychol Med, 42*(7), 1343–1357. doi: 10.1017/s0033291711002236

Johnson, J. G., Cohen, P., & Kasen, S. (2009). Minor depression during adolescence and mental health outcomes during adulthood. *Br J Psychiatry, 195*(3), 264–265. doi: 10.1192/bjp.bp.108.054239

Joiner, T. E., Jr. (1997). Shyness and low social support as interactive diatheses, with loneliness as mediator: testing an interpersonal-personality view of vulnerability to depressive symptoms. *J Abnorm Psychol, 106*(3), 386–394.

Joiner, T. E., Jr., Lewinsohn, P. M., & Seeley, J. R. (2002). The core of loneliness: lack of pleasurable engagement—more so than painful disconnection—predicts social impairment, depression onset, and recovery from depressive disorders among adolescents. *J Pers Assess, 79*(3), 472–491. doi: 10.1207/S15327752JPA7903_05

Joiner, T. E., Jr., & Metalsky, G. I. (2001). Excessive reassurance seeking: delineating a risk factor involved in the development of depressive symptoms. *Psychol Sci, 12*(5), 371–378. doi: 10.1111/1467-9280.00369

Joormann, J., Gilbert, K., & Gotlib, I. H. (2010). Emotion identification in girls at high risk for depression. *J Child Psychol Psychiatry, 51*(5), 575–582. doi: 10.1111/j.1469-7610.2009.02175.x

Joormann, J., Talbot, L., & Gotlib, I. H. (2007). Biased processing of emotional information in girls at risk for depression. *J Abnorm Psychol, 116*(1), 135–143. doi: 10.1037/0021-843X.116.1.135

Kahn, J. S., Kehle, T. J., Jenson, W. R., & Clark, E. (1990). Comparison of cognitive-behavioral, relaxation, and self-modeling interventions for depression among middle-school students. *School Psychol Rev, 19*(2), 196–211.

Kaufman, J., Birmaher, B., Brent, D., Rao, U., Flynn, C., Moreci, P., . . . Ryan, N. (1997). Schedule for Affective Disorders and Schizophrenia for School-Age Children–Present and Lifetime Version (K-SADS-PL): initial reliability and validity data. *J Am Acad Child Adolesc Psychiatry, 36*(7), 980–988.

Keenan, K., & Hipwell, A. E. (2005). Preadolescent clues to understanding depression in girls. *Clin Child Fam Psychol Rev, 8*(2), 89–105.

Keenan, K., Hipwell, A., Feng, X., Babinski, D., Hinze, A., Rischall, M., & Henneberger, A. (2008). Subthreshold symptoms of depression in preadolescent girls are stable and predictive of depressive disorders. *J Am Acad Child Adolesc Psychiatry, 47*(12), 1433–1442. doi: 10.1097/CHI.0b013e3181886eab

Kessler, R. C., Avenevoli, S., & Ries Merikangas, K. (2001). Mood disorders in children and adolescents: an epidemiologic perspective. *Biol Psychiatry, 49*(12), 1002–1014.

Klerman, G. L., Weissman, M. M., Rounsaville, B. J., & Chevron, E. S. (1984). *Interpersonal psychotherapy of depression.* New York: Basic Books.

Klomek, A. B., Marrocco, F., Kleinman, M., Schonfeld, I. S., & Gould, M. S. (2007). Bullying, depression, and suicidality in adolescents. *J Am Acad Child Adolesc Psychiatry, 46,* 40–49.

Kovacs, M. (2004). Children's Depression Inventory 2 (CD-2). Toronto: Multi-Health Systems.

Kovacs, M., Feinberg, T. L., Crouse-Novak, M. A., Paulauskas, S. L., & Finkelstein, R. (1984). Depressive disorders in childhood. I. A longitudinal prospective study of characteristics and recovery. *Arch Gen Psychiatry, 41*(3), 229–237.

Kovacs, M., Feinberg, T. L., Crouse-Novak, M., Paulauskas, S. L., Pollock, M., & Finkelstein, R. (1984). Depressive disorders in childhood. II. A longitudinal study of the risk for a subsequent major depression. *Arch Gen Psychiatry, 41*(7), 643–649.

Kovacs, M., Gatsonis, C., Paulauskas, S. L., & Richards, C. (1989). Depressive disorders in childhood. IV. A longitudinal study of comorbidity with and risk for anxiety disorders. *Arch Gen Psychiatry, 46*(9), 776–782.

Kovacs, M., Paulauskas, S., Gatsonis, C., & Richards, C. (1988). Depressive disorders in childhood. III. A longitudinal study of comorbidity with and risk for conduct disorders. *J Affect Disord, 15*(3), 205–217.

Leadbeater, B. J., Blatt, S. J., & Quinlan, D. M. (1995). Gender-linked vulnerabilities to depressive symptoms, stress, and problem behaviors in adolescents. *J Res Adolesc, 5*(1), 1–29.

Lereya, S. T., Copeland, W. E., Costello, E. J., & Wolke, D. (2015). Adult mental health consequences of peer bullying and maltreatment in childhood: two cohorts in two countries. *Lancet Psychiatry, 2*(6), 524–531. doi: 10.1016/s2215-0366(15)00165-0

Lewinsohn, P. M., Rohde, P., Seeley, J. R., Klein, D. N., & Gotlib, I. H. (2000). Natural course of adolescent major depressive disorder in a community sample: predictors of recurrence in young adults. *Am J Psychiatry, 157*(10), 1584–1591. doi: 10.1176/appi.ajp.157.10.1584

Lifford, K. J., Harold, G. T., & Thapar, A. (2008). Parent-child relationships and ADHD symptoms: a longitudinal analysis. *J Abnorm Child Psychol, 36*(2), 285–296. doi: 10.1007/s10802-007-9177-5

Lipsitz, J. D., & Markowitz, J. C. (2013). Mechanisms of change in interpersonal therapy (IPT). *Clin Psychol Rev, 33*(8), 1134–1147. doi: 10.1016/j.cpr.2013.09.002

Magnuson, K. M., & Constantino, J. N. (2011). Characterization of depression in children with autism spectrum disorders. *J Dev Behav Pediatr, 32*(4), 332–340. doi: 10.1097/DBP.0b013e318213f56c

Mazzone, L., Ruta, L., & Reale, L. (2012). Psychiatric comorbidities in Asperger syndrome and high functioning autism: diagnostic challenges. *Ann Gen Psychiatry, 11*(1), 16. doi: 10.1186/1744-859x-11-16

McLachlan, J., Zimmer-Gembeck, M. J., & McGregor, L. (2010). Rejection sensitivity in childhood and early adolescence: peer rejection and protective effects of parents and friends. *J Relation Res, 1*(1), 31–40. doi: 10.1375/jrr.1.1.31

Meyer, A. (1957). *Psychobiology: A science of man*. Springfield, IL: Charles C. Thomas.

Mufson, L., Dorta, K. P., Wickramaratne, P., Nomura, Y., Olfson, M., & Weissman, M. M. (2004). A randomized effectiveness trial of interpersonal psychotherapy for depressed adolescents. *Arch Gen Psychiatry, 61*(6), 577–584. doi: 10.1001/archpsyc.61.6.577

Mufson, L., Pollack Dorta, K., Moreau, D., & Weissman, M. (2004). *Interpersonal psychotherapy for depressed adolescents* (2nd ed.). New York: Guilford Press.

Mufson, L., Weissman, M. M., Moreau, D., & Garfinkel, R. (1999). Efficacy of interpersonal psychotherapy for depressed adolescents. *Arch Gen Psychiatry, 56*(6), 573–579.

Muris, P., Van Brakel, A., & Meesters, C. (1998). Coping styles, anxiety, and depression in children. *Psychol Rep, 83*(3 Pt 2), 1225–1226. doi: 10.2466/pr0.1998.83.3f.1225

Nelson, E. E., & Guyer, A. E. (2011). The development of the ventral prefrontal cortex and social flexibility. *Dev Cogn Neurosci, 1*(3), 233–245. doi: 10.1016/j.dcn.2011.01.002

Nelson, E. E., Leibenluft, E., McClure, E. B., & Pine, D. S. (2005). The social re-orientation of adolescence: a neuroscience perspective on the process and its relation to psychopathology. *Psychol Med, 35*(2), 163–174.

Nolan, S. A., Flynn, C., & Garber, J. (2003). Prospective relations between rejection and depression in young adolescents. *J Pers Social Psychol, 85*, 745–755.

Nomura, Y., Wickramaratne, P. J., Warner, V., Mufson, L., & Weissman, M. M. (2002). Family discord, parental depression, and psychopathology in offspring: ten-year follow-up. *J Am Acad Child Adolesc Psychiatry, 41*(4), 402–409.

Olino, T. M., Lopez-Duran, N. L., Kovacs, M., George, C. J., Gentzler, A. L., & Shaw, D. S. (2011). Developmental trajectories of positive and negative affect in children at high and low familial risk for depressive disorder. *J Child Psychol Psychiatry*, *52*(7), 792–799. doi: 10.1111/j.1469-7610.2010.02331.x

O'Shea, G., Spence, S. H., & Donovan, C. L. (2015). Group versus individual interpersonal psychotherapy for depressed adolescents. *Behav Cogn Psychother*, *43*(1), 1–19. doi: 10.1017/s1352465814000216

Ostrander, R., Crystal, D. S., & August, G. (2006). Attention deficit-hyperactivity disorder, depression, and self- and other-assessments of social competence: a developmental study. *J Abnorm Child Psychol*, *34*(6), 773–787. doi: 10.1007/s10802-006-9051-x

Ostrander, R., & Herman, K. C. (2006). Potential cognitive, parenting, and developmental mediators of the relationship between ADHD and depression. *J Consult Clin Psychol*, *74*(1), 89–98. doi: 10.1037/0022-006x.74.1.89

Polanczyk, G. V., Willcutt, E. G., Salum, G. A., Kieling, C., & Rohde, L. A. (2014). ADHD prevalence estimates across three decades: an updated systematic review and meta-regression analysis. *Int J Epidemiol*, *43*(2), 434–442. doi: 10.1093/ije/dyt261

Posner, K., Brown, G. K., Stanley, B., Brent, D. A., Yershova, K. V., Oquendo, M. A., . . . Mann, J. J. (2011). The Columbia-Suicide Severity Rating Scale: initial validity and internal consistency findings from three multisite studies with adolescents and adults. *Am J Psychiatry*, *168*(12), 1266–1277. doi: 10.1176/appi.ajp.2011.10111704

Posner, K., Melvin, G. A., Stanley, B., Oquendo, M. A., & Gould, M. (2007). Factors in the assessment of suicidality in youth. *CNS Spectr*, *12*(2), 156–162.

Poznanski, E., Freeman, L. N., & Mokros, H. B. (1985). Children's Depression Rating Scale–Revised. *Psychopharmacol Bull*, *21*, 979–989.

Puig-Antich, J. (1982a). Major depression and conduct disorder in prepuberty. *J Am Acad Child Psychiatry*, *21*(2), 118–128.

Puig-Antich, J. (1982b). The use of RDC criteria for major depressive disorder in children and adolescents. *J Am Acad Child Psychiatry*, *21*(3), 291–293.

Puig-Antich, J., Blau, S., Marx, N., Greenhill, L. L., & Chambers, W. (1978). Prepubertal major depressive disorder: a pilot study. *J Am Acad Child Psychiatry*, *17*(4), 695–707.

Puig-Antich, J., Goetz, D., Davies, M., Kaplan, T., Davies, S., Ostrow, L., . . . Ryan, N. D. (1989). A controlled family history study of prepubertal major depressive disorder. *Arch Gen Psychiatry*, *46*(5), 406–418.

Puig-Antich, J., Lukens, E., Davies, M., Goetz, D., Brennan-Quattrock, J., & Todak, G. (1985a). Psychosocial functioning in prepubertal major depressive disorders. I. Interpersonal relationships during the depressive episode. *Arch Gen Psychiatry, 42*(5), 500–507.

Puig-Antich, J., Lukens, E., Davies, M., Goetz, D., Brennan-Quattrock, J., & Todak, G. (1985b). Psychosocial functioning in prepubertal major depressive disorders. II. Interpersonal relationships after sustained recovery from affective episode. *Arch Gen Psychiatry, 42*(5), 511–517.

Robin, A. L., & Weiss, J. G. (1980). Criterion-related validity of behavioral and self-report measures of problem-solving communication skills in distressed and non-distressed parent-adolescent dyads. *Behav Assess, 2*, 339–352.

Rohde, P., Beevers, C. G., Stice, E., & O'Neil, K. (2009). Major and minor depression in female adolescents: onset, course, symptom presentation, and demographic associations. *J Clin Psychol, 65*(12), 1339–1349. doi: 10.1002/jclp.20629

Rohde, P., Lewinsohn, P. M., Klein, D. N., Seeley, J. R., & Gau, J. M. (2013). Key characteristics of major depressive disorder occurring in childhood, adolescence, emerging adulthood, adulthood. *Clin Psychol Sci, 1*(1), 41–53. doi: 10.1177/2167702612457599

Rossello, J., & Bernal, G. (1999). The efficacy of cognitive-behavioral and interpersonal treatments for depression in Puerto Rican adolescents. *J Consult Clin Psychol, 67*(5), 734–745.

Rossello, J., Bernal, G., & Rivera-Medina, C. (2008). Individual and group CBT and IPT for Puerto Rican adolescents with depressive symptoms. *Cultur Divers Ethnic Minor Psychol, 14*(3), 234–245. doi: 10.1037/1099-9809.14.3.234

Ruble, D. N., Greulich, F., Pomerantz, E. M., & Gochberg, B. (1993). The role of gender-related processes in the development of sex differences in self-evaluation and depression. *J Affect Disord, 29*(2–3), 97–128.

Rudolph, K. D. (2002). Gender differences in emotional responses to interpersonal stress during adolescence. *J Adolesc Health, 30*(4 Suppl.), 3–13.

Rutter, M., & Graham, P. (1968). The reliability and validity of the psychiatric assessment of the child: I. Interview with the child. *Br J Psychiatry, 114*(510), 563–579. doi: 10.1192/bjp.114.510.563

Shaffer, D., Gould, M. S., Brasic, J., Ambrosini, P., Fisher, P., Bird, H., & Aluwahlia, S. (1983). A Children's Global Assessment Scale (CGAS). *Arch Gen Psychiatry, 40*(11), 1228–1231.

Shanahan, L., Copeland, W. E., Costello, E. J., & Angold, A. (2011). Child-, adolescent- and young adult-onset depressions: differential risk factors in development? *Psychol Med, 41*(11), 2265–2274. doi: 10.1017/s0033291711000675

Sheeber, L. B., Davis, B., Leve, C., Hops, H., & Tildesley, E. (2007). Adolescents' relationships with their mothers and fathers: associations with depressive disorder and subdiagnostic symptomatology. *J Abnorm Psychol, 116*, 144–154.

Silk, J. S., Davis, S., McMakin, D. L., Dahl, R. E., & Forbes, E. E. (2012). Why do anxious children become depressed teenagers? The role of social evaluative threat and reward processing. *Psychol Med, 42*(10), 2095–2107. doi: 10.1017/s0033291712000207

Silk, J. S., Shaw, D. S., Skuban, E. M., Oland, A. A., & Kovacs, M. (2006). Emotion regulation strategies in offspring of childhood-onset depressed mothers. *J Child Psychol Psychiatry, 47*(1), 69–78. doi: 10.1111/j.1469-7610.2005.01440.x

Silk, J. S., Siegle, G. J., Lee, K. H., Nelson, E. E., Stroud, L. R., & Dahl, R. E. (2014). Increased neural response to peer rejection associated with adolescent depression and pubertal development. *Soc Cogn Affect Neurosci, 9*(11), 1798–1807. doi: 10.1093/scan/nst175

Spence, S. H., O'Shea, G., & Donovan, C. L. (2016). Improvements in interpersonal functioning following interpersonal psychotherapy (IPT) with adolescents and their association with change in depression. *Behav Cogn Psychother, 44*(3), 257–272. doi: 10.1017/s1352465815000442

Stanley, B., & Biggs. (2014). Safety planning to prevent suicidal behavior (pp. 366–371).

Stanley, B., & Brown. (2012). Safety planning intervention: a brief intervention to mitigate suicide risk. *Cog Behav Pract, 19*(2), 256–264. doi: 10.1016/j.cbpra.2011.01.001

Stark, K. D., Streuand, W., Krumholz, L. S., & Patel, P. (2010). Cognitive-behavioral therapy for depression: the ACTION program for girls. In J. R. Weisz & A. E. Kazdin (Eds.), *Evidence-based psychotherapies for children and adolescents* (2nd ed., pp. 93–109). New York: Guilford Press.

Steinberg, L., & Silverberg, S. B. (1986). The vicissitudes of autonomy in early adolescence. *Child Dev, 57*(4), 841–851.

Sullivan, H. S. (1953). *The interpersonal theory of psychiatry*. New York: Norton.

Swartz, H. A., Cyranowski, J. M., Cheng, Y., Zuckoff, A., Brent, D. A., Markowitz, J. C., . . . Frank, E. (2016). Brief psychotherapy for maternal depression: impact on mothers and children. *J Am Acad Child Adolesc Psychiatry, 55*(6), 495–503 doi: 10.1016/j.jaac.2016.04.003

Swartz, H. A., Frank, E., Zuckoff, A., Cyranowski, J. M., Houck, P. R., Cheng, Y., . . . Shear, M. K. (2008). Brief interpersonal psychotherapy for depressed mothers whose children are receiving psychiatric treatment. *Am J Psychiatry, 165*(9), 1155–1162. doi: 10.1176/appi.ajp.2008.07081339

Szigethy, E., Bujoreanu, S. I., Youk, A. O., Weisz, J., Benhayon, D., Fairclough, D., . . . DeMaso, D. R. (2014). Randomized efficacy trial of two psychotherapies for depression in youth with inflammatory bowel disease. *J Am Acad Child Adolesc Psychiatry, 53*(7), 726–735. doi: 10.1016/j.jaac.2014.04.014

Thomas, R., Sanders, S., Doust, J., Beller, E., & Glasziou, P. (2015). Prevalence of attention-deficit/hyperactivity disorder: a systematic review and meta-analysis. *Pediatrics, 135*(4), e994–e1001. doi: 10.1542/peds.2014-3482

Tompson, M. C. (2008). Adolescent mood disorders and familial processes. In N. B. Allen & L. B. Sheeber (Eds.), *Adolescent emotional development and the emergence of depressive disorders* (pp. 280–298). Cambridge, UK: Cambridge University Press.

Tompson, M. C., Boger, K. D., & Asarnow, J. R. (2012). Enhancing the developmental appropriateness of treatment for depression in youth: integrating the family in treatment. *Child Adolesc Psychiatr Clin N Am, 21*(2), 345–384. doi: 10.1016/j.chc.2012.01.003

van Hees, M. L., Rotter, T., Ellermann, T., & Evers, S. M. (2013). The effectiveness of individual interpersonal psychotherapy as a treatment for major depressive disorder in adult outpatients: a systematic review. *BMC Psychiatry, 13*, 22. doi: 10.1186/1471-244x-13-22

Visser, S. N., Danielson, M. L., Bitsko, R. H., Holbrook, J. R., Kogan, M. D., Ghandour, R. M., . . . Blumberg, S. J. (2014). Trends in the parent-report of health care provider-diagnosed and medicated attention-deficit/hyperactivity disorder: United States, 2003–2011. *J Am Acad Child Adolesc Psychiatry, 53*(1), 34–46. doi: 10.1016/j.jaac.2013.09.001

Vostanis, P., Feehan, C., & Grattan, E. (1998). Two-year outcome of children treated for depression. *Eur Child Adolesc Psychiatry, 7*(1), 12–18.

Vostanis, P., Feehan, C., Grattan, E., & Bickerton, W. L. (1996). A randomised controlled out-patient trial of cognitive-behavioural treatment for children and adolescents with depression: 9-month follow-up. *J Affect Disord, 40*(1–2), 105–116. doi: 10.1016/0165-0327(96)00054-7

Weissman, M. M., & Bothwell, S. (1976). Assessment of social adjustment by patient self-report. *Arch Gen Psychiatry, 33*(9), 1111–1115.

Weissman, M. M., & Klerman, G. L. (1992). Depression: Current understanding and changing trends. *Annu Rev Public Health, 13*, 319–339.

Weissman, M. M., Markowitz, J. C., & Klerman, G. L. (2007). *Clinician's quick guide to interpersonal psychotherapy.* New York: Oxford University Press.

Weissman, M., Warner, V., Wickramaratne, P., Moreau, D., & Olfson, M. (1997). Offspring of depressed parents: 10 years later. *Arch Gen Psychiatry, 54*, 932–940.

Weissman, M. M., Wickramaratne, P., Merikangas, K. R., et al. (1984). Onset of major depression in early adulthood. Increased familial loading and specificity. *Arch Gen Psychiatry, 41*(12), 1136–1143.

Weissman, M. M., Wolk, S., Wickramaratne, P., Goldstein, R. B., Adams, P., Greenwald, S., . . . Steinberg, D. (1999). Children with prepubertal-onset major depressive disorder and anxiety grown up. *Arch Gen Psychiatry, 56*(9), 794–801.

Weisz, J. R., McCarty, C. A., & Valeri, S. M. (2006). Effects of psychotherapy for depression in children and adolescents: a meta-analysis. *Psychol Bull, 132*(1), 132–149. doi: 10.1037/0033-2909.132.1.132

Weisz, J. R., Thurber, C. A., Sweeney, L., Proffitt, V. D., & LeGagnoux, G. L. (1997). Brief treatment of mild-to-moderate child depression using primary and secondary control enhancement training. *J Consult Clin Psychol, 65*(4), 703–707.

Wesselhoeft, R., Sorensen, M. J., Heiervang, E. R., & Bilenberg, N. (2013). Subthreshold depression in children and adolescents—a systematic review. *J Affect Disord, 151*(1), 7–22. doi: 10.1016/j.jad.2013.06.010

Whalen, D. J., Dixon-Gordon, K., Belden, A. C., Barch, D., & Luby, J. L. (2015). Correlates and consequences of suicidal cognitions and behaviors in children ages 3 to 7 years. *J Am Acad Child Adolesc Psychiatry, 54*(11), 926–937. doi: 10.1016/j.jaac.2015.08.009

Whitlock, J., Eckenrode, J., & Silverman, D. (2006). Self-injurious behaviors in a college population. *Pediatrics, 117*(6), 1939–1948. doi: 10.1542/peds.2005-2543

Wickramaratne, P. J., Greenwald, S., & Weissman, M. M. (2000). Psychiatric disorders in the relatives of probands with prepubertal-onset or adolescent-onset major depression. *J Am Acad Child Adolesc Psychiatry, 39*(11), 1396–1405. doi: 10.1097/00004583-200011000-00014

Willcutt, E. G. (2012). The prevalence of DSM-IV attention-deficit/hyperactivity disorder: a meta-analytic review. *Neurotherapeutics, 9*(3), 490–499. doi: 10.1007/s13311-012-0135-8

Williamson, D. E., Birmaher, B., Brent, D. A., Balach, L., Dahl, R. E., & Ryan, N. D. (2000). Atypical symptoms of depression in a sample of depressed child and adolescent outpatients. *J Am Acad Child Adolesc Psychiatry, 39*(10), 1253–1259. doi: 10.1097/00004583-200010000-00012

Woodman, A. C., Mailick, M. R., & Greenberg, J. S. (2016). Trajectories of internalizing and externalizing symptoms among adults with autism spectrum disorders. *Dev Psychopathol, 28*(2), 565–581. doi: 10.1017/s095457941500108x

Young, J. F., Benas, J. S., Schueler, C. M., Gallop, R., Gillham, J. E., & Mufson, L. (2016). A randomized depression prevention trial comparing interpersonal psychotherapy--adolescent skills training to group counseling in schools. *Prev Sci, 17*(3), 314–324. doi: 10.1007/s11121-015-0620-5

Young, J. F., Mufson, L., & Davies, M. (2006). Impact of comorbid anxiety in an effectiveness study of interpersonal psychotherapy for depressed adolescents. *J Am Acad Child Adolesc Psychiatry, 45*(8), 904–912. doi: 10.1097/01.chi.0000222791.23927.5f

About the Authors

Laura J. Dietz, Ph.D. is a clinical and developmental psychologist whose research focuses on the study of family risk factors for depression and the development of psychosocial interventions for mood disorders in youths. Dr. Dietz completed her graduate work at the University of Pittsburgh, a predoctoral internship at Children's Memorial Hospital, Feinberg School of Medicine, in Chicago, IL, and a postdoctoral fellowship at Western Psychiatric Institute and Clinic. For the past 10 years, Dr. Dietz has developed, manualized, and tested the efficacy and putative treatment mechanisms of Family Based Interpersonal Psychotherapy (FB-IPT) for Depressed Preadolescents. She is an Assistant Professor of Psychology at the University of Pittsburgh at Johnstown, and trains clinicians in Interpersonal Psychotherapy for Depressed Adolescents (IPT-A) and FB-IPT.

Rebecca J. Weinberg, PsyD, is a clinical psychologist at the Women's Behavioral Health program of the Allegheny Health Network, specializing in the treatment of women with perinatal mood and anxiety disorders. Dr. Weinberg completed her graduate studies at the Ferkauf Graduate School of Psychology, Yeshiva University and a predoctoral internship at Allegheny General Hospital. Dr. Weinberg completed her postdoctoral training at Western Psychiatric Institute and Clinic and participated in the development of Family Based Interpersonal Therapy (FB-IPT) for Depressed Preadolescents, assisted in writing the treatment manual and provided this psychotherapy to preadolescents and their families.

Laura Mufson, Ph.D. is a Professor of Medical Psychology in Psychiatry at Columbia University Medical Center (CUMC), Co-Director of the Office of Clinical Psychology at CUMC, and Director of the Department of Clinical Psychology at New York State Psychiatric Institute. In addition, she is Director of Clinical Child Psychology in Child Psychiatry at Columbia University College of Physicians and Surgeons. Dr. Mufson developed the adolescent adaptation of Interpersonal Psychotherapy for Depression

(IPT-A) and has published extensively on interpersonal psychotherapy and its adaptations for treating youth in diverse settings. Through her own work as well as through mentoring and collaborating with other researchers, Dr. Mufson has contributed significantly to the evidence base for IPT for depressed youth. Her areas of expertise include the evaluation of empirically-supported intervention outcomes in clinical trials conducted in research and community settings, and the transportability and implementation of treatments in the community. Dr. Mufson conducts training workshops on IPT-A throughout the United States and internationally.

Made in the USA
Monee, IL
13 September 2026

63138397R00184